COMPANY OF VOICES

COMPANY OF VOICES

Daily Prayer
and
the People of God

GEORGE GUIVER CR

PUEBLO PUBLISHING COMPANY

New York

Cover design: Frank Kacmarcik

First published in Great Britain by the Society for
Promoting Christian Knowledge.

Printed in the United States of America

ISBN: 0-916134-97-0

To
Shepherd's Law

Contents

Acknowledgements

My deepest debt is to a person and a place which must both remain anonymous. If anything is of value in this book its inspiration is traceable to that source. If it proves to be of help to anyone, as I hope it will, then it is merely because I have shown them what I have been shown already by another. Wherever I err or mislead, that is my fault alone.

My thanks are also due to many who have helped me at various points along the road. To the people of the Bishop's Frome group of parishes, through whose generosity I was able to sustain a year's study in Germany. To the Diocesan Liturgical Institute in Trier, Professor Andreas Heinz and its staff, and Dr Lucas Brinkhoff, the librarian, for enabling me to carry out the necessary research, and encouraging me further. To Professor Balthasar Fischer for his advice and encouragement, and to the brethren of St Matthias' Abbey for their hospitality and their splendid worship. Also I wish to thank Mgr J. D. Crichton for his interest and help over the years, and particularly with this present work; the Revd Paul Bradshaw for much helpful comment; and Sister Benedicta Ward SLG for salutary advice. I am grateful to various members of my community who have read the manuscript at its various stages of development, especially Fathers Simon Holden, Denys Lloyd, Norman Blamires, Peter Allan and Antony Grant, and to Fathers Mark Tweedy and Vincent Girling for the reading of proofs. I have been kindly helped by so many people that I am sure I have omitted others who deserve thanking. I hope they will understand that any such omission is purely due to the distractions of a not very commendable busyness, and that I am truly grateful for all their help. I have not always been able to acknowledge my indebtedness on particular points, and I record here my gratitude where that is so.

Last but not least, I must thank my community for having enabled me to write the book at all. All opinions are purely my own and should in no way be seen as reflecting the community's views. I thank them for that freedom too.

GEORGE GUIVER C.R.
Mirfield
1987

Publisher's Acknowledgements

The extract from *Selected Writings on the Spiritual Life* by St Peter Damian, translated by Patricia McNulty, is reprinted by permission of Faber and Faber Ltd.

Extracts from *Ramsa: An Analysis and Interpretation of the Chaldean Vespers* by S. Pudichery are reprinted by permission of Dharmaran Publications, Bangalore.

The extract from 'Ghetto or Desert . . .' by Charles Davis is reprinted from *Studia Liturgica* 7.2–3 (1970) by permission of the publisher.

Extracts from *Alexandrian Classics*, vol. 2 in the Library of Christian Classics, edited by J. E. Oulton and H. Chadwick, are reprinted by permission of SCM Press and Westminster Press.

The extract from 'Bishop Taylor's remedies against tediousness of spirit' by David Scott is reprinted from *A Quiet Gathering* (1984) by permission of the author and Bloodaxe Books.

The illustration of the church of the Holy Sepulchre, Jerusalem, is reproduced from the publication *Il Santo Sepolcro di Gerusalemme* by P. L. H. Vincent and others, by permission of Nuovo Istituto Italiano Arti Grafiche, Bergamo.

Abbreviations

ALW	*Archiv für Liturgiewissenschaft*
DACL	*Dictionnaire d'Archéologie Chrétienne et de Liturgie*
EL	*Ephimerides Liturgicae*
GILH	*General Instruction on the Liturgy of the Hours*
JEH	*Journal of Ecclesiastical History*
JTS	*Journal of Theological Studies*
LMD	*La Maison-Dieu*
LO	*Lex Orandi*
NT	New Testament
OC	*Oriens Christianus*
OCA	*Orientalia Christiana Analecta*
OCP	*Orientalia Christiana Periodica*
OT	Old Testament
PG	J. P. Migne (ed.), *Patrologia Graeca*
PL	J. P. Migne (ed.), *Patrologia Latina*
RB	The Rule of St Benedict
SL	*Studia Liturgica*

The Hebrew numbering of the Psalms is used throughout, except in patristic references, where it is added in brackets.

The term *mattins* is used throughout to denote the morning office (known as 'lauds' in the Roman tradition).

Numbers in **bold type** refer to the corresponding sections in Part V: *Sources*.

Introduction

Many Christians today do not pray, and this is something that is true both of laity and clergy. The cause is a mystery. This book has been prompted by a desire to understand why there is a problem, and what can be done about it. It is, first of all, a history of the 'divine office', those acts of prayer which are offered several times a day all the year round in cathedrals, parish churches and monasteries, as well as by individuals and clergy. It tries, not without a few surprises, to paint a picture of what people actually have done in the past, what they felt and thought when they did it, and what it would have been like to be present. It attempts, too, an outline history of people at their private prayer, rich and poor, educated and uneducated, particularly where their prayer shows links with the daily office. Many themes recur, including such daunting questions as the nature of the Church, the nature of our relationship with God, the problems Christian believers have with prayer, and problems of parish ministry today. This is, therefore, more a history of *practice* than of *content*, and wherever possible I have put technical detail and quotation from sources in a separate section at the end of the book. We do look at content also, however, with a view to learning from the past for the needs of today.

All of this is preceded by seven chapters which ask: 'Why pray in this way? Why pray daily at special times? Why pray liturgically? Why, in fact, a daily office?' These first chapters tackle head-on something which emerges throughout the history of this way of prayer: the sheer humanity of it. The message that comes clearly from its extraordinary history is that this way of prayer is nothing less than essential to all Christians.

1

On Earth as in Heaven

'As the eyes of servants look to the hand of their master, as the eyes of a maid
to the hand of her mistress, so our eyes look to the Lord our God.'[1] If all that
the Christian religion claims about life and living is true, then prayer ought to
be the most natural thing in the world: like the attention of the servant, or the
child looking spontaneously to its mother. However, due to God's hiddenness
and man's sin, prayer is not at all like that, but rather something which we have
to learn through suffering and struggle, and through remaining alive to the
question: 'How should we pray?'

There are occasions, such as times of crisis, when prayer arises spontaneously,
but most of the time we know prayer more as an added extra to the business of
daily living, something we have to struggle to make time for. The world in
which we live feels enclosed and entirely self-sufficient, and although religious
inclinations can arise in us naturally and spontaneously, we have to make an
effort to stay faithful to them in the long term. 'The world' sets its own agenda
and the agenda of faith fails to harmonize with it, so that faith exists in a state
of tension with the world. The New Testament makes a juxtaposition between
the Kingdom of God and 'the world'. We are to be not of the world but of God.
This is not a simple question of turning from the world. God does not call us
out of it, but calls us to live the faith and wrestle with it *within* 'the world'. This
is inevitably difficult, because there will always be a difference between the
faith we seek to hold, and the way we do in fact hold it; a difference between
the way we should be believing and the way we are in practice believing. The
reason the exercise is difficult is that there is a seemingly insuperable imbalance
in favour of *this* world. The world in which we live has given birth to us,
nurtured us and formed us. We see it, hear it, touch it and suffer its effects
every moment of our lives. Our faith on the other hand is abstract, and God we
cannot see. Charles Davis says:

Our faith and worship are not part of the modern secular world in which we live, not
part of its socially shared and confirmed reality. As believers and worshippers we step
outside the dominant secular culture as social deviants.

Men are the product of society ... The individual comes to be as a person only in and through the action of the social environment upon him. From infancy onwards by socialization he internalizes the social reality that surrounds him. That social reality is drawn into his consciousness and is built into him as the structure of his inner life. His thought and imagination, his emotions and activity are ordered into a pattern given by the culture in which he has been formed, and he depends upon society for continuance of his attitudes and activity, which otherwise would disintegrate and become meaningless ... consider how the language an individual receives from his culture patterns his thought and emotions ...

What most men take as real is what is accepted and confirmed by society as a whole. The reality of the everyday world in which men live has a taken-for-granted quality, which comes to it from being socially shared and socially confirmed. Social institutions and social activities constantly presuppose and reinforce what society understands as real; this 'knowledge' and this 'reality' are difficult to question, and by most are unquestioned. Whatever lies outside this socially shared and socially confirmed knowledge does not have the same accent of reality. It seems to lack solidity and does not impose itself with the same matter-of-fact clarity upon the mind. What is confirmed generally by society conveys a sense of unmistakable reality; what is held only as private opinion has the feel of a fugitive and tenuous reality.[2]

Therefore the position of a minority which attempts to perceive the world differently 'is not easy, either socially or psychologically'. Our world is so convinced of the reality of certain aspects of life as it perceives them that it is quite blind to others. For example, the individual's *rights* are exalted to a revered position, while concepts of duty which are needed to put this in balance are regarded with suspicion and distaste. Another example from the recent past would be the newspaper article in the 1950s which referred to a popular entertainer as 'admitting' that his son was mentally retarded, as if this were a social sin. Thomas Kuhn, the historian of science, can thus speak of how 'the large-scale pictures of reality, or "paradigms", held by a culture can render most people blind to important features of the world which conflict with their preconceptions'.[3]

All of this is, of course, as old as the eternal hills. It is *the* grand theme of the Old Testament, the zig-zagging of the chosen people between faithfulness to their God and forgetfulness of him in favour of the things of this world. The New Testament wrestles with it in various ways, always held to it by the incarnation, crucifixion and resurrection of Jesus, man and God. In the subsequent history of the Church the problem obstinately refused to go away. When Christianity was against the Roman consensus it was persecuted, and when it became part of the establishment under Constantine it had a perpetual problem in staying faithful to the gospel's values. Committed Christians in all ages have found it difficult not to be diverted off course by the prevailing consensus. Even in the ages of faith, say in the fourteenth century, such people as English bishops and parish priests must be forgiven for not having always discerned clearly between what was of the gospel and what was of fourteenth-century England.

The Christian is in a difficult situation because of all this. In order to know the gospel as it really is, not only do we have to set one foot outside our culture, but we also have to decontaminate that foot. In distancing ourselves from the modern world we have to remember that we have been formed by it, steeped in it, and are, far more than we can see, thoroughly 'pickled' in it, through to our very heart. If some attempt is not made to undo this, our faith will end by merely being co-opted by the consensus, becoming a mould into which are poured all the prejudices of a very particular culture. So the operation required is a double one. We need to be able to discern some of those major prejudices of our society which twist our understanding of the gospel, and on the basis of that learn how to maintain an essential minimum of detachment from our society in favour of closer attachment to the God who is the Truth. First, we need to become conscious of the reality of our situation – if we can borrow a term which was coined in a very different context, we could speak of the necessity for 'conscientization'.[4] Secondly, we need a means of maintaining that awareness so that it can inform the whole of our life.

To help us see what this implies, we can take a parable from the natural sciences. Peter Berger, in his book *A Rumour of Angels*, speaks of a similar situation, with the anthropologist involved in fieldwork. An anthropologist wishing to study some primitive tribe will need to live among them, learn their language and share their life, seeking to enter, as far as possible, into their thoughts, assumptions, emotions and hopes, as they are in reality. However, such anthropologists have to be very careful: if they go too far, something can happen to them which is sometimes known as 'going native'. They can become so identified with their hosts that they are no longer capable of studying them. If the essential toehold of detachment is lost, they will no longer be able to do anthropology. Therefore anthropologists in the field have to observe certain rituals and routines which will guard against their 'going native'. These include 'staying in the company of, or at least in communication with, fellow outsiders to the culture being studied, and best of all by going home from the field after a relatively brief period of time'.[5] The problem is one of relationships, of the bonds between people within a group, and the power such bonds can wield over our ability to relate to other groups. Therefore the anthropologist needs to maintain human contact with the home group in order to be able to remain an anthropologist. The Christian's situation is similar. If our Christianity is not to be a travesty of the real thing, we need rituals capable of maintaining living links with our home base, which is God himself. These we find in the Christian traditions of prayer and liturgy.

'The act of praying', says Archbishop Anthony Bloom, 'is an act of rebellion against slavery.'[6] Prayer is not escape from reality, as some may believe, but the pursuit of the *real*. Modern society is, by many people's admission, not fully real. It lacks reality. 'Life has no meaning.' The Christ whom we seek in prayer, however, is the real man, the Kingdom is the real place, and the Christians' search has any sense only if it is a quest for what is most *real*, most true.

Such a quest cannot entail turning our backs on the world. We cannot have the Kingdom of God on its own. God so loved the world that he entered into it. Indeed, many of our false beliefs need to be challenged by it. We have to be committed to the world, and yet prepared to stand in the place where two worlds meet – the realm of this world to which we are inevitably attached by an unbreakable umbilical cord, and the Kingdom of God, of whom we are sons and daughters by adoption, by means of our baptism.

There is a modern insight which is of tremendous importance in getting this right, and that is the rediscovery of the immanence of God in his creation. We are not seeking a Kingdom of God *rather than* a Godless world: we are seeking God in both places simultaneously, both in his mysterious transcendence 'in heaven' and in the everyday world. This recognition of the holiness of all of life can be found in all ages of the Church and is rooted in the New Testament. But in a particular way today it has come into its own. It is difficult to overestimate the strength with which this vision of the holiness of the world has impressed modern Christians, accompanied not on the whole by a spurning of personal religion and the life of prayer, but by a subtle shift whereby they drop into a supporting role. Many Christians do pray. But there is an assumption that God does not want us to waste too much time on this private affair when we should be out living life to the full and helping our brothers and sisters to get more out of life. There is an inability to hand over to God, due deep down perhaps to an inability to believe that such a thing could be possible.

Nevertheless it is as much a denial of the doctrine of the incarnation to opt too much for this world as it is to opt too much for the other. The two have come together in all their fullness in Christ's incarnation. Christian activists engaged in human affairs in the name of the gospel still have to set prayer and worship at their highest possible value, and submit all they do absolutely to the transcendent God. The monk on the other hand 'abandons the world', according to Thomas Merton, 'only in order to listen more intently to the deepest and most neglected voices that proceed from its inner depth',[7] voices which our materialistic, trivial culture seeks constantly to suppress. An absolute handing-over to God in prayer is essential to any attempt to live the Christian life. Without it the Church will become a poor imitation and a parody. How are we to recognize the Lord in daily life if we have not first sought him 'neat' in the direct encounter of prayer? We may as well expect a tracker-dog to trace a burglar without having first sniffed a piece of his clothing. Our calling is to be immersed in the world, but we can only recognize God there if we also stand apart to be exposed to the equally uncomfortable challenge of prayer. It is through this that we, the Church, can be freed from ourselves. In the words of Alexander Schmemann,

The Church is never more present to the world and more 'useful' to it than when she is totally free from it, free from it not only 'externally', i.e. independent from its structures and powers, but also and primarily internally, i.e. free from her own spiritual surrender to its values and treasures. To accomplish such liberation, however, is not easy, for it presupposes that our hearts find the only true treasure, the experience of the Kingdom of God, which alone can restore to us the fullness of the Church and the fullness of the world, which alone makes us capable of truly fulfilling our calling.[8]

The world is real, and prayer is real. If both are brought together, both will be more real still. The unity between this world and God is proclaimed in the incarnation; through that it was possible for a human being to say, 'I and the Father are one'. It is therefore inevitable that Christian prayer, no less than Christian service, will demand a living-to-the-full of the incarnation. Prayer requires the participation of all our emotions, hopes, thoughts and urges: it has to be rooted in our very entrails. It has to feel real and not eccentric; it has to be incarnated in life as it is.

We shall now look at some of the incarnational aspects of the prayer which the Church has handed on to us.

2

Myth

Religious belief is not what it was. Even if we believe in God, our perception of the world and our behaviour in it will usually be much less religious than would have been true for people in earlier centuries. Faith requires much more of an effort, and religious behaviour has a very limited place in the ordinary affairs of our daily life, either in public or in private.

The transition from a supposedly religious primitive man to a non-religious modern man has been traced in various disciplines including anthropology, psychology, sociology, philosophy and the study of history. A good example of such an analysis is found in the writings of Mircea Eliade, whose work straddles several of these disciplines. He has traced how the religious attitudes in primitive peoples have passed through various phases to what he regards as the poverty of the modern approach to the universe.

In his book *The Sacred and the Profane* he shows how ancient people found orientation and meaning to their life by means of myth, and through it found meaning and order in the cosmos. Eliade takes an example from an Australian nomadic tribe:

According to the traditions of an Arunta tribe, the Achilpa, in mythical times the divine being Numbakula cosmicized their future territory, created their Ancestor, and established their institutions. From the trunk of a gum tree Numbakula fashioned the sacred pole (*kauwa-auwa*) and, after anointing it with blood, climbed it and disappeared into the sky. This pole represents a cosmic axis, for it is around the sacred pole that territory becomes habitable, hence is transformed into a world. The sacred pole consequently plays an important role ritually. During their wanderings the Achilpa always carry it with them and choose the direction they are to take by the direction toward which it bends. This allows them, while being continually on the move, to be always in 'their world' and, at the same time, in communication with the sky into which Numbakula vanished.

For the pole to be broken denotes catastrophe; it is like 'the end of the world', reversion to chaos. Spencer and Gillen report that once, when the pole was broken, the entire clan were in consternation; they wandered about aimlessly for a time, and finally lay down on the ground together and waited for death to overtake them.[9]

Eliade shows that, in order to feel ourselves to be truly real, we need to stand at the central point where we are closest to the gods. This fixed point enables us to find *orientation*, and is also a point of ontological *passage* from one world to the other. The myth associated with this point has constantly to be re-entered into and renewed. Liturgy was born from the need regularly to relive, re-enact the myth, and to recover now in reality the primordial time when the world began. In primitive peoples this is an eternally cyclic process, as the myth is periodically renewed in a circular rhythm. In the Judaeo-Christian tradition, however, the circle is replaced by a straight line, and life is seen to be travelling forward through a series of unique events towards a goal or goals set in the future. Myth will no longer do – the story has now become history. The orientating 'myth' is no longer a fantastic legend, but real historical events involving ordinary people. Through reliving it in liturgy we see history to be united with the sacred. Like primitive man, the Christian participating in liturgy recovers what Eliade calls *illud tempus* ('that time'), but in the context of a historical time sanctified by the incarnation. We are no longer pumping new life into an old and too-remote legend, but entering into a forward-flowing stream to relive once again in their immediacy the saving historical events. We experience passage into another kind of time, liturgical time. 'When a Christian in our day participates in liturgical time, he recovers the "that time" in which Christ lived, suffered, and rose again – but it is no longer a mythical time, it is the time when Pontius Pilate governed Judaea.' This historical story, while losing many of the characteristics of myth, has not, however, lost them all. It continues to perform some of myth's most enduring functions.

In all that follows it should be remembered that the word 'myth' is used as a technical term for a particular use we make of story. It is not intended in any way to cast the slightest doubt on the historicity of the biblical events. It is a technical term perfectly applicable to historical and true events.

Anamnesis

At the Last Supper Jesus said: 'Do this in *anamnesis* of me.' The full meaning of the Greek word *anamnesis* is remembrance, done in such a way as to call forth the actual presence here and now of the person and deeds commemorated, in the kind of way that liturgical re-enactment of myths has always done. In the Eucharist it is effected in a very special way, but it is also true that the foundation of all Christian prayer and worship is anamnesis. When we pray, we inevitably do it in the context of all of those things which make up the gospel, and our prayer will be an incarnating of them. In addition the Lord promised his presence to those who pray together in his name. Even in our private prayers we are not speaking out of a vacuum to a figure of the past. We are remembering in such a way as to be aware of his presence here and now. So in the daily offices of the Church anamnesis is made as we hear the 'myth', salvation-history, recounted and reflected on, and then move on from that to pray to the risen, living Christ who is in the midst. It is in this way that we can speak of the real presence of Christ in the Church's daily liturgical prayer.

Now experience shows that further layers to this anamnesis emerge in practice. It is not simple but cumulative, for we pray conscious not only of the saving events up to and including the earthly Christ, but also his work in the Church after his resurrection. In this way we are in effect making anamnesis of the history of the Church. I will give an example. In the Paschal Vigil we light a candle and perform other ceremonies which recall the Lord's resurrection. But the commemoration of the resurrection is further heightened and redoubled by the fact that we are conscious at the back of our minds of all those people who have done the same things on this same night since very early times. We are conscious of how the primitive Church kept the *Pascha*, of how it was celebrated in all the ages leading up to today. This fact of cumulative anamnesis helps to explain why it is important not to make unnecessary changes in liturgy – for we are doing it as it has been done in order to make anamnesis of Christ's work in his Church since his resurrection. We are making anamnesis of all past anamneses. This helps to explain the importance of tradition.

This is not all. At the Paschal Vigil, not only are we recalling all of the past until today, but we are also very conscious of all the people the world over who are doing the same thing together with us at the same time. At the back of our minds we are conscious of them, and are in this way making anamnesis of all that the Lord is doing in his Church today. This helps to explain why some basic things must be held in common in the Church's prayer, in order that the contemporary unity of the one Body may find expression. This anamnesis of the present Church is another way of expressing the notion that in liturgical prayer we are praying 'with the Church'.

In these ways the 'myth' which is the basis of our prayer includes all that followed from the primordial story, and the Church's prayer acts as an evocation of the ongoing life of the Church in time and space. Anamnesis is dynamic and all-embracing, and this is well brought out in the famous 'purple passage' in the last chapter of Dix's *Shape of the Liturgy*,[10] where he stirs the reader with evocations of the multitude of times and places where the Eucharist has been celebrated, in the most different ways and by the most different people in all sorts of circumstances, implying that when we make anamnesis of the 'myth' of Jesus in the Eucharist, we also make anamnesis of all the people who have ever celebrated it and are celebrating it now. This is true of baptism too, where the Body of which the candidate is becoming a member is reckoned to be present. It is certainly true also of ordination, and to a greater or lesser extent of the other sacraments. It is, finally, one of the great leitmotivs of the history of the daily office, the recalling of the living Christ in his living Church, both in the Church of the past and in the Church of the present moment. We shall see, indeed, that the Church's daily prayer of the offices has borne very much the stamp of the paschal mystery, as it constantly acknowledges the presence of the living Lord who leads us in that 'ontological passage' through the waters from death to life.

ß. Orientation

Making anamnesis of the 'myth' in liturgy illuminates the quest for orientation. We each have our myths, and by them we orientate ourselves. They give shape and meaning to our world, and help us to feel our place in it. One perennial myth is that of the 'good old days', the backward reference to the time of childhood, or the previous generation, as the *normal time*, when all was best. So commercial advertising knows how to exploit such legends as the rural England of the 1930s, and similar ages when all was thought to be 'golden'. For all of us there are events in our life which are sacred, human achievements which we individually revere (a local football team, or former models of motor cars which bring tears to the eyes), hobbies and interests of our own, and, perhaps supremely, myths about ourselves. Our myths about ourselves can be so wrong as to be comical to others (such as illusions about personal beauty or abilities). I remember sitting in a farmhouse kitchen when the death of Bing Crosby was announced on the television news. Clips from his shows and films appeared on the screen, as well as scenes of emotion among mourning fans. My slightly ironical attitude was not well received by the other person in the room, who I then realized had tears in his eyes. Our myths are sacred. No one can live without myth. In *Myths, Dreams and Mysteries* Mircea Eliade shows how deep and varied this need is, and describes the various ways in which we meet it. Psychoanalysis, taking the patients back to their childhood, recovers their personal primordial time when all began. Even modern historical study helps to perform this function for society as a whole. At the family level, myths are relived, for example, in photograph albums and keepsakes and well-loved furniture. Without such things time becomes bland and shapeless, pastless and futureless, a meaningless 'now', an unbearable, imprisoning time which has to be escaped from by means of distractions. We use myth in order to understand our place in the world. Without it we are adrift.

For Christians the history of Jesus operates in this way. It becomes the foundation-stone from which we relate to the world and find its meaning, though in a much deeper and more unfathomable way than with any of our other myths, because to such a unique degree it is larger than us.

So it is that the Church developed disciplines of prayer, liturgy and Bible-reading which fulfil the purpose of keeping us alive to the 'myth'. Anthropologists and historians of religion agree in seeing the function of religious rituals as making anamnesis, bringing the life of the myth once again into the midst, realizing its real presence. So Christians have sought to keep up a perpetual walk through the story, in prayer, liturgy and Bible-reading. One of the most vivid ways in which this is achieved is through the calendar, and the scriptural themes of the Sunday eucharists and the greater and lesser feasts. Frame by frame the story is held before our eyes, and little by little it becomes more real to us, and through it the world becomes more real, because we see it much more in connection with eternal reality.

Why should we need this constant reminding? Is it not enough to have read the story and then try to put its message into action? The problem is that we all suffer from a chronic forgetfulness. As Dr Johnson is supposed to have said, 'people need to be reminded more often than they need to be instructed'. C. S. Lewis comments: 'The real job of every moral teacher is to keep on bringing us back, time after time, to the old simple principles which we are all so anxious not to see; like bringing a horse back and back to the fence it has refused to jump or bringing a child back and back to the bit in its lesson that it wants to shirk.'[11] We are too much at the mercy of all that assails us in everyday life, and of the moods which assail our inner being, to be able to stay with the 'myth' without some effective technique. Lewis says later in the same book:

... moods will change, whatever view your reason takes – Now that I am a Christian I do have moods in which Christianity looks very improbable: but when I was an atheist I had moods in which Christianity looked terribly probable – unless you teach your moods where they get off, you can never be either a sound Christian or even a sound atheist, but just a creature dithering to and fro, with its beliefs really dependent on the weather and the state of its digestion – The first step is to recognize the fact that your moods change. The next is to make sure that, if you have once accepted Christianity, then some of its main doctrines shall be deliberately held before your mind for some time every day. That is why daily prayers and religious reading and churchgoing are necessary parts of the Christian life. We have to be continually reminded of what we believe. Neither this belief nor any other will automatically remain alive in the mind. It must be fed. And as a matter of fact, if you examined 100 people who had lost their faith in Christianity, I wonder how many of them would turn out to have been reasoned out of it by honest argument? Do not most people simply drift away?[12]

The oddest thing about our forgetfulness is how it affects even the things which mean most to us. We can experience a marvellous, converting act of worship in church and half an hour later be doing somebody down or kicking the cat. Mircea Eliade sees this to be all bound up with the role of the 'myth'. 'One of the most difficult things to comprehend is the fact that a man can forget even those events and revelations on which his happiness and salvation depend.'[13] That is a parable of the Christian life if ever there was one – we simply *forget*. The children of Israel forgot their dramatic rescue by God once they were in the wildnerness, and in the centuries which followed they constantly re-enacted the cycle of forgetting and being recalled. The new Israel, the Church, has hardly shown itself to be much better. The human capacity to forget is so strong that special measures have to be taken to counteract it. We forget even those things which are most important to us, or abandon them to a shadowy superficial state at the back of our minds, so that they constantly need to be reawakened to life. The things we receive from our prayer, Bible-study and other aspects of the continual experience of life in Christ glow for a moment and then fall partly or totally asleep. So a daily celebration of the 'myth' will patrol the corridors of our mind, waking up one by one a throng of truths and perceptions which we have the incredible inclination to forget. Liturgy at its best keeps us in living contact with the 'myth' by steeping us ever deeper in the story of salvation, which includes the Scriptures in which it is recorded, and by converting our inadequate apprehension of time, and graining life with the 'myth', so that we come to *see* the world more as God sees it. Balthasar Fischer has found a parallel in modern literature:

Franz Kafka says that a book must be 'a hatchet for the frozen sea inside us'. The poet wants to say that every man bears within himself a reality which is as limitless, mysterious and marvellous as the sea. Every man has the painful experience that this interior sea is always beginning to freeze up, and what should flow in waves becomes like ice. The axe is needed here to break the ice and allow it once more to flow.[14]

Unless we are able to do this, we shall constantly tend to fall back on more comfortable, unreal myths which merely confirm us in our own forgetful preferences.

Entering below the surface of the 'myth'

All of this might imply that daily prayer aims to keep us up to a fixed standard that we have the tendency to slip away from. It is not concerned with mere maintenance, however, but with growth. We can read a passage from a book on two different occasions and find to our astonishment that it seems completely different the second time. How far we get below the surface of a text depends very much on our state of mind at the time. Repeated reading, however, will have the overall effect of taking us deeper and deeper, as far as the particular text will bear it. Otloh, a tenth-century monk, wrote that by reading Scripture

the eyes of the inward man are opened, and understanding what heretofore he had not understood of Scripture and the rest, he is astonished at having been so heavy and so blind. Then he goes even further in holy reading, and what at first he read from fear and a longing for forgiveness, now that he has begun to love he reads that he may also know the wonders of the Wisdom and Mercy of God. He tastes how sweet the Lord is, he meditates on his law day and night; he no longer stops at the historical meaning or the superficial value of the words themselves; he searches out the secrets of mysterious truths which are hidden, especially in the Old Testament.[15]

The 'myth' becomes real to us through a gradual process of conversion, as Scripture is spun out in Bible-study and liturgy. Gregory the Great, whom Otloh must have read, summed it up when he said that Scripture '*crescit cum legente*' – Scripture grows as the reader grows, or, Scripture grows as you read it.[16] It becomes more real the longer and more consistently and determinedly you stay with it and grow with it. We shall expect the 'myth' to change before our eyes as we persevere in courting it. We can never possess the gospel. It is always greater than us.

D. Time

As well as changing our perception of the 'myth', regular worship also changes our perception of the world. The liturgical round, and the daily office in particular, sharpen our sight by doing something with time. Modern technology, which issues us all with digital, bleeping watches, has stripped time of its subtle layers – now passing at an equal rate, it is steadily extruded in neatly packaged units. Time for modern man tends to be bland and featureless. It is the 'measurement, which we express in numbers, of a restless activity which embraces not only the bustle of our work time, but even more the restlessness of our free time. We measure the amount of this activity with the numbers of the hours... So we have the tendency to combine activities in one uninterrupted race. Once we are harnessed by time in this manner, then every moment we say: "I have no time". And this is exactly because a particular *kind* of time has got *us*, that is, has imprisoned us, so that we have become something like slaves.'[17] Having lost the capacity to live without looking at the time, we have become blind to the infinite variety of textures it can possess.

Even today we can still sometimes perceive time to flow at varying rates. A visit to the theatre can take away all sense of time, so that when the play ends and we step back into the street, we are disoriented at returning to ordinary time. Holidays always pass very quickly because we are enjoying ourselves. The time can shoot by. But if a relative is in intensive care after an accident, the time drags so heavily that days are like weeks, while we wait to know if he or she will pull through. Newly-weds can live in a no-time, where there is no morning and evening, no living and dying, and the people on the street are not going to anything so mundane as work – time has slipped into the eternal.

There are also special times for special things, such as April Fool's Day. Only then can pranks be played, and not the next day or the next week. At Christmas, northern Europe experiences an especially powerful irruption of the eternal into time. We do not simply hear the same old story again. It becomes *real.* On that night Mary and Joseph *are* in the stable and the baby *is* in the manger. It is as if they are always there in an eternal time, and once a year we drop into it. Time does not just stop, it disappears, and we are with them in an eternal time. Easter too is Easter, and cannot be put off if the vicar is ill, or celebrated on any other Sunday in the year but that one. Entertainment, pleasure, celebration, drama and suffering all affect the flow of time. The more fully we are living, the more marked is the change in our apprehension of time. This was discovered by a young officer in the First World War and expressed in a letter he wrote home, in which he contemplated 'the virtual certainty' of his own death – he was in fact killed almost exactly three months after the letter was written:

We make the division between life and death as if it were one of dates – being born at one date and dying some years after. But just as we sleep half our lives, so when we're awake, too, we know that often we're only half alive. Life, in fact, is a quality rather than a quantity, and there are certain moments of real life whose value seems so great that to measure them by the clock, and find them to have lasted so many hours or minutes, must appear trivial and meaningless. Their power, indeed, is such that we cannot properly tell how long they last, for they can colour all the rest of our lives, and remain a source of strength and joy that you know not to be exhausted, even though you cannot trace exactly how it works.[18]

These few examples perhaps show how our perception of what we call 'time' is open to great variations, of which we have become less aware than our forefathers. We are so preoccupied with manipulating a material world that we are unable to value the *quality* of time. We are too obsessed with its quantity.

It is perhaps in reference to this that the daily office has been spoken of as 'redeeming the time'. Daily prayer imposes a pattern on time, creating the kind of framework to daily living which human nature naturally responds to. It enables us to get a grip on time, setting it in relief by patterning its surface. But by plunging us daily into the Christian 'myth' the Church's daily prayer is also a door between historical time and the *real* time of eternity. This is no escapism, but the quest for what is most *real*. It acts like stitching along the join between the two dimensions, each stitch forcing us to hold together both history and the eternal in our daily lives. It will not let us forget that other time – the time of the 'myth', the undying history of Jesus which is ever present in the eternal time of God. Prayer should bring us to what is *real*, not only in heaven, but on earth too. The Church's vocation is to be totally *present*, and to see the world as God sees it. Far from being any kind of escapism, it is an entering deeper into the world. Prayer and liturgy texture the time, putting a grain in it: that grain is the living story of salvation which culminates and presses forward in Jesus. As the scanning ray of the radar screen shows up objects in regular flashes, the daily prayers regularly flash up a matrix which we put against the world in which we live our daily lives, and this gives us orientation, so that we discover where we are. Time is no longer bland and shapeless, but an oriented time with a life of its own. Sometimes we say, 'Isn't it funny how you get up, go to work, eat, rest, and go to bed, and get up again day after day?' The daily discipline of the Church's prayer and liturgy enables us to see *meaning* in this apparent mastery which time has over us, because it is transformed by the saving story rolling us forward into the present moment and bearing us on to its own proclaimed, if hidden, goal. An Orthodox speaking of the daily office can therefore say:

Above the rhythm of the day's prayer there arches the greater rhythm of the day by day, month by month conformity to the given pattern. Prayer is cumulative. 'The repetitive rhythmic reiteration takes us up into the flow of centuries of tradition, out of the past into the present, and out of the present into the future. And, with this sense of timelessness within time, we are naturally drawn into the awareness of the transcendent, into the incomprehensible no-time of God.'[19]

3

Form and Rhythm

The returning, again and again, to the 'myth' which gives orientation, is a returning ultimately to him who calls us. It is a returning which is constant and regular, and as it is about a personal relationship it will probably be of help to see if we can recognize similar repetitive patterns in our relations with each other: in the family, let us say.

Love needs pattern and structure. Without such foundations there can be no freedom to love. Jack Dominian, claiming the same for marriage, says: 'Predominantly, sex conveys love in such a unique and precious way that it needs an appropriate relationship to safeguard it, characterized by continuity, reliability and predictability.'[20] Commitment to another person involves the evolution of symbols and rituals which give expression to the relationship, which are strongly characterized by continuity and regularity. In particular, most married people, on reflection, would be able to say that *time* for them bears strong patterns. There are certain hours of the day when certain things tend to happen, when particular things have to be done. Failure to keep the patterns can lead to trouble. For example, it is common today for both partners to become so busy that, without realizing it, not only do they spend little time together, but such time is experienced as a 'one-off', and not within a greater rhythm. And so even the times they do manage to spend together have lost their penumbra of equivalent times of meeting, and are exposed and bare. A couple of my acquaintance, having come to realize that they were in this sort of situation, responded by signing up for a twelve-week course in ballroom dancing. To their relief they found that this restored the bonds which were being loosened through the loss of regular time together. It is a part of love to plot against ourselves, devising schemes against our weaker nature, and against any drift into being dominated by circumstances.

Two sides to our personality show up here: the moods of the moment on the one hand, and their complementary partner, that capacity of the intellect for seeing all sides of an issue and planning accordingly. One side of our personality has to work against the other. In the days when I was a parish priest I used to ring the church bell daily when I sang mattins and evensong, usually alone, in church, partly so that people who lived nearby would come to regard it as part of the daily round, and notice the times that I missed. Without that small subterfuge I would have fallen short much more than I did. A covenant relationship such as marriage or baptism brings with it a submission to the patterns which any relationship with another must impose on us. Emotion has to be disciplined by the planning which arises from a thought-out commitment. Every relationship needs its own mix of both love and covenant. Regular disciplines of prayer and liturgy are a covenanting of prayer, and, by rewording Dominian's statement on marriage, we could say that 'Christian prayer mediates love in such a unique and glorious way that it needs an appropriate covenanted relationship characterized by continuity, reliability and predicta- bility', in order that it may be free to be itself. It is a paradox that through being circumscribed we are enabled to transcend the ordinary.

Marriage and its rhythms bring their own cost, but are entered into by our own choosing. So rhythms of prayer bring their own cost, essential as they are to the living-out of the covenant relationship. We are, however, also governed by rhythms which are not of our own choosing. Externally, these are the cycles of day and night, the seasons with the changing weather and the fruit and vegetables peculiar to each season, the phases of moon and tides, and all the varied rhythms of the cosmos. Internally, they are our rhythms of eating, sleeping, our bodily functions, moods, work, rest and play, and the social rhythms of visits to relations, weekly nights out at some club or hobby, periodical celebrations, holidays, school and working hours, regular television programmes, and the endless, boring repetitions of advertisements and news bulletins.

Through the ages daily prayer has reflected the texture of the day as we experience it. Dawn, midday and dusk, even in the modern city, mark cardinal turning-points. The Hindu prays three times a day at similar moments, and so does the pious Jew. This arises naturally in the most diverse and unconnected religions.

However, even for the country dweller today these rhythms have lost much of their power. Gone are the mystery and fear of the night, and the fearsome shadows cast by candle and lamp. Heat, cold and wet have lost their domination over us, and seasonal foods sit all year round in the freezer. Most of us are far from the rhythms of the natural world and have a much weaker general sense of the rhythms of the cosmos than our ancestors. These are overshadowed now by the confused rhythms of the complex world we have created for ourselves, rhythms which refuse to fit the Church's simple matrix evolved in pre-modern times. Weekends out in the car, shift work, commuting and the television timetable play havoc with Sunday and weekday worship as well as with any attempt to keep up disciplines of prayer. The churches have done comparatively little to come to grips with modern patterns of living, and much experimenting remains to be done.

We have to be careful, however, of simply adapting to the ways of society.

The Church conserves things which society has lost and needs to recover, and without which it is disoriented; one such great loss in modern life is the replacement of appropriate patterns of living with other patterns which bring stress, anxiety and dislocation. For any who have distanced themselves from these jarring patterns by entering a religious community, journeys back into the daily world can seem to have a similar effect to that of radio jamming, that meaningless din aimed at obliterating the transmissions of foreign stations. How can anyone believe and pray in the midst of the modern cacophony? Only by getting out of it can we suddenly recognize it for what it is. Only by stemming it can we pray in it. Some religious orders have deliberately set out to found houses in the midst of the modern city, and they show that it can be done – outposts of peace can be set up in the chaos. And they would all agree that the mainstay of their life is the rhythm of prayer.

The pure rhythm of liturgical prayer is a primeval channel of grace, and while it is necessary to look for ways of adapting the Church's patterns of prayer to modern life, there is much that the old patterns have to give us, even at the cost of forcing our lives to adapt to *them*, rather than vice versa.

Within the daily rhythm which governs any serious prayer there are more complex rhythms of structure and form.

Few of us realize the governing role played in many aspects of life by underlying form. To take a musical example: for well over 100 years 'sonata form' was a stock pattern for instrumental works, yet people are able to enjoy Mozart or Schubert symphonies without needing to know about this or recognize it. In principle extremely simple, such forms as this nevertheless allow the composer to stretch his creative powers, and at the same time give unity and shape to pieces of considerable length; and for ordinary listeners this is achieved at a completely unconscious level. Form can do its work in a very roundabout way so that even the expert hardly traces it. A good example is Bach's *Goldberg Variations*. In traditional baroque variations a theme is stated and then elaborated on in a series of short movements. The theme can always be recognized, and gives a strong unity to the work. The *Goldberg Variations* reduce reference to the theme to a very indirect minimum. Sometimes even the bare sequence of harmonies of the theme can only be recognized with difficulty, and yet at some buried level the brain registers the links, and the hearer feels the underlying diaphanous unity of the whole work. The chemistry of form is a strange thing, evidence of the power of hidden regions of the mind to respond to underlying patterns in things in a way the conscious, rational mind does not perceive. In music, it could be said that form arises from the need to ensure unity and coherence in a piece, that limitation to some given framework is necessary for creativity if the effort is not to be dissipated, and that the challenge of a given form imposing strict and characteristic limitations can call forth deeper resources of the spirit which only emerge in situations of limitation and challenge. Even a game of football has its own very stylized form (the rules).

Otherwise the players would spend their time aimlessly kicking a ball around. Fixed forms of prayer and worship, far from being death to the spirit, present the kind of obstacle course on which in art, sport, marriage and many other fields the human spirit rises to its best.

Within these forms and rhythms come still smaller ones, which make up the moment-to-moment texture. Music and dance have an ancient place in worship, not least for their capacity to induce ecstatic states. Just as the ticking of a clock can pacify an uneasy mind, so rhythmical breathing in Buddhism and Christianity has been a basic technique for prayer, inducing peace and receptivity. Recent discoveries suggest that the ecstatic states caused by prolonged rhythmic music and dancing are caused by a chemical released into the blood as a result. It is important to recognize that mental states associated with prayer can spring from something which in itself is purely physiological. Worship can induce a reflective mood purely through its rhythm. We should beware of thinking that we can generate communion with God by such techniques. Rather we should realize that such states of well-being are to be seen as the starting-point, and not the end. If the rhythm of the Church's worship opens us up and makes us receptive, its purpose is simply to prepare the mind so that it may attend to God.

Sigmund Mowinckel draws our attention to rhythmical prayer, observing that in most parts of the world the ritual word has the tendency to assume rhythmic and poetic forms. Poetry is the 'speech of the gods'; hence the Hindu Vedas, the Gathas of the Persians, the hymns and lament songs of Sumeria, Babylon and Assyria, the Egyptian cult-psalms, the cultic songs of the Greeks, the magic songs of shamans and medicine-men, and the Hebrew psalms themselves, as a natural and 'right' form of cult prayer.[21] In the daily liturgical prayer of Christianity the Psalter in particular, when recited or sung slowly and rhythmically, quietens and calms, reducing tensions and restlessness, and opening us up to prayer.

In the light of all this it therefore comes as no surprise to see that the prayer of Christians has been very strongly characterized throughout history by regular rhythms, weekly, daily, and within the day, and that the finer texture of the prayer itself consistently sticks to the use of basic forms, and the greater and lesser pulses of rhythmic language.

4

Formula

Verbal formula

The way we use language is much more complex than we usually assume. A word is never merely a capsule carrying a precise 'meaning' from speaker to hearer. We use words in a variety of ways. Sometimes we treat them like confetti, strewing them around in gay abandon. Children love to use repetitions and formal phrases, and even meaningless sounds. Jesus criticized vain repetitions as hypocrisy, on a level with the witch-doctor's babble which aims to manipulate the divine, or the priests of a temple in Rome who held services in a language neither they nor anybody else understood, believing all would be well merely if they repeated the formulas. The Lord's stricture was rightly against such vain repetitions as these, but he held no objections to those repetitions he would have met in his worship in temple and synagogue, and which can always be met in everyday life – repetitions which are far from vain. We are to be persistent and repetitive in our prayer, he said, like the woman who pleads with the unjust judge, or the man who pesters his neighbour for a midnight loaf of bread. A baby babbles nonsense for the fun of it; the boy opens the window to his father approaching, and shouts 'Daddy, daddy, daddy ...' Boy and girl speak for hours on the phone, repeating many things and saying nothing in particular.

The simple act of speech can be a vehicle for communion without the presence of 'meaning' in the lexical sense. H. Mühlen says that we are wrong to think that words should always have a meaning in this way. The mere sounds can be valid forms of expression in their own right, as in speaking in tongues, long melismas on one vowel in plainsong, expressive words such as Alleluia, Zion, Om, the Jesus Prayer, the Rosary and other repetitions where the formal meaning recedes into the background, and Alpine traditions of yodelling during the canon of the Mass.[22] There is indeed an old tradition for Swiss menfolk to go on to the mountainside to say morning or evening prayers and then yodel at length. Communication through words in which the meaning largely falls away, or comes and goes in waves, is nothing out of the ordinary. 'In the villages of South American Indians or Negroes,' wrote Friedrich Heiler, 'delightful chatter is accustomed to last far on into the night, but its intellectual substance could be expressed in a few short sentences.'[23] We do not need to go to South America to find that! Any garden fence or street corner will know it well enough. In a slightly more exalted mood, Werner Pelz has described an evening spent with a friend: 'We had a long discussion all to ourselves. It was one of those rare, slow discussions where every phrase is significant while it lasts, every sentence pregnant, every rejoinder an antiphone, because the words are only the foam of a wave that rocks you together, only the outward and visible sign of a hidden, only half-suspected consummation.'[24] When taking part in a service we cannot concentrate on every item of meaning in it – indeed, it may be wrong to do so. All we may need to do is simply make sounds. Words function in many ways, and often the simple physical act of making sound is effective expression in itself. The Egyptian hermits recited the psalter endlessly night and day. It was a way of keeping the mind trained on the right things. But it was also surely because they simply could not stop talking. They were like parents with a new baby, a man in trouble, or a soldier due to go on leave, filled with an involuntary need to talk about the same thing, over and over again. The long monastic night office later acquired its many readings in a similar way, meeting the need for material, for more words in the word-bank to spin out in an unending progress of praise. The curious appropriateness of the Psalms, despite the considerable limitations of their literal content, must lie partly in this: they provide rhythmic noises for us to make, whose content is sufficiently relevant to the matter in hand. It can be enough that they are poetry. 'Somewhat as the lover is caught', says J. D. Crichton, 'and breathes out names that add nothing to that beauty, names that are in a sense useless and yet are necessary to sustain the love, so the Christian who has caught a glimpse of the glory and beauty and love that is God, utters his praise and adoration in "useless" words which in fact reach the lover through Jesus Christ, our Advocate and Mediator.'[25] An old Russian proverb says, 'A beloved child has many names', for its mother is always inventing new nicknames. For Louis Bouyer,

Across the necessary multiplicity of words and ideas, as heart speaking to heart, our prayer must tend to the ineffable communication of the one to the One: beyond the exchange of words, to the exchange of looks, where we rediscover at a single glance all that we have said to each other, and realize all that we are unable to say.[26]

Often in history monks have been criticized for rushing too quickly through an office, but even that is not so self-evidently bad as we might assume. A traveller in Greece, reporting on Orthodox worship there, once described how

psalms, hymns, *troparia*, *kontakia*, readings, unfold upon the newcomer at the rate of an Orient-Express; before his eye has been able to grasp one or two notes of the text, the experts are already five lines further on. The Greeks find it all natural, and I think they find it beautiful. They are anyway convinced that the angels themselves must fall asleep in heaven listening to the psalmody of the Latin monks.[27]

While the Church of England has tried various ways of shortening the Benedicite, it never seems to be considered that to rush through the whole thing at speed can be an exhilarating offering of celebration. In old Byzantium, as we shall see shortly, worshippers sang it as they poured in from the narthex, coping all at the same time with doors, steps, pillars, and a general pressing throng of celebrating bodies. Speed of recitation, or the doing of other things while we speak, are not inevitable obstacles to the valid use of the words.

A characteristic of Orthodox worship is the continual vocal recitation of texts for hours at a time. The modern temperament can find this very difficult to cope with – we prefer our use of language to be more rational. One of the results of the Reformation was a desire that every word used in worship should be authentic and 'meant', said in full consciousness of its meaning. This, which we could call the *prayer of careful concentration*, was one of the positive fruits of the Reformation, and has become an established expectation of prayer among many traditions. It does, however, have its own pitfalls (excess individualism, piousness and dependence on feelings, leading, in their absence, to their fabrication) and needs the strong counterweight of formal, onward-moving liturgy; and we could call this forward-pressing recitation of texts *stream prayer*. Texts, mainly from Scripture (although in Protestantism and Orthodoxy hymns and poetry loom large too) are read through without much pause for thought. The effect is that of a stream, slowly wearing away stones and banks; or like the swiftly moving beam in a cathode-ray tube, darting from top to bottom of the television screen many times a second to keep an intricate comprehensive picture before our eyes. It is like a newspaper photograph, building up a picture from a panorama of tiny dots which are appreciated not individually, but as part of the whole. The *prayer of careful concentration* moves consciously from detail to detail. *Stream prayer* stands us in a panorama, taking our eyes off the details, and enabling us to see through an impressionistic web of words to broader vistas. Sometimes it can hold before us whole sweeps of the Creed or salvation-history. It is vistavision as opposed to the microscope.

Stream prayer builds up deposits over a long time. Its under-the-skin working in liturgical prayer is similar to the experience of learning a language in a foreign country. Anyone who has had that experience will know how the language builds up inside quite imperceptibly. A stream of incomprehensible talk pours over you all day long and you seem to be getting nowhere. But all the time the back of your brain is quietly digesting and processing it all so that after a few months you find you can converse and begin to feel at home in a way which seems miraculous. The daily office works by accumulation over the years. As far as its effect on us is concerned, it all piles into the unconscious, fermenting away, working its imperceptible transformation. The individual occasions are usually unremarkable – the lasting fruit is not there but in the accumulation of the years. A person moving out of a house he has lived in for years takes one last look before closing the door for the last time. That will not add anything; it is purely symbolic. The meaning is not in that individual moment or in any of the others in the past, but in the accumulation of the sum total. So Macrina, the sister of Gregory of Nyssa, was pleased to have celebrated the evening prayer at the lighting of the lamps for the last time before she died.[28] The ritual in itself was not much to speak of, but it had behind it a lifetime of its celebration which was ingrained in her experience. It is missing the point of the exercise always to expect a pay-off on the nail. Prayer is a long-term undertaking whose principal fruits are born at subliminal levels beyond our notice.

Hearing, as opposed to silent reading, makes an important difference. There is an ancient tradition of the necessity to *hear* the Scriptures or read them aloud. All Scriptures were originally oral. Buddhism, for example, has been averse to writing its Scriptures down – they must be heard. The early Christians only began to make written records when forced to. The initial impulse is to pass on the living message, and for the word truly to live it must be spoken out loud. If one reads a passage first silently and then rereads it aloud, the difference in apprehension can be striking. In ancient times all reading was done aloud, as people did not have the faculty to read silently. Someone has said of Scripture that we need to get our jaws round it. At international conferences distinguished speakers are invited to give lectures which are printed and distributed in advance. There is evidently some point in paying out large sums to have the lecturer there in person to read it. The living voice is as important as that. There is a world of difference between silent reading and prayer, and that which is spoken aloud. Scientists and scholars need to get their jaws round their subjects and so does the Christian. According to Jean Leclercq, two things result: 'a muscular memory of the words pronounced and an aural memory of the words heard'.[29]

The *spoken* word, indeed, exercises a psychological power which has been feared ever since we lived in caves. To *name* something vocally is to exercise power over it, but also to be subjected to its power. For primitive people, to name a good or evil thing is to call it forth. If we do not pray, we have nothing to 'name' God with when we need to. In Umberto Eco's novel *The Name of the Rose* we understand only too well the pain of Adso who, not knowing the name of the girl with whom he has built up a relationship, is horrified that he can call out nothing as she is taken away to suffer death at the stake. Conversely, speech is so powerful that there are certain things we do not name. Modern civilized man has not lost this at all. Tensions within a group of people can be expressed subtly, obliquely, but to mention them directly is to unleash forces so potentially destructive that they are to be avoided at all costs. Someone's habits may annoy us, but to tell them baldly is such an act of power that people can spend whole lives together without daring to name things between them. The iteration of the names of God and the reading aloud of his Scriptures will never be empty or meaningless, for whenever we name someone or something we give them a place in the objective reality of the world.

In liturgical worship, words are woven in formulas. But even 'spontaneous' prayer is composed of formulas, for language works by means of formula, and the phrases we utter are almost totally made up of standard formulas we have received from other people, although our selection from them will often be characteristic to us, and an inventive frame of mind can create new turns of phrase which still, however, are bound by the language's formulaic patterns. Prayer and language are so dominated by form and formula, that the difference between liturgy and extempore prayer can only be one of degree, not of kind. To heighten the element of formula is to put in concentrated form one of the basic factors of the way we communicate. A German writer, Emmanuel von Severus, sums up much of the Church's wisdom on liturgical prayer when, reflecting on experience in the hard wartime years in Germany, he says:

Man needs formula as a model, to practise saying his own prayer as an answer to the God who speaks to him, just in the same way as a child learns. . . . In formulas which are common to all Christians . . . the borders of prayer widen out, and it becomes a gift offered by brothers together. Words expressed in a formula . . . prove to be enduring when earthly structures collapse. We will even be able to express in formulas what is the frequent experience of those who pray in the school of Christ and his saints; he who knows that he is praying has not yet begun to pray. But to pray in fixed formulas means to recognize that we are poor, and our hands are empty, and only God can fill them, and that what we offer him are gifts which he has put into our hands.[30]

To these uses of formula we should add something which has attracted the attention of modern psychology: the fact that all our speech has more than one level of meaning. Most of what we say is a veil over the 'hidden agenda' of what we really want to say. This is a familiar fact of life once we think of it. The special contribution of psychology has been to show the depth and extent of this trait in human nature. Below the surface of all human conversation there are further layers of the *real* thoughts and *real* feelings which are going through the hearts and minds of the speakers. The various ways we communicate with each other through words, gestures and actions, form part of a subtle game, whether we like it or not, which is partly intentional and partly involuntary. Even with people as close as husband and wife, such games play an important part in communicating obliquely. In our relations with God, however close we may feel to him, and however open we are trying to be, much that we try to say in our prayers is operating differently from the way we imagine it.

For a start, while we are happily having our say in our prayers, God is seeing through it all to what is really going on. I am asking for this and that, confessing this sin, hiding that one, praying for this person to improve and that one to have better fortune, and all the while God is watching this performance, encouraging the good and looking for ways to help me see the truth about myself, and in his humility trying, as he promised, to be of service to me. But if all our prayer is like that, growth in spiritual maturity is likely to be slow. The advantage of the use of formula is that it does not allow us the delusion that we have necessarily spoken 'sincerely', heart-to-heart to God; for indeed it is unlikely that we very often can, so mixed are our motives and urges, and so deep some of our fears and pains. It is a serious mistake to see prayer as a test of our ability. We can be discouraged by the feeling that we are hopeless at it, or we can feel pleased at having done well. Either way we have not yet turned our regard away from our self, and this self-regard is as obstructive in the person whose Christian faith and prayer are for ever confident and rosy as it is in those of us who find prayer difficult. Personal extempore prayer is of course important for us, but the regular use of formula enables us to have in addition the experience of prayer which is not so dependent on, or limited by, our personal capacities. It provides the 'surface' conversation, but deprives us of the credit for the words and thoughts. And yet still, below the surface of the conversation, the agenda of the real me is the same, and this hidden agenda of my true self colours the prayer of the Psalms and the Scriptures as I speak to God, and as I try to understand what he is *really* saying to me. The words may not be our own, but they will carry on their backs the searchings, questionings and deepest movements of our inner selves as surely as any 'personal' prayer, but in a different and complementary way. Formal prayer is in this way a necessary counterbalance to 'personal' prayer.

In daily life communication through formal phrases has an important place. When two people meet in the street and stop to chat they perform a commonly shared ritual. 'Good morning', 'How are you?' and comments on the weather, politics and personal aches and pains draw on a tool-kit of formulas, clichés and sayings within a range of topics considered to be suitable. Yet real communication takes place beneath the surface of the stereotyped dialogue, as the participants breathe life into the stock phrases. Each will say the same things to the next person he or she meets, and much the same again tomorrow. Little or no information is conveyed, but communion takes place, in the same way as when we stroke the cat or embrace one another.

Physical formula, gifts and tokens

Controlled expression can be seen not merely in words, but also in physical rituals which divert the potentially chaotic emotions and urges behind human encounters into channels which render them manageable and capable of bearing fruit. In various ways rituals and small ritual acts meet a great need to mark occasions, to plant what we could call 'markers'. For example, someone calls on a neighbour that she is not so familiar with. The neighbour offers a cup of tea, which is gratefully accepted. Now both can relax. Without the tea the meeting would be formless and uneasy, if not threatening. Part of the importance of the meeting has been transferred to the cup of tea. The tea becomes the occasion for sitting down and talking, so the visitor can relax, for the spotlight has been taken off her and deflected onto the cup of tea; the duration of the conversation has been fixed to comprise the period the tea-drinking lasts. The tea 'marks' the occasion, giving anchorage, shape, and an exterior motive for staying, which frees the visitor from the need to make it known that 'I want to stay for a moment'. It is also of course a simple act of generosity. Hospitality by its nature involves giving and receiving.

Another very common use of 'markers' is to enable subjective feelings to have objective expression. When someone dies, great importance is attached to putting flowers on the dead person's grave, and perhaps having him or her commemorated at services in church. These things do more than give comfort to the mourners. They enable them to demonstrate to themselves the reality of what has happened, and to enact in physical form the drama of their experience. They provide something physical to relate to, an anchorage, fulfilling the need for something to be done. They mark and give significance to what otherwise is a mere absence. This is why such distress can be caused when a dead person's body is for any reason irrecoverable. There is nowhere to put the body or the ashes, nothing to incarnate the person's departure and establish it as visible fact, nothing on which to direct the emotions. Nothing has been *done*.

These are only two examples of symbolic games we need to play all the time in our daily life and naturally we will need to play the same games with God. Daily disciplines of prayer, and especially the daily office, are important for us – contact is made with God and is seen to be made. They are ways of marking, incarnating, what can feel to be an elusive relationship with God. They anchor what can be anxiousness about our relationship with him, and establish at the back of our mind the fact that we have made contact, however slight. The daily office is a procession of markers – marking, proclaiming to us and to the world that something has been done. The communion shared in this daily prayer works partly at the unconscious level, colouring the day and shaping the state of mind of the participants. When we miss, we notice it. Like the man who got up early and did not speak to his wife before going to work, it seems a long time since they last met, by the time evening comes. When we have been to evensong we feel it is a job well done: something offered. We might have been tired and inattentive, but the need to relate to God has been duly marked, the apparently insignificant handshake or peck has been given and received. We have to beware of thinking that that is enough, and lapsing into a round of cold formalities, but the principle remains sound that daily liturgical prayer has the ability to mark something which needs marking and leaves us restless until it is marked, while at the same time relieving us of the burden of being at the mercy of our own inadequacy. In the Church's liturgy the spotlight is taken off our faltering individual struggle and focused on the prayer itself, allowing us to tag along and relax, in an exercise shared by the community and the whole Church.

The symbols and 'markers' which we use in daily life also spring from the need to give, to offer something, to sacrifice. The gift to a friend, the flowers on the grave, the vegetables given to a neighbour over the garden fence, the candle in church, come from the natural impulse to generosity. For W. H. Vanstone, God is profoundly sensitive to our generosity or lack of it. The Church itself is an offering, our offering, and a part of this offering is our prayer. The daily prayer of the Church is in the last resort given as a disinterested gift, the least that love can do. God makes himself vulnerable by allowing himself to be dependent on our love.[31] The daily office, if seen as a gift offered without any thought of return, assumes a God who is not remote and unfeeling but sensitive to, and in a way dependent on, our capacity to love him; a God who is only too ready to respond to this daily proffering of 'markers' of our faltering love.

Such an idea of prayer as pure gift without any thought of return is quite alien to the spirit of the modern age. We cannot believe in a God who would want us to spend time on him alone, time which is unlikely to produce any practical results. In our worship we are the real ones in command. That is clear from the way services are so often conducted today. But we find it so difficult to believe in God anyway that we cannot connect pure worship with reality. Our worship often seems to be more like the meetings of a mutual help society in which God hovers in the background as a very important helper. The understanding of worship as pure gift, however, can only reduce us to silence as we realize we are in the presence of the living God.

Another trait of ours is to judge the value of services by the number of people who attend. If a priest wants to celebrate all the traditional liturgical services in Holy Week, but nobody comes, the notion of worship as disinterested gift by and on behalf of the whole community would make it entirely right, fitting and worthy for him to go ahead with the services on his own. Our worship finds it so difficult to rise to moments of totally disinterested offering without thought of any pay-off. Yet it is precisely those moments which are a proclaiming and a celebration of the fact that God is there. Worship offered as pure gift to the beloved is worship indeed.

To sum up, prayer shares with ordinary everyday encounters between human beings a dependence on objective formula; this applies not only to words, but also to symbol and gesture.

5

Work and Play

Work

The players in a string quartet sit in a circle, concentrating on the score and playing their instruments. Their mental and physical activity is skilful, interpreting a code and transmitting it into corresponding sounds. They also give of themselves, and there are times when the music 'takes off' and becomes something greater and more powerful than the mere sum of their activities, as if they have enabled a flame to burst spontaneously into their midst which has a life all of its own, catching them up in itself. The framework is mundane: an ordinary room, four chairs, four music-stands, some dog-eared music-sheets, four well-worn instruments, four human bodies with their imperfections and ailments, and four minds perhaps preoccupied with family and financial problems, and, finally, behind the music hours and years of careful practice. The heights the music reaches will be the fruit of dogged, unromantic preparation and humdrum discipline.

Perhaps in a similar way the daily liturgical prayer of the Church functions as a framework or apparatus within which the Holy Spirit makes himself known, a framework consisting largely of work. Any practice missed debilitates the musician or sportsman, and any unit of prayer-discipline which is missed takes us time to recover from. The spiritual muscles have been allowed by one degree to lapse into flabbiness.

Marriage has to be worked at. So does friendship. Sigmund Mowinckel points out the semantic connection between 'cult' and 'cultivation'. Even in Hebrew it is there. The word for service – '*abodah* – can mean the servant serving his lord, the man serving God, the beast of burden doing its work, and the farmer cultivating, ploughing his field.[32] The Latin *servitium* – service, the Germanic *Dienst*, and the Slavonic *slujba* can all mean both serving and working, and also a religious act of worship. In the cult, Mowinckel continues, man is concerned with a 'someone' who is 'served', who must be cultivated, attended to, whom man needs, to whom he is bound and with whom he maintains and preserves this association, and with whom he 'cultivates' intercourse.

Such cultivation, whether of music, sport, fields, or of God himself, is *work*.

Being a Christian is no fairy-tale romance. It has to be worked at, and sometimes we have to work hard. The concert pianist knows that for good or ill he is landed with his daily practice, husband and wife know they are landed with each other, and Christians know in just the same way that such is their commitment to God. There is no justification for escape from the daily sacrifice, the effort of giving, or for time off when we feel like it. A test of the healthiness of our daily relationship with God is how comfortable it is. If our religion fits like a perfect shoe, if it runs smoothly without too much trouble, these may well be signs that we have not yet found the way from the broad road which leads in the wrong direction, and on to the strait and narrow. Christ offers us a yoke, a burden, which will become light only by taking it up. Therefore the Christian way of prayer is a way of testing, a drawing forward through exercise which stretches us, exercising our spiritual muscles somewhat more than is comfortable. The New Testament speaks not of coasting along in prayer, but of *persevering* in it (for example Acts 6.4; Rom. 12.2; Col. 4.2), implying keeping our nose to a grindstone which we would rather like to have a rest from, and presupposing reaching forward, effort and cost. This is part of what St Benedict must have been angling at when he referred to daily prayer by a name which seems to have been traditional: *Opus Dei* – the Work of God. As if to illustrate it, a Cistercian monk has been moved to utter these words:

When I think of the five hours I spend in choral prayers every day they seem like a huge mountain of sand I drag over to God.[33]

However beautiful, moving and rich the worship might be, day-by-day repetition eventually takes us through the top layer of the 'onion' to more intractable layers beneath. Even those who are attracted by the majesty and beauty of Orthodox worship find the eventual result to be this. Aesthetic feelings and the apparent *experience* of receiving God's grace eventually fall away, and one has to soldier on regardless, accepting the fact that such things may from now on only be granted intermittently. If we persevere in faith, however, we find that with time deeper, less readily identifiable fruits have been granted. Thomas Merton, speaking of the writers of the 'Benedictine centuries', says:

They see, quite realistically and altogether in the spirit of St Benedict himself, that all life on earth must necessarily combine elements of action and rest, bodily labour and mental illumination. It is sometimes necessary to practise a laborious, arid and unconsoling form of prayer; at others one may receive grace and light almost without effort, provided that one is sufficiently well disposed. This *vicissitude* (the term is from St Bernard) or variation between labour and rest cuts across the dividing line between communal and private prayer, and is found, quite obviously, in both.[34]

Play

Work is inseparable from play. A musician will not practise unartistically; nor can he play for fun without having to work physically. The string quartet, by means of hard work and a formal framework, *plays*. The framework is essential. J. Huizinga, in his famous book *Homo Ludens*, comments on the importance of rules for any sport. It is important that everything should be provided. This allows the participants to cope with the one essential, to give of their best. For athletes the ground is clearly mapped out, the rules are clear, if arbitrary, even senseless in themselves. But they set the participants free to *be* – they do not have to worry about practical details – all is settled for them, just as in daily liturgical prayer everything is previously fixed and ready for use. Sportsmen have described the heights that this liberty-to-be can take them to. Cricketers can speak of moments when the batsman feels a sense of oneness with the bowler, as if they have found a wavelength where their opposition becomes unity. Runners have described similar experiences of a sense of transcendence, and of unity with all things. People at the height of the sporting profession can sometimes use language similar to that of the mystics. For Huizinga, the sportsman plays with devoted seriousness and with the courage of inspiration, but he plays, and knows that he plays. The violinist experiences the holiest excitement, a world outside and above the usual, and yet her work remains play.

But all of life is play. When children play at being doctors and nurses or cowboys and Indians, they so enter into their play that it becomes real. We never lose this faculty – it figures much more in our lives than we realize. In football, intense emotions go into a struggle which seems to be of life-and-death proportions, but a short while later it is forgotten. The emotion that can go into overtaking a car when driving is often pure play, and out of all proportion to the life-and-death risks involved. Our homes are pure theatre. There is no practical need for wallpaper on the walls, or even plaster, but this scenery is essential to the elaborate play which expresses home life. Even our job, our commitments, the layout of our towns and their systems of government can all be understood as an elaborate game, the creation of a world around us which we need as a framework within which to be ourselves. Back in the heady days of the 1960s a Frenchman was able to write:

All society is a theatre. Whether one is lawyer, doctor, porter, minister, or labourer, each plays a role. It is not enough to do one's work. One must also conform to the appropriate ceremonial. All society is made up of a mythic representation of human relations...[35]

Strikes are therefore not simply economic or political, but a 'violation of the sacrosanct rules of the social theatre. It is as if the theatre technicians ... interrupted the play of the actors, in order to put on another play in their very own style.'

The human spirit needs to act and to play, and dangers arise if we begin to take all this theatre as if it were itself serious reality, rather than a game through which we approach the truly serious mystery of what it means to be alive and human on this earth. Modern Western society tends to see *itself* as a simple goal, rather than an elaborate game by confused human creatures looking for security. So material well-being, security and personal 'freedom' become ends in themselves, and we avoid looking below the surface to the true agenda.

This failure to see the extent to which all of life is a game has its own baleful effect on liturgy. Game and reality are inseparable. One without the other results in shallowness. We can take liturgy so seriously that we have to perform it meticulously and correctly, indifferent to whether those present are enabled to relate with heart, mind and soul to the Lord. We are unable to celebrate it sensitively and release that in it which is of the height or depth of joy, sorrow and all that is at the vital heart of life and the Christian gospel. We cannot throw our whole being into it because we can only do that when we *play*. Conversely, we can take daily life as serious reality and see liturgy as 'mere' game and therefore only of limited worth. Prayer and liturgy fail to be as serious a business as daily life, except when they can be connected to its 'real' concerns. This, too, leaves us far from the heart of reality.

Play and serious reality cannot be put into separate compartments. They are inseparable. So when Christians celebrate the day's prayers with candles, flowers, incense, gestures and singing, with the full awareness that this is a game, and with the intention, as far as possible, of playing the game to the full, we are being fools in the best biblical understanding of the term, shaming the serious wisdom of a world which believes it is not playing games, and exulting in play as the most potent means for living life and the gospel to the full.

Play needs utter self-giving, and a half-hearted game will be a disappointment for everybody. Yet self-giving cannot be demanded, but only sought and encouraged. In a good game the players become completely lost and forgetful of themselves and of the time. But when they were first introduced to the game they may have been diffident and unsure, having to go through a kind of courtship before they reached the point where they could abandon themselves to it. Prayer needs a persevering courtship too, before we can begin to feel we are getting anywhere. But even then, if daily prayer 'feels good', it is not much like our idea of a good game of football. A growing sense of the benefits of the Church's daily worship will always be accompanied by the sense of hard work whose rewards are perceptible but not easy to put one's finger on. For many people it could best be described as a game based on work, which only makes sense over a long time-span, and within the context of the whole of the life it gradually comes to inform.

We always have to be careful, however, not to approach prayer with an intention of inducing some kind of religious experience. To take an example from piano-playing, earnest concentration on a particular goal can completely block the way to it. Continuous practice of a difficult passage can end in angry frustration. We believe we can tame the music by force, but in the end find that the road through the difficulty lies in abandoning ourselves to the music. In an off-hand performance on a later occasion we notice to our surprise that we have played the passage perfectly. This happens to us all the time in all kinds of activity, from typing to driving a car, from adding up figures to trying to remember somebody's name. The advice we need is, 'You are trying too hard'. We put too much faith in achieving things by manipulation, and are reluctant to abandon ourselves without thought of reward. So we are always tempted to specify the outcome of prayer in advance. Perhaps C. S. Lewis had this in mind when he wrote:

As long as you notice, and have to count the steps, you are not yet dancing but only learning how to dance. A good shoe is a shoe you don't notice. Good reading becomes possible when you do not consciously think about eyes, or light, or print, or spelling. The perfect liturgy would be one we were almost unaware of; our attention would have been on God.[36]

Proper piano practice follows a balanced, regular rhythm which stretches the player without being overtaxing. In Christian prayer this has been called 'discretion'. Only gradually can we learn to give of ourselves. In learning to do so in a discipline of daily prayer we may well have to start, not with very lofty intentions, but precisely at the humble level we are at; not with hopes of being taken up into the seventh heaven and of transfiguring all the problems of the world, but with very simple forms of prayer which we can enter into and enjoy. Starting here, we later allow the pressure to be put on, as the game becomes more demanding and challenging, fun cedes more ground to work, and we learn, gradually, to give. Prayer is a mirror and symbol of Christian living. In following Christ to the top of the mountain there comes a point where we have to exchange our soft slippers for stouter boots, which, in the course of much work and play, we will have to grow into.

6

Habeas Corpus

The word 'prayer' immediately evokes the thought of language. Some branches of the Reformation tried to reduce prayer to words, spoken with the voice, printed in books, and cogitated with the mind. All the churches of the Reformation, however, have been dominated by a simple association of the mental with the spiritual, and a reduction of physical and material ways of worship at best to the mere role of helpful back-up. Yet Protestantism only took to an extreme a common characteristic of all Western Churches, Reformed and Catholic: a tendency to see the ultimate essence of prayer as mental and 'spiritual' – 'interior prayer' is the best sort of prayer. Modern insights into human nature, however, force us to question such a naive division between spiritual and material. I am a psychosomatic unity. My mind, my body, and the environment in which they are set form between them an organic whole. Any search for the roots of prayer will therefore have to give attention to the part that our bodies and the physical world need to play in it.

The ancient legal principle of habeas corpus, which goes back at least to Saxon times, assumes that I am my physical body. This remains a basic principle of law today, so that if for some reason I am thrown into permanent coma, my sleeping body still constitutes the legal me, enjoying full legal rights. This body which is me wants its place in prayer. Physical expression and gesture are essential to integrated prayer, and one of the bones chewed over by the Liturgical Movement between the wars was this one. 'He who in liturgy stands, prays, offers up and acts is not the "soul", not the "inward", but "the man",' asserts Romano Guardini. 'Our nature means being Man; embodied spirit, ensouled body ... Our goal can only be to become a complete human being.' We express what is within us through outward things, and we receive into our inner selves things which are outwardly expressed. 'Human behaviour is symbolic behaviour', and the 'first task of liturgical education is that man must have once more the knack of the use of symbol.'[37] This symbol is no mere token, like a traffic-sign or a cigarette with a diagonal line through it. In true symbol, diverse levels of reality can be simultaneously held together in a counterpoint of meanings which can never be achieved by words alone. Symbol can, indeed, sometimes function alone, for words are not indispensable to worship. We can mime the Lord's Prayer, for instance, very effectively. Orthodox worship still retains much of its content when the language, to a visitor, is incomprehensible. There are without question times when words are unwelcome, or inappropriate. We can come to prayer so tired of the inane talk of modern life, or so empty inside, that any reciting of prayers, psalms or Bible-passages is beyond us. We have to persevere, but as a very last resort may have to close the book and sit in silence. Or we can be so full of what we want to say that words fail us. There are times in life, and hence in prayer too, when the right and sufficient thing is simply to be present. The notion of the significance of bodily presence at worship is an old one, based on a natural understanding of the value of our simply being in a place. Mary's physical presence was sufficient to Jesus, who felt it achieved more than Martha's exertions at the sink. The woman with a haemorrhage felt totally incapable of speaking to Jesus. All she could rise to was a momentary presenting of her body by touching his robe. He accepted it as a sign of faith, and encouraged her for her positive act. All she could give was her minimum, her body. Some of us have relatives or friends we feel we should visit now and again. We may not always be in the mood, and would prefer to be doing something else, but we go along and make the best of it, and they are pleased. Our physical presence is perhaps the most important thing we can give. We have presented our bodies, which can mean more than any amount of letters or phone-calls. Anatole France tells the story of an acrobat who went into a cathedral to pray and, not knowing how to use words, did what came naturally and stood on his hands before the altar.

Jungian psychology has a lot to teach us in this area, and one good introduction to this is to take part in a 'Myers Briggs workshop'. This provides a method for identifying our dominant preferences, and can reveal things which are surprisingly obvious once we have had them pointed out.[38] A striking example of this is relevant to our present discussion. Wide experience has shown the following traits in clergy and laity:

Dominant preferences in roughly 90 per cent of clergy	Dominant preferences in 75 per cent of the population
Interest in internal reactions	Interest in external events
Hunches	Experience
Speculation	Realism
Possible	Actual
Head-in-clouds	Down-to-earth
Imaginative	Sensible
Mental	Physical
etc.	etc.

The Church is run on the whole by people who are on a quite different wavelength from the majority of the population. This means that while clerics tend to talk about interior prayer, silence and meditation, about principles, ideas and future possibilities, most of the population can best respond to material, practical, present realities. While people represented in the first column live in a world of *possibilities*, those in the second column are engrossed in the present moment, as it is, *now*, before their eyes, touchable and usable by their hands. Neither is better than the other, just different. This is a caricature, to be sure, but it helps us to see why for most people the way in to prayer and the interior life will be via the physical, through having something to *do*. This does not mean that things stay there. Most of Jung's clients belonged to the second column, where there is a tendency to fail to work on one's inner life. This seems to suggest that, yes, Christians are called to seek the inner life, but in most cases it will start with physical, objective realities, and with very practical and matter-of-fact forms of prayer, moving on from that point to foster the inner life.

The first-column people do not emerge as angels: their problems are the reverse. They have to learn to live in the present moment, to be attentive to objective realities, and to pray objectively without always expecting internal 'experiences'. All Christian prayer, then, will have its subjective and objective strands usually woven together in a complex way. Yet it will not be surprising to find that sometimes prayer will seem to be totally subjective and internal, and that there will be other times when to all appearances it is entirely external and without 'feeling' or 'thought'. While both will be present in each of us, one or the other will tend to predominate.

Ritual and gesture are quite capable of functioning without an imprimatur from our conscious mind. So long as our prayer is 'interior' some of the time, the other times when it seems to be more 'exterior' are perfectly valid tracts of our long pilgrimage. When a mother kisses her children as they go off to school she may well be thinking about whether she will catch the bus to work in time, or about what to get for dinner. It certainly will not usually be like a scene from *Gone with the Wind*, and there would be something wrong if it were. We relate to each other quite sincerely at various levels of vacancy and simultaneous thought, and this is quite natural in prayer too. Mental wandering in prayer, so long as it is not chronic, should be accepted as quite natural, and understood as a part of the offering we are making to God, an offering of ourselves as we are.

We cannot be human this side of the veil without our body, and neither can we be Christian. We cannot love our neighbour or bring in the Kingdom. Even if my body is ill or housebound and apparently of little use, it is the sacrament of me to others, and through it come my words and gestures which are potential instruments of the Kingdom. It is a great mistake to believe we can leave our body out of prayer. Even sitting as still as a statue, there will be times when we are conscious of having to hold our body down. Even in very simple prayer by a group in a front room, small rites such as the use of candles, kneeling, the sign of the cross and the peace, can enable us to evoke the peace of God with our mortal bodies.

However we pray, sitting in a front-room chair, celebrating the liturgy in church, praying in a small group, or walking the fields, there will always be a sense that we are surrendering sovereignty over our body, as Jesus did every time he prayed and finally in Gethsemane and on the cross. When I walk into the times of prayer I am handing over the keys to God, who says, 'In your daily life you are the master and make all the decisions; here I am the Master.' Sometimes we are like a bucking bronco, and our daily discipline of prayer sits on us until we are quietened and attentive. Daily prayer includes the presenting, surrendering, of our bodies.

When I present my body to God in the liturgy, the setting is likely to be taken up with it. 'To express the spiritual to the full, the expressive abilities of the body, with its surfaces, lines and movements, its limbs and its form, are not enough. The human being spreads these out by taking the things around him into the sphere of his body.'[39] The parachute is an extension to the soldier's body, enabling him to fly, after a fashion. The violin is an extension of the musician's body through which the inner person is expressed in music; the house is the same thing to the family. We shall see below that the history of daily prayer frequently shows a joyful grasping of these facts, and we need not only to rediscover them but also to be convinced of their importance. A vicar in his study can hardly be expected to stage an audio-visual, psychosomatic experience twice a day, but even where the possibilities are limited, it is part of the wholeness of prayer to be conscious of the body and of its surroundings as part of the offering. The service celebrated in a circle in someone's living-room involves the room in its action, the family who live there, the immediate neighbours (whose television can be heard faintly through the wall), and all the aspects of daily life associated with the room.

The Church can pray anywhere, and has prayed in some strange places in its time, but at the heart of this prayer it needs to have symbolic places as points of reference, places which, like the violinist's instrument, become an extension of our body. There has been a necessary reaction in recent years against attaching too much importance to church buildings, but at some time we shall have to return to the proper balance, for the church building is consciously symbolic space which heightens and enriches the Church's prayer in a unique way: perhaps something like a concert hall, whose acoustics bring out resonances in the music which are lost in any ordinary room, so that the sound is richer and truer. A good concert hall enables the music to speak with a special freedom and be more than usually true to itself. A prayed-in church does the same with the prayers of those who pray.

Romano Guardini has analysed the meaning of special space in secular life. The home, with all its spaces, walls, furniture and decoration is interiorized by those who live there and is a part of them. The houses, streets and squares of their neighbourhood and home town come in next, and finally all that makes up their native country.[40] All these things help to make up what is me. They are part of me, and I am penetrated by them. This happens not only with individuals but with groups too. Not only is the family somewhat adrift if the house is temporarily unusable and they have to stay elsewhere: the scouts are lost without their own hut, a school would be greatly diminished if its lessons had to be held in a strange building, and a pub can lose its customers if it moves elsewhere. For any activities of significance, human nature needs characteristic spaces, where special symbols can be hung on the walls and stood on the floor, holding in a complicated, many-layered *presentness* what it all means. So in school the activities are enriched by a counterpoint with the pictures on the walls, the books, equipment and eccentricities in each classroom, and the richness or poverty of these symbols in a school can be a sign of how alive it is. The church building, similarly, is no optional extra like a weekend cottage. It amplifies and extends through specific symbol the prayers we offer in it. It will be as alive as we make it, and a church which is loved and prayed in proclaims it to the visitor immediately he walks in at the door.

In a sense the church building is the symbolic *body* of the Christians who use it. The daily office, seen as presenting our bodies as a living sacrifice, is not only an individual presentation of my body, but a presenting of the whole Body of Christ, and when celebrated in church the sense of that is greatly heightened.

Prayer, then, is something which commands the participation of the whole person, body, soul and setting, and includes the use of physical gesture and symbol. Our stock of such things is terribly depleted, and it will not be easy for us in our particular culture to recover the rich vocabulary of symbol and gesture which is required, and which can be found in other parts of the Church and in other religions. But at least if we can recognize the need, that is a beginning, a step towards liberation from that mental imprisonment which seems to overtake us whenever we pray, as if the incarnation had never happened.

7

One Body

We come now to a subject which will crop up frequently in this book: the relationship between private and public prayer. Making a distinction between them can be misleading. There are times when we pray alone and times when we pray with others, certainly. But the activity is always Christian prayer, one thing, not two. 'Private' prayer, in the strict sense of the word, is impossible for a Christian. So Cyprian was able to say:

Before all things the teacher of peace and master of unity would not have prayer to be made singly and individually; so that when one prays, he does not pray for himself alone. For we say not '*My* Father which art in heaven', nor 'give *me* this day *my* daily bread' ... Our prayer is public and common; and when we pray, we pray not for one, but for the whole people, because we the whole people are one.[41]

When we became Christians we ceased to be able to live entirely as private individuals. The hand cannot be a real hand apart from the body to which it belongs. In this way, all prayer is offered as part of the Church's prayer, and can never be a totally private thing. In the words of an Orthodox,

Nobody is a Christian by himself, but only as a member of the Body. Even in solitude, 'in the chamber', a Christian prays as a member of the redeemed community, of the Church.[42]

Whenever I am praying to God, millions of others are praying too. My prayer cannot possibly be in solitude. In his book *Towards the Unknown God* Petru Dumitriu describes the pilgrimage of unbelievable physical and mental suffering through which he has come from atheism towards a tentative belief in the God of Jesus. He arrives, independently of any doctrine, at this sense of the unity of all prayer:

Perhaps at this very moment, on other earths, in other solar systems belonging to other galaxies, other beings are turning in the same way as we do, or in an equivalent way, towards God: the silence of the abyss contains, perhaps, an infinite murmuring of prayers.

I do not know. But I do know that human beings are praying at this very moment, and always have been. I do not believe there is one single second of time in which there is not one human soul at prayer ...

... Let us think of those who think of us without knowing us, let us think of those who pray, of all the silent multitude of souls at prayer. We are not alone. In solitude, silence, forsakenness, in the sleep of matter, the sound and the fury of suffering, of birth, of coupling, of despair, of evil and of good, there is everywhere the peace of prayer, everywhere glimmers of grace; there is the Church of souls.[43]

The prayers of this throng, this company of voices, are seen by the author of Revelation as the praise rendered to God by the whole of creation:

Then I heard every created thing in heaven and on earth and under the earth and in the sea, all that is in them, crying: Praise and honour, glory and might, to him who sits on the throne and to the Lamb for ever and ever! And the four living creatures said, Amen, and the elders fell down and worshipped.[44]

Not only do all our prayers focus in on God, and become united there, but their source also is one. 'I live no longer, but Christ lives in me' (Gal. 2.20). It is the one Christ who prays in all of us. So Augustine could say:

When the Body of the Son prays, the head is not separated from the body. It is the one saviour of his body, our Lord Jesus Christ, who prays for us, prays in us, and is prayed to by us.[45]

This notion of all prayer being the prayer of the Church was particularly well expressed by Peter Damian (1007–72) in a little book entitled *The Lord be with you*, written for the guidance of hermits in their recitation of the daily office.

The hermit life is somewhat different from what is popularly imagined. It is the practice of withdrawing into solitude, alone or with a small group, for short or longer periods, in order to direct all the attention to prayer. (Permanent withdrawal into absolute solitude is very rare.) The frontiers of life will always find individuals wanting to challenge them: people 'crazy enough' to climb mountains, sail round the world in tiny boats, or explore potholes or the mouths of volcanoes. It is therefore only to be expected that some will be 'mad enough' to throw all their energy into exploring the frontiers of prayer. 'The hermit is simply a pioneer ... in the way of the desert which the whole of humanity must follow of necessity one day, each one according to his measure and his desire. This eremitical vocation, at least embryonically, is to be found in every Christian vocation, but in some it must be allowed to come to its full flowering in the wind of the Spirit. It is not enough to affirm that the thing is good in itself, it is necessary that Church and society do something, so that this life may be realizable, so that each may at least touch it, be it only with the tip of his little finger.'[46] The eremitical life has something to say to all of us, and certainly to those of us who pray alone. Peter Damian writes:

... the Church of Christ is united in all her parts by such a bond of love that her several members form a single body and in each one the whole Church is mystically present;

so that the whole Church universal may rightly be called the one bride of Christ, and on the other hand every single soul can, because of the mystical effect of the sacrament, be regarded as the whole Church . . .

If we look carefully through the fields of the Holy Scriptures we will find that one man or one woman often represents the Church. For though because of the multitude of her peoples the Church seems to be of many parts, yet she is nevertheless one and simple in the mystical unity of one faith and one divine baptism . . . Holy Church is one in all her members, and complete in each of them; her many members form a single whole in the unity of faith, and her many parts are united in each member by the bond of charity and the various gifts of grace, since all of these proceed from one source . . .

If, therefore, those who believe in Christ are one, then wherever we find a member according to outward appearances, there, by the mystery of the sacrament, the whole body is present. And so whatever belongs to the whole applies in some measure to the part; so that there is no absurdity in one man saying by himself anything which the body of the Church as a whole may utter, and in the same way many may fittingly give voice to that which is properly said by one person . . .

Whatever is reverently offered up in God's service by any member of the Church is sustained by the faith and devotion of the whole body, since the Spirit of the Church, which gives life to the whole body which is preserved by Christ its Head, is one . . . And so it is good that whatever action in the holy offices is performed by any one section of the faithful should be regarded as the common act of the whole Church, joined in the unity of faith and the love of charity . . .

Now just as the Greeks call man a microcosm, that is to say a little world, because his body is comprised of the same four elements as the universe itself, so each of the faithful is a little Church . . .

[The priest] sees as present with the eyes of the spirit all those for whom he prays, whether or not they are actually there in the flesh; he knows that all who are praying with him are present in spiritual communion. And so the eye of faith directs the words of his greeting and he realizes the spiritual presence of those whom he knows to be near at hand. Therefore let no brother who lives alone in a cell be afraid to utter the words which are common to the whole Church; for although he is separated in space from the congregation of the faithful yet he is bound together with them all by love in the unity of faith; although they are absent in the flesh, they are near at hand in the mystical unity of the Church.[47]

The individual as a microcosm of the Church, as someone who, even in solitude, prays with the Church, is a theme which can be detected through the history of Christian liturgical prayer. One thing it achieves is to support the efforts of the one who prays. Knowing that we are not alone, we realize that our small effort, poor as it seems, does not stand or fall by its own apparent success or failure. We know that we are part of an infinitely larger operation which is shared, and therefore we are supported. Attention is taken away from me and my struggle, so that God seems much less enormous and forbidding. It is as if I were a homely but not very brilliant violinist. If asked to perform on stage before a critical audience, I would play stumblingly and with a great sense of inadequacy. But if I were to play in an orchestra, I would not only be happier to play, but would do it much better in the more reassuring circumstances. Knowledge that the Church is praying with me also enables me to cope with the times when I find it impossible to pray through fatigue or 'dryness' – I will know the prayer in which I have a stake is still going on. It is said that Russian churches are built to be seen from afar because once the snows come there will be little chance of getting there. The parishioners will still be able to see the church, however, inside which the priest is saying the prayers.[48] The prayer of Christ in his Church conjures up the image of Jacob's ladder – angels and people go up and down it perpetually, and we step on to it whenever we want. John Macquarrie puts it thus:

The cosmic significance of prayer has been recognized in various ways in the Christian tradition. The prayer of the Church has been understood as part of the response of all creation to God and as joined 'in a wonderful order' with the adoration of angels, who may be taken as representative of the whole range of rational and spiritual beings who have existed or do exist or will exist in this universe in addition to the race of men. 'The real significance of the divine office', wrote Evelyn Underhill, 'is that in its recitation the individual or group enters the ancient cycle of prayer, by which day by day and hour by hour the Church in the name of all creation adores and implores the eternal God.'[49]

We have to be careful not to misunderstand this. Such talk of praying with the Church can be misleading if it suggests that we must have a grand mystical experience of angels whenever we pray. In practice it does not necessarily mean any direct sensation of praying with others. Romano Guardini explains that 'the individual has to become quite detached from the need to "feel" the togetherness – we are dealing here not with experiences but with training, with a conscious state of mind *which must be learnt*' (my italics).[50] As we persevere with this training in shared prayer, we will reach a stage where it means a lot to us and becomes very real. From there it passes down into the less conscious mind where it becomes 'part of the furniture'. These stages vary according to our situation. A solitary priest in a difficult town parish will be very conscious of the support and strength he receives from knowing he is praying with the Church. It will be central to his approach to all prayer and worship. But it will be very different for the monks or nuns in a monastic choir, where all centres on 'The Life', whose most concrete expression is *this* community and *this* tradition. For them the sense of praying with the Church will be just as important, but different, hidden among a whole range of understandings, and not specially emphasized.

In either case we are not talking about a crude whipping-up of some feeling which does not come naturally, but something like the player in a football team who will naturally fall into saying 'we' rather than 'I', or married people who will without any prompting talk of 'us' rather than 'me'. They use the singular too, of course, but constant 'I' and 'me' will be evidence that all is not well, and in the Church it is just the same, not least with prayer.

If football and marriage throw light, so can other areas of common endeavour. In trying to explain the point of the daily office, comparison is sometimes made with the soldier's drill. The image of the Christian as soldier has had a long and rich history, from St Paul to Ignatius of Loyola and the Salvation Army. It can no longer be so attractive in an age more sensitive to the brutality and senselessness of war, but if we make allowances for that, we can still find it a helpful image.

There are two basic modern types of drill. *Close-order drill* rehearses the movements and formations of formal marches, parades and ceremonies. *Combat drill* is used to train small units in the looser, more extended formations and movements necessary in battle. There are some parallels in both with what goes on in prayer and liturgy. First, drill aims to form reflex actions so that the soldier can respond without wavering in circumstances which can be difficult and disturbing, and where it is essential to move with confidence. A long-maintained discipline of prayer can have a similar effect, giving us a foundation in Scripture and prayer which will come into its own in times of difficulty. Prayer ought never to be approached as a mere means to some practical end; but a common characteristic of those who pray is that they can be a source of strength when those around them can no longer cope, and that they will have resources within them which otherwise they would not have had. It is not possible either to generalize or to claim any Christian monopoly on goodness or heroism, but the least we can say is that many of us who do pray within the Church's discipline of prayer are better equipped for the crises of life than we otherwise would have been.

Secondly, the soldier's drill, as well as shaping reflexes, develops character. The individual learns to control every action in order to co-ordinate them with the actions of others. It enables one to accept both the discipline laid on one from outside and that self-discipline which stems from within. Prayer, if it is to have any backbone to it, will include an element of submission, of staying faithful to that which has been commonly decided, regardless of the moods of the moment, and a committed self-discipline which will in the long run permeate other parts of our Christian life. So the nun or monk finds that submission to the burden of the daily office helps to cultivate a self-discipline and a commitment to respecting the common will, which in the world would be seen as intolerable slavery, but to those who live it is a doorway to life in all its fullness. Except, that is, if the person is not really made for the monastic life, or is going about it in the wrong way. Then the daily office can be a fruitless exercise.

Wise guidance and the monastic traditions of 'discretion' are necessary for any who undertake Christian disciplines of prayer. The athletic training of which St Paul speaks in 1 Corinthians 9 can easily be distorted into a binding of people with burdens which the gospel came to abolish.

Thirdly, drill develops an army's corporate spirit, and its members' allegiance to their unit, their regiment, and through them to the whole force. It helps to instil a sense of corporate pride. This is particularly true of close-order drill, and the pride engendered and expressed in common effort and spit and polish is potent in any army, stirring its members to a spirit of confidence and good cheer. Daily liturgical prayer can be a morale-builder, encouraging confidence and pride in the Church – not as the power-seeking human institution which it so often is, but as the mystical Body of the Christ who desires to lead his Church out of all its imperfections. Pride in him is poles apart from that churchy jingoism which sometimes deforms his Body. It is a pride which springs out of reverence, and is grounded in worship.

The greatly revered Eucharist and the frequent daily prayers of the early Christians enabled them to maintain a sense of solidarity in a hostile or uncomprehending environment. As we shall see, the daily office itself quickly became an important means of keeping priest and community together in the kind of framework which they needed, and maintaining a corporate sense of the Church. It has the capacity to build up such a sense, and to produce an interior formation which will affect the way we respond to life and its incidents. It also puts the local Body of Christ in proportion: most of us gain our primary experience of the Church from our local Christian congregation. This experience can be limiting, and needs to be set in its wider context, the household of the Church Universal, in past, present and future, militant here on earth and glorified in the presence of God.

Our individual prayer is put in its due proportion too. In the music of Christian prayer there may be occasional solos, but none of the instruments is ever played 'privately' or 'personally' in a narrow sense. All are taken up together in a symphony of immeasurable beauty and sorrow, struggle and joy, illuminated from within and above by the quickening fire of the eternal Son. R. P. L. Thomassin (1619–95) has put it this way:

The thought which occupies us most during the Divine Office and should bring about in us the most deepfelt love, is this: Jesus Christ lives in us, his members. He quickens us with his Holy Spirit; for us and in us he continually brings to his Father a sacrifice of praise. He unites us with himself and his Sonship, so that we are ... children of God.[51]

Now all of these insights, from everyday experience, from the fruits of suffering, from the experience of hermits, from music, marriage, football, life in the army, and the day-to-day prayer of the divine office, witness in their very different ways to certain truths about the nature of life as we actually experience it, and truths which are, even more strikingly, at the heart of the gospel. The blessed Trinity stands at the centre of all things, at the place where love is eternally shared in an eternal circle of relating, where the one is many, and many become one. It was the purpose of Christ that we should be taken up into the life of the Trinity – 'Father, may they be one in us, as you are in me and I am in you.'[52] In this way Christ was able to speak of himself as the vine and ourselves as the branches. St Paul elucidated this further in his image of the Body with its many members, none of which lives unto itself, but all are taken up in the life of the whole Body, of which Christ is the head.[53] In another way Christ is the entire Body itself, we are his hands and his voice on earth, the Church is the continuance of his incarnation and resurrection. When we pray, therefore, it is not simply we who pray, but Christ prays in us, takes us up into the eternal circle of the divine love. These themes are frequently taken up by the Fathers and by spiritual writers down the centuries, and have only dimmed in our sight with the comparatively recent advent of our excessive individualism. We are not here talking about a negating of the individual in favour of the mass – it is simply that we have got the balance wrong. We talk so incessantly about *my* faith, *my* ministry, *my* needs in worship, my everything, that we are like a listing ship. It needs a profound change in our consciousness, so that we may come to pray from our hearts in such words as these by Charles Wesley, who was steeped in the Scriptures and the Fathers:

> See where our great High-Priest
>   Before the Lord appears,
> And on his loving breast
>   The tribes of Israel bears,
> Never without his people seen,
> The head of all believing men.

> With him, the corner-stone,
>   The living stones conjoin;
> Christ and his Church are one,
>   One body and one voice;
> For us he uses all his powers,
> And all he has, or is, is ours.[54]

In all too brief a way we have described how it is possible to see the peculiarities of liturgical, formal daily prayer as no peculiarities at all, but facts of human everyday life. If such use of myth and story, form, rhythm, formula, work and play, physical gesture and symbol, and a sense of common endeavour are all so important, we must now turn to examine the role they have played in the history of Christian prayer.

PART II

The History of Daily Prayer

8

The Beginnings

The birth of the Christian Church was a hectic event. The Church of Pentecost was a message rather than an organization, springing green from its Jewish soil in a reckless, energetic outpouring of the Spirit. The Church's leaders and missionaries got on with what they burned to do, but had they stopped to consider, they might well have frozen in their tracks at the thought of the task before them. With an immense and ancient tradition behind us of communally recorded experience, we can hardly imagine what the difficulties must have been for the Church's pioneers in evolving structures, clarifying the truths to be held, and keeping together a popular movement spreading through the known world, in the absence of any adequate means of communication to co-ordinate the effort. There were no New Testament, no church buildings, no precedents to turn to in solving unexpected problems, no way of foreseeing misunderstandings, wrangles and dilemmas that would arise. This is the situation out of which Christian liturgy was born, very far from the serene, idealized picture we sometimes imagine.

In the effort to hold things together liturgy will have played a vital role. Converts needed simple, urgent formation in the faith if they were to put down roots in this still inchoate body, the Church, and it is perhaps in such a fervent and crash-programme atmosphere that we should see the origin of the discipline of praying at fixed points throughout the day. The initial gusto could eventually fizzle out. So we hear calls to persevere, to pray without ceasing, to conserve by frequent prayer the flame of faith. Christians are to strain forward like the athlete, lest they should slip back. As enthusiasm began to lose its head of steam, discipline stepped in for the husbanding of spiritual resources, and to provide structures for what enthusiasm could not indefinitely maintain.

The evolution of disciplines within the Church was related to a powerful sense of *belonging*. In a world where the individual was held to be of little account, Jesus' vision of the one Body, of the vine with its branches, must have come up to ordinary people like a Rolls-Royce car to a footsore tramp. Suddenly each person learned they were somebody, because made in the image of a God who numbers even the hairs of our head, and they learned that the Kingdom of heaven itself was their inheritance. 'Once you were no people, but now you are God's people' (1 Pet. 2.10).

The New Testament (3) is steeped in this sense of belonging, and this permeated people's worship and prayer no less than their thoughts. Instances of prayer with others far outweigh those of people praying in solitude. Even alone in the wilderness the Lord will hardly have forgotten the people he came to save. In Gethsemane it was tragically important to him to know if the disciples were awake and praying with him. Peter on the housetop at Joppa prayed not as an 'individual' – even if he had understood that idea, he would have rejected it. Christ and his Body the Church will have coursed through all his prayers and determined his sense of himself as a person. Any parish priest today knows how much that is true. In his study of worship in the New Testament, D. G. Delling remarks that 'from the common worship there proceeds an energizing over the whole range of the life of the "individual" (who indeed is no longer an individual): he is ... always joined with the brethren by the ties of the life of worship'.[1] In New Testament times the Church will have run in restless counterpoint through the prayers of the Christian individual.

Our information on how the first Christians prayed is very piecemeal. We can deduce with moderate certainty that there was an early break with the synagogue, by AD 90 at the latest in Palestine. People met instead for regular meals, at which on the Lord's Day at least the Eucharist was celebrated. As they evolved their own ways of worship they were inevitably conditioned by what they were used to. Jesus gave them an example in the Last Supper, but also in various pieces of guidance on how to pray, and in the habits of common prayer he built up with the disciples. He was not one to go into the finer points of detail, however, and seems to have left his followers to find their own way in matters of practical organization. They, either Jewish or Gentile in upbringing, brought all their cultural-religious baggage to bear in finding their way.

We can find many Jewish elements in the forms of worship which eventually arose, but it is difficult to say how far these are a direct inheritance from the synagogue (1). Until the end of the first century Jewish belief and practice varied so much from place to place, and group to group in any one place, that talk of inheritance from 'the synagogue' as some homogeneous entity is not really possible.[2] Obviously, some continuity was inevitable, the mere retention of the Old Testament being of colossal importance before anything else, and liturgical continuity is clearly to be seen in the eucharist. But the practices of daily prayer which gradually developed show no cast-iron evidence for continuity with any practices in the first-century synagogue. We are not at all certain that Jewish public services took place daily on any scale outside the Temple, and if they did, the Christians seem to have given them up rather than take them over, for we have no reference to daily public worship in the Church before the fourth century. Even the Psalter was only gradually discovered, and in the early period we only have evidence of its use at table – for ordinary and religious meals.

It is likely that the Christians' daily prayers followed fairly stereotyped patterns, though evidence on 'private' prayer is thin in most periods of history, and it is impossible to say with any certainty what form these daily prayers of the early Church would have taken. They were offered mainly in the home, or by individuals wherever they happened to be. Later evidence implies that in the home there was a rich prayer-life in which, where possible, all the family shared.[3] Mealtimes were surrounded by prayer. Thanksgiving (*berakah*) was given over the food, and psalms and hymns were sung before and after the meal. All our references to psalms in the first century are connected with meal- *biblical* times. Clement of Alexandria describes people singing psalms to each other at table,[4] a practice earlier alluded to in Ephesians 5.19 and Colossians 3.16.

The hours of prayer reported in Acts are problematic (3). At most they could reflect only local practice at the time of writing, but these random references to prayer at the third, sixth and ninth hours are not enough in themselves to establish that Luke was used to daily services or private prayer at these hours. Indeed, it is by no means certain that there were universally recognized, publicly marked divisions of the day under the Romans,[5] and the incidence of these hours of prayer occurs so early and so widely in Christian history that it is very tempting to read them that little bit further back to apostolic times, something for which available evidence gives little justification. They could just as easily have grown up later as devotional practices to mark the stages of the passion, and to imitate the apparent practice of the apostles in Acts – in the early centuries terce, sext and none in particular were regularly associated with both.

It may seem unhelpful to be so cautious, but with a subject as enigmatic as Christian daily prayer we must have the poverty of the evidence clear in our *2nd century* minds before resorting to conjecture. The history of liturgy is often muddied by anachronistic tendencies to read back into the past developments which only arose later. While it may possibly be true that the hours of prayer go back to apostolic times and the synagogue, we should be clear in our minds about the fact that very little can be said on this subject with certainty. Not until the second century does evidence begin to appear of a pattern of daily prayer-times. From then on we receive fairly consistent references to prayer in the morning, at the third, sixth and ninth hours, in the evening, in the middle of the night, and at cockcrow (4 onwards). (The final two hours of prayer need some clarification. It was an acceptable and widespread custom for people to get up in the middle of the night to pray for a while and then return to bed. Distinct from this was a practice of rising some time before the light in order to greet the dawning day with prayer, as the Lord did in Mark 1.35. The proportion of direct and oblique references in the New Testament to prayer in the hours of darkness is large (3), and this preoccupation with the night was to endure until the monks came to specialize in it in the fourth century. Then it declined among the laity, who resented later attempts to revive it.) People would have prayed vocally, standing with their hands raised. Origen and Tertullian tell us in addition that there were 'prescribed prayers' (7, 8) but we have no information on the content of such prayers until much later. All of these times of prayer were usually, as far as we can see, private or domestic. They were obviously observed by many, especially bishops, clergy and devout people, but it is impossible to say how far ordinary people kept them.

It seems obvious to seek a connection between these early Christian hours of prayer and the fixed prayer-times observed by devout Muslims. While it is difficult to find positive evidence of an inheritance by Islam of prayer-disciplines known to Christians, the idea of saying prayers at certain hours of the day was a part of the common background of Judaism and Christianity. Muhammad had contact with both Jews and Christians in Arabia, and similarities in prayer customs with some Middle Eastern Christian groups are remarkable enough to suggest a link. The influence may well have come from monasticism, for there are traditions which mention contact between Muhammad and a Christian hermit. Research on this subject could well throw light on the Christian side of the story.[6]

The public cult

Morning and evening prayer were the principal prayer-times, and at some stage they were transformed into public services. Eusebius of Caesarea (?260–340) is the first to mention this (11), and from the advent of Constantine and the peace of the Church this public daily office became a universal norm. Christianity suddenly found itself donning the shoes of the old gods, and mass conversions brought in people of varying commitment, more likely to be sanctified by attractive and imaginative services than by a private discipline which no longer had the strong back-up of the small, committed sect. So the daily prayer-times went public, which is not to say that some people did not still observe some of them at home, for we know that they did. These new public services did not attempt to keep to the old private scheme of six or seven hours of prayer. They homed in on those natural turning-points of the day, the morning and evening. The 'morning and evening hymns', as the services were known, rapidly became an institution everywhere in East and West, popular services attended daily by people in large numbers. Staged in the large new churches being erected in the towns and cities, these services made all the use they could of music, ceremony, visual effect and audience-participation. They were strictly hierarchical, each order from bishop downwards having its allotted part. There were no books, so the content had to be simple, most of it being fixed and invariable, the people joining in through the use of simple refrains, both in the psalmody (known, confusingly, as 'hymns') which made up the body of the service, and the litany which concluded it.

Ever since Anton Baumstark's coining of the term, the public office which arose at this time has been referred to as a 'cathedral office' to distinguish it from the daily offices of the monks. This presents problems in so far as the public office of the Church was not long confined to cathedrals. The word 'office', while failing to reflect the air of celebration of these services, is useful in indicating a public service which is liturgical and part of an ordered daily round; the problem is, rather, in finding an appropriate adjective. The services are 'public', 'ecclesial', 'community', 'congregational', 'parish', 'secular'; but perhaps they are above all worship for the people, and in two senses: (a) the worship of the assembled people of God, the *ecclesia*, and (b) worship for ordinary people, the *plebs*. A term which seems to suggest itself therefore is 'people's office'. None of the eligible terms is entirely satisfactory, but on balance this appears to be most adequate, and I shall use it from now on.

The people's office has to be distinguished from the monastic office which arose out of it (not vice versa). While the subject of this book is the people's office, it is impossible to understand it without giving some attention to its monastic counterpart: for the story which unfolds is one of a dialectic between the two, each quickly coming to be indebted to the other. At this point, therefore, we need to look briefly at the distinguishing characteristics of the people's office and the monastic office.

9

Monasticism

The monastic ideal finds its roots in the primal experience of the Christian Church, and the close-knit, committed life of communities of believers in the apostolic era. In any period Christian congregations have had some members who are more committed than the majority, and from very early on there were those who wished to live a life of particular asceticism and commitment, even to the extent of renouncing marriage and family ties. Such people came to be known by various names, one of the most common being the devout or *devoti*.[7] Things later thought to be typical of monasticism were part of normal life in local Christian communities. Only subsequently did those who led a more rigorous life, consecrated entirely to the Church, begin to separate off from the congregation. By the third or the fourth century such *devoti* had begun to evolve strong liturgical characteristics of their own, especially in Syria, and were beginning to live in community rather than as individuals, while they continued to worship in the local church.

Into this current came a strong injection from the side, arising from the eccentric flight of hermits to the desert in the third and fourth centuries, especially in Egypt. This considerably sharpened the whole picture, raising the business of commitment to a more dramatic and aggressively challenging plane. The enduring legacy of the Egyptian hermits was twofold. They left behind them a tradition of ripe wisdom with a sharp cutting edge, to remain a fundamental source of inspiration in the future history of the religious life. In the second place they brought a new and surprising approach to prayer and worship. The Egyptian hermits had no daily office, but centred their whole waking life on perpetual recitation of the Psalter. As far as we know, this had had no place in Christian worship until then.

When the hermits came to be organized in centralized communities under Pachomius (*c.* 290–346), their times of common prayer developed from this tradition, taking no account of the secular hours of prayer. Their 'services' were in essence simply communal meditation on the Psalter, read through, as the hermits were accustomed, in numerical order. There were only two of them, in the morning and the evening (36, 37). The day was given over to work, the monks continuing on their own the recitation of the Psalter as they worked.

These services were daily in Pachomius' monasteries, but in lower Egypt they normally seem to have taken place on Saturdays and Sundays. Otherwise they were prayed individually in the monks' cells.

It seems fair to say on the basis of this that two types of monastic office were to be found in these early years: the daily services of the *devoti* centring on the services of the local church, and the rigorous ascetic labours of the Egyptians, perpetually running off the whole Psalter in their desert exile. This Egyptian type of monasticism was to spread to Europe, finding particularly sympathetic soil among the British and Irish Celts, but in the end fading out with no direct heirs outside Egypt itself (42). The *devoti* were to be the model for the future, heavily impregnated, however, with the ideals, and in part the practices, of the Egyptian monks, for as these *devoti* began to distance themselves from their 'parish' base they came to discover some of the virtues of the Egyptian way of prayer. It was in this type of monasticism that a hybrid daily office thus developed, a mixture of people's and monastic prayer which was to set the parameters for monastic worship in the future.

It will probably help at this point to list the distinguishing characteristics of the two poles of prayer, people's and monastic. First, however, it needs to be said that it is misleading to talk of a 'monastic office' as if it were some independent species. All we can speak of are trends to which the epithet 'monastic' can reasonably be applied. These trends cannot simply be assumed in monastic worship, and we must be careful to distinguish in any case between Egyptian monasticism and the other types which evolved in Palestine and elsewhere. Indeed, the question of whether the Egyptian gatherings can be called 'offices' as such is an open one. Adalbert de Vogüé contends that they cannot, but were merely opportunities for performing together the continuous psalmody which the Egyptians would be reciting continuously throughout the day anyway.[8] Bearing these qualifications in mind, the table overleaf lists some typical preferences in the two strands.

The bases on which these distinctions can be made will emerge as we proceed, but it will be helpful to elucidate one or two of them here:

1, *Principal services*: the 'lesser hours' were in origin a discipline for all Christians (in theory), as we have seen. They failed, however, to become general public services until the early Middle Ages, when the people's office came under monastic influence; and they never succeeded in becoming popular public worship. They soon became essential to monastic prayer, however – even, with the passage of time, in Egypt.

4, 5, 6, *Ceremonies, music and clerical order*: early monks were very suspicious of the use of music and ceremonies. In the fifth century Abba Pambo admonished a monk who had been beguiled by church music he had heard in Alexandria: 'What kind of contrition does the monk have when he . . . raises his voice like the oxen?' Another abbot was moved to point out that 'singing . . . and melodious tones may be appropriate for secular priests and others, as a

Early people's office	*Early monastic office*

1 Principal services:
    'morning and evening hymns'; res-
    urrection vigil on Sunday mornings
	Principal services:
	    seven or more daily, including during
	    the hours of darkness, aiming at
	    'prayer without ceasing'

2 Small number of fixed psalms	Whole Psalter in numerical order
3 No readings (except at special vigils, and gospel at resurrection vigil)	Systematic Bible-reading in night office
4 Ceremonies, processions, incense, vest- ments, etc	Minimum external observance
5 Much music and hearty singing	Music very restrained (or even absent altogether)
6 Hierarchical ordering of liturgy	No special place given to ecclesiastical orders, except that the abbot presides
7 Important place given to intercession	Often no intercession

8 Conscious of celebrating the prayer of
    the Church
	Praying in the tradition, as part of that
	    particular community's way of life

means of attracting people to the church, but monks live far from the noise of
the world, and such things are not good for them . . . let all melodious singing
be far from the monk who desires to be saved'.[9] This reticence towards music
has remained in the monastic strands of the Byzantine services, and is especially
evident there in the lesser hours, which are recited by a single reader. In the
West the elaborate musical system which developed is difficult to categorize, as
the plainchant can trace its origins via the *devoti* and their 'parish' links to the
music of the ancient secular Church. This chant eventually came to be seen in
itself as an ascetical exercise.[10]

The only offices in monastic tradition which can normally make use of
ceremonies and the clerical order are the morning and evening offices when
they are solemn. This is because, like the Eucharist, their essential form has
always been the same in both monastic and people's worship. They are pivotal
and ecclesial in character, part of the parish round which was simply continued
by the *devoti*. The question of ceremonies is complicated because the more
monasticism has become involved with 'the world' the more it has naturally
gravitated towards splendid ceremonies, or at least has become more interested
in the seemly performance of liturgy. There are plenty of positive and negative
examples of this from history, but that should not be allowed to obscure the
fact that any single-minded following of the monastic way will naturally tend
towards simplicity.[11]

These two different approaches to daily prayer, secular and monastic, were
quite clearly defined in the early period, and stand for fundamental differences
of emphasis which have always continued to be valid. But each side borrowed
from the other to such an extent in subsequent centuries, often to the detriment

of the original understandings, that today we are faced with the problem of teasing out these strands from each other, as if trying to separate two bushes whose branches have become intertangled. For in looking at the forms of daily office which eventually established themselves in the various traditions, we shall usually find ourselves faced with a mongrel.

Western Europe

The various monastic currents made their way to Western Europe in the fourth century, and the early story there is therefore one of great variety. John Cassian brought Egyptian monasticism to Marseilles about 415. Perhaps by a different route it also strongly informed the monastic rules of the Celtic Church in the British Isles (42), as it did to some extent all the earliest Western rules, which are mostly of a dour and disciplinarian spirit, making for heavy work in church (and out of it). Bishop Caesarius of Arles wrote one which envisaged nine or more services every twenty-four hours, and on Fridays his monks had to cope with at least thirty-seven readings and ninety-eight psalms (44).

The *devoti*-type of life from Palestine and Cappadocia on the other hand found a strong base in Rome. The forms of office used by the quasi-monastic communities at the Rome churches were by the sixth century close to the form they were to retain for 1500 years, and from them we inherit the office of the Roman or 'Western' liturgy (32). The undoubted crux of the monastic story in the West is the Rule of St Benedict, written about 540 (46). Benedict signalled the wane of the old monasticism, and the arrival of a new development, a balanced and humane rule which it was possible for anyone to follow. The form of daily office prescribed in the Rule became the basis of all Western monastic prayer in the succeeding centuries, as the old variety was gradually swept away. It is most probable that Benedict took the office of the old Roman communities as his model, though he was also heavily indebted to the *Rule of the Master* (45), of which his Rule is partly an ingenious adaptation.

The effect of Benedict's Rule was not immediate, but as it gained ground it brought with it a subtle revolution in monastic living. Sunday mass had rarely been celebrated in religious houses up until then. The community attended the nearest convenient church. It now became more common for priests to be monks, and the monastery to become a self-sufficient family, independent of the outside world. All these characteristics were entrenched and magnified in that decisive rewriting of the Rule which was undertaken at Charlemagne's behest by another monk, Benedict of Aniane (*c.* 750–821).

The history of the Western monastic office in a sense starts and ends with St Benedict, even though developments over the following centuries make a complicated story. The shape of the Western monastic office was now fixed for good and all, the Rule remaining the fundamental point of reference for all monastic orders which arose after it.

Retracing our steps from Benedict to the fourth century once more, we can now pick up the story of the people's office where we left it. There is one place whose liturgy stands out from all others at this period – the church of the Holy Sepulchre in Jerusalem. Not only did it play a very important role in the development of liturgy; it is outstanding too because of the unusually detailed information we have on its services, thanks to that precise and formidable nun, the lady Egeria, who presents us for the first time with a vivid picture of the people's office in full operation.

10

Jerusalem

Somewhere on the Atlantic coast of southern France or northern Spain was a community of devout ladies (nuns?) which in the fourth century had the enterprise to send a sister to report on worship in the Holy Land. This was quite the thing to do at the time; many pilgrims travelled to Palestine from all over Christendom, taking back with them reports on the worship there for the benefit of communities at home. Jerusalem had great influence in this period, and there were many attempts to introduce elements of its liturgy into local rites in East and West. This borrowing played an important part in the development of the Eastern rites, and anyone familiar with Eastern worship will quickly recognize some of the things described in the report sent back by this Western nun.

Her name, it is now thought, was Egeria (16, 22). She tells us that at the church of the Holy Sepulchre there were five daily offices: a service from cockcrow until dawn (a monastic vigil), a dawn service which followed without a break (people's morning office), and services at noon, three p.m. and evening. On Sundays there were fewer but longer services and at festivals and special times there were considerable variations.

Four groups of people were associated with the basilica: the bishop and his clergy; the monks and nuns; the local laity; the pilgrims. The *Anastasis* was therefore no ordinary church, and its worship falls into no simple category. But it does give us a picture of what popular worship could be like.

Morning office

The weekday service at cockcrow was monastic, with few laity present. 'From that time till dawn hymns are recited and psalms with their refrains, and antiphons too; and after each hymn there is a prayer, for two or three presbyters, and deacons also, are present by rota each day with the monastics (*monazontes*) to say the prayers after each hymn and antiphon.'[12] Prayers can only be said by a priest if the bishop is not present. No one else may recite prayers of any sort (maybe because the prayers were improvised, and the speaker needed to know what he was doing). A principal function of the deacon was to announce the biddings in the prayers, a function he still has in certain litanies in Orthodox worship. As soon as it begins to get light the morning office begins. 'They begin to recite the morning hymns. Then the bishop comes with his clergy and immediately enters the cave, and from inside the screen he first recites the prayer for all, and he himself commemorates any names he wishes; then he blesses the catechumens, recites another prayer and blesses the faithful. After this, the bishop comes outside the screen, and all come to his hand, and he blesses them one by one as he comes out, and so the dismissal takes place when it is already light.'[13]

Several details in this account are curious. First, Egeria gives no information on what she means by 'hymns' and 'the morning hymns'. The word 'hymn' is frequently used in contemporary accounts to refer to psalms, and the phrase 'morning hymns' has a double use, indicating both the morning office as a whole and the fixed psalms and canticles which formed its nucleus. Egeria's matter-of-fact mention of the morning hymns implies that they are identical with what she is used to in Gaul, and it seems very likely that they included some or all of the following: Psalms 51, 63, 148–150, the Benedicite and Gloria in Excelsis.[14] The fact that Egeria never sees fit to give details of the material used in services is typical of all early authors, and may imply a general uniformity of practice, but seems more readily to be explained by a simple lack of interest in liturgical detail. All contemporary writers are uniformly exasperating, including the greatest among the fourth- and fifth-century Fathers. Egeria evidently does not think her community would be interested in learning about psalm-cycles and lectionaries. Such detail is not of major importance in the matter of daily prayer!

Another curious fact is the entry of the bishop and his clergy after the service is well under way. Here we have a concept of liturgy offered to God as something in its own right. Neither clergy nor people are there first and foremost to pray their private prayers, but to play their particular part in the whole offering. In the bishop's entrance there is perhaps a hint of the theatrical, but it heightens the solemnity of the offering which the people in their entirety are making to God. Africa often provides interesting parallels which throw light on early church history. In the Anglican Church in Africa Sunday worship often begins with mattins, led by the churchwardens or catechists. After it has finished, the congregation fills the time waiting for the arrival of the priest by hearing a sermon or singing hymns. It can never be certain when the priest will arrive, so the gathered faithful are used to carrying on for half the morning until he should show up. In a society with plenty of time, things can work quite happily like this. There are parallel practices in churches of various traditions. Among Roman Catholic Red Indians there has been a custom of the chief leading a service of a catechetical sort while the priest's arrival is awaited. In the Presbyterian Church of Scotland there was the so-called 'reader's service' which preceded the main service of the day. In Orthodox Russia the entrance

The rotunda of the church of the Holy Sepulchre as it appears in a seventeenth-century engraving. It was here that the offices were celebrated in the fourth century. By the time of this engraving the *Anastasis*, as it was called, had undergone many vicissitudes and transformations. It was all destroyed in a disastrous fire in the nineteenth century and rebuilt to a different design. The structure in the middle is the sepulchre (Egeria refers to it as the 'cave').

of the clergy in the middle of vespers was a tradition on Sundays and feasts. 'All the priests of the city, as well as any who from the suburban periphery happened to be on hand, were obliged to participate. In order to be at the cathedral church on time for the singing of the vesperal psalms, the priests of the other churches in the city had to celebrate vespers in their own places a little earlier.'[15] In fourth-century Jerusalem all the clergy would have been based on the cathedral, but the services were such that had they not served by rota they would have spent most of their time in church. The bishop had no one to share his contribution, and so, unless he were to be in and out of church around the clock, he had to content himself with attendance at the principal moments.[16]

Evening office

In vespers, the principal service of the day, the psalmody is divided into two parts. First, all the lamps are ceremonially lit from a flame in the Holy Sepulchre and then the Lucernare Psalms are sung. In the second part, the bishop arrives and sits down for the second set of psalms and canticles. Then a litany follows in the typical Eastern manner, with a deacon reciting the biddings and a choir responding: '*Kyrie eleison*'. Then, as in the *Apostolic Constitutions* (13), there is a blessing of catechumens and another for the faithful, each following the form of the 'Prayer of Inclination'.[17]

The service proper begins with psalmody. The origin of such preliminary psalmody, which is found in all the Eastern rites (except the Maronite, which dropped it) has never been fully established. It usually takes the form of groups of psalms, mostly in numerical order, each group having its own antiphon or popular refrain. It is part of a wider question which still waits to be clarified – the origin of psalmody *in course* in the people's offices of both East and West, generally presumed to be of monastic origin. Egeria gives no definite indications that her psalmody is of this sort, and indeed it is far from being a mere preliminary – it accompanies the lucernarium, the ceremonial lighting of the lamps.

The lamplighting ceremony was once an almost universal observance at vespers, and normally understood not, as some suppose, as a mini-Paschal Vigil, but simply as a thanksgiving for the light. The moment for lighting-up was an important turning-point of the day for pre-modern man, and something of the feel of it can still be experienced by the motorist on a long journey, a moment of truth which reveals how the day is passing. It was natural to associate prayers with it. In the *Apostolic Constitutions* (13), an early Christian document, such a ceremony preceded the agape, and this may in fact be the origin of the vesper ceremony in the people's office – as an agape rite. But there are also pagan precedents, not to mention too the ceremonial lighting of lamps in the Jerusalem temple at morning and evening (Exod. 30.7f.).[18] It is out of this lucernarium tradition that the paschal candle arose, and not vice versa –

significantly, few early liturgical texts or commentaries associate the lucernarium itself with the resurrection. It was a thanksgiving for the light, and a celebration of Christ our light, performed at home as well as in church. The theme of resurrection was much more associated with the morning office, and particularly with the vigil which preceded it on Sundays.

The service at Jerusalem ends with a special devotion at the cross, which was in another place in the same building, on the reputed site of Golgotha. This additional devotion found its way into all manner of local liturgies, always in the people's office.[19]

Vigil of the resurrection

A vigil of the resurrection was held every Sunday morning at cockcrow; the first part of it was for the whole community, the second part monastic. The people apparently went back to bed while the monastics kept things going until dawn. The psalms seem to have been a basic popular devotion, and while the great crowd waited for the doors to open, clergy were on hand to organize the psalmody and, as far as we can see, people joined in as spontaneously as a crowd at Lourdes breaks into saying the rosary. Such a people's vigil as this is also mentioned in the *Apostolic Constitutions*, and was a widespread observance throughout the Church, still preserved in the Eastern rites. The climax was the reading of the resurrection gospel (which at Jerusalem may have included the passion narrative).

There were important changes in the programme of services in special periods such as Lent and Holy Week, but what I have said above should give a good idea of how the daily office was approached. We do not know how far this was the creation of Bishop Cyril (*c.* 315–86) who, partly through a need to make the services more vivid for pilgrims, had embarked on revision a few years before. Egeria records more than once how impressed she is that psalms, prayers and readings were always appropriate to the time, place and theme of the service. Cyril's reform aimed at making maximum use of evocative and vivid worship, ceremonies and processions which engaged the emotions of a highly emotional clientele. The very different monastic services wove in counterpoint through the scheme, as shade to the light, and sober reflection behind the spectacle.

Much of what Egeria saw was akin to the worship she was used to in Gaul, or whatever Western region she came from. This unity of practice between East and West was to endure longer than is generally realized, even though the two halves of the Church early began to feel their separate identity.

Before we can begin to consider the Western liturgy, it is essential to have some idea of how daily worship developed in the East. First, what happened to the liturgy of Palestine – did it produce any direct descendants? Further afield, yes, but on the territory of Palestine itself, destined to a turbulent history with many breaks in continuity, there was to be no simple handing-on of liturgical traditions.

Where, then, should we look? There is a whole range of rites which are historically of great importance in the East, the principal families being the Armenian, east and west Syrian, Maronite, Coptic, Ethiopian and, of course, the Byzantine. While the latter came to predominate, the others are equally important for the history of liturgy: they all owe a great debt to Jerusalem, and all of them preserve elements we can find in Egeria's account. We do not have space here to consider them all, but let us take the road north-east from Jerusalem to the home of a rite which was first described little more than two centuries after Egeria's visit, and has changed little in essentials since then.

11

After Egeria

The Christians of eastern Syria have a remarkable history. Known variously as Chaldeans, Assyrians or Nestorians (though they hold no Nestorian views), their Church once extended from its Mesopotamian centre, beyond Persia, through Afghanistan, Turkestan, Mongolia and Tibet to China, where they enjoyed royal favour in the seventh and eighth centuries and remained important throughout the Middle Ages. Their greatest missionary success, however, was along the Malabar coast of South India, where the church has flourished right down to the present day. 'It is no exaggeration to contend', writes A. S. Atiya, 'that, in the early Middle Ages [this church] was the most widespread in the whole world.'[20] Many aspects of the liturgy and church life in general are so primitive that they take us back to the very early centuries of the Church, and in many ways back to Judaism. The *Apostolic Constitutions* were probably written in the vicinity in the fourth century, and we know that by the seventh century the liturgy had reached a stable state, its many Jewish features suggesting at least some preservation of first-century Christian practice.

The story of the east Syrian daily office is closely bound up with political events. Through the disaster of the Islamic conquest the Christians, reduced to poverty, were to endure centuries of maltreatment and deprivation. There was some small compensation for future generations, however, in that this meant the preservation of many very ancient churches, and a fixing of liturgy and the layout of churches in a primitive stage of their development. Innovation was a luxury not to be afforded in such hard circumstances, and established tradition was to be held on to at all costs. The greatest descent in the fortunes of the east Syrian Church seems to have come after the Middle Ages, perhaps beginning with the Mongol invasion in the fourteenth century. At some point between then and the nineteenth century a dramatic decline ensued, and while this affected the performance of services, it left their content unaffected. The internal arrangement of churches was drastically simplified, and reduced to a level of utter poverty and simplicity. Only in recent years has any improvement in the situation been possible.

In order to understand this daily office we need to be aware of the peculiarities of the traditional east Syrian church building. The altar is screened off by a solid wall, with a central doorway giving access. Across this a veil is drawn. In the midst of the nave used to be a large platform, the *bema*. This was semicircular in shape, like a reversed apse, with a central throne for the bishop and curved benches on either side for the clergy. In ordinary churches the bishop's throne was replaced by a stone stand on which the Gospels were enthroned. Also on the *bema* was a table known as Golgotha, on which were placed a cross and the gospel-book, and on either side of this were often two lecterns. The main part of the daily office was led from the *bema* while the men crowded round, the women having to occupy the back of the church. The *bema* is also known in the modern synagogue, and may be an inheritance from Jewish worship, although its precise origins remain a subject of controversy. Ancient examples have been found as far away as West Germany.[21] In the early centuries of the Church there was a good deal of experimenting with chancel furniture, and the *bema* was one solution to the problem of where to put the clergy and singers, the square 'chancel' at San Clemente in Rome, the large ambo in Hagia Sophia in Constantinople, and the three-sided rectangle of western cathedral choirs all being obscurely related. By the nineteenth century at the latest the use of the *bema* had disappeared in the Syrian liturgy – the poverty-stricken people now crowded into small, dark, bare churches where furniture and ceremonial were reduced to a minimum, and the clergy, even bishops, to leading weekday services in ordinary laymen's clothes.

I shall base the following account on the daily office as it was performed in the heyday of the east Syrian liturgy, before the period of decline and before the attempts at revival in the present century. There is evidence that some of the lesser hours may have had an important place in the past, and various forms of monastic-type night prayer are also described in liturgical books, but standing proud of everything else is a classic people's office scheme of daily morning and evening prayer, with a resurrection vigil at weekends and festivals.

Vespers

The evening service is a very primitive form of vespers to which has been added preliminary 'monastic' psalmody (17). The opening kiss of peace is not mentioned in the service-books, but is practised by tradition, and we can assume it originally took place during the arrival of the people before the service began, as it does today in English country parishes, where people feel it is important to greet each other before the service starts, and again at the end, when they may make a point of shaking hands with the priest. In Coptic monasteries, too, the monks greet each other with the Peace before each service and more formally at the end. After this comes the psalmody. It is performed in numerical order, *in course*, and is therefore probably of monastic origin. After this psalmody, vespers proper begins, with lighting of lamps and the offering of incense. A flame was brought from the altar (in Egeria's Jerusalem, from the

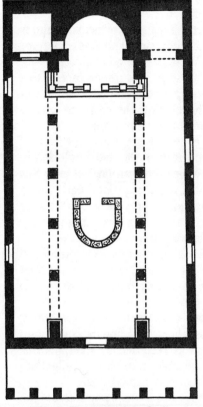

Kharab-Shems, northern Syria.

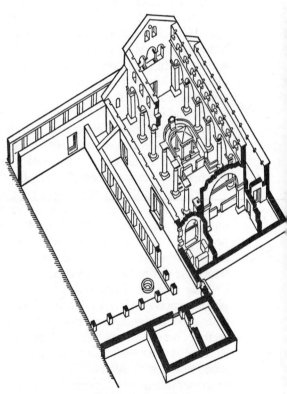

Behyo, northern Syria

The *bema* of Syrian churches, a kind of reversed apse in the middle of the nave, varied in design from a simple horseshoe to a grandiose structure with high walls and a canopied table ('Golgotha') in the midst.

Sepulchre), and with it a lamp standing before the sanctuary was lit, and then all the lamps in the church, and incense was offered.

The main part of the office was celebrated at the *bema*. Its principal psalm is Psalm 141, which is found too in all the other Eastern rites, and is as important to Eastern vespers as the Magnificat is in the West. It is an odd choice, having earned its position purely on the strength of verse 2. The importance of this psalm, however, in the Church's evening worship since very early times, can hardly be overestimated – for half of the Church over the best part of two millennia it has typified what the Church means by its daily vespers.

That concludes the 'evening hymns'. Now come the prayers, in the form of three litanies. The first one asks for comparatively little, and is gloriously doxological.[23] The second has simply 'Amen' after each petition, but even this is sometimes omitted. The refrain is not essential to a litany. Some early forms simply have silence after each petition. Having led the prayers before the altar the deacon cries: 'Raise your voices and glorify the living God', and all sing, 'Holy God, Holy and Strong, Holy and Immortal, have mercy on us'. The Trisagion here is very much a people's song, for in no other rite is it introduced with a bidding from the deacon. The prayer of inclination[24] is in origin the final blessing. All bow to receive it, and the lights are extinguished and the veil is drawn in front of the altar.

But that is not the end. On Sundays and feast-days there follows something more for the people: a procession. In it the cross is honoured, and the connection with the procession to the cross after vespers as recorded by Egeria seems irresistible.[25] The cross used to be taken from the table on the *bema* ('Golgotha') and placed in the sanctuary. During Paschaltide it was carried outside.

On ferial days, however, after the psalm-verses and more prayers, comes the anthem of the martyrs. In earlier times there was here too a procession to an outdoor cross, or to a martyr's tomb at one side of the sanctuary. After it each priest present says a proper prayer (everybody is 'given something to do') and the service closes with final prayers, the blessing and the peace, to the end of which the Creed has been tacked on.

This additional material after the prayer of inclination illustrates a phenomenon much in evidence in Eastern liturgy, and no less in the West, the addition of bits and pieces to the end of a service. It certainly has many familiar features for Anglicans, whose Sunday evensong, after the Grace, carries on again with intercessions, sermon, and often a procession of clergy and choir, all interspersed with hymns. They tend to obscure the fact that the essential shape of the service is very simple. The service could be described as psalmody plus intercessions, and we shall see later that there is cause to suggest that this is in fact the essential basic framework of any form of the morning and evening offices.[26]

B Resurrection vigil

Before considering the morning office it is necessary to mention the vigil which takes place on Sundays and feast-days. The service begins while it is still dark. The veil is opened as the psalmody begins. This used to be led from the *bema* in former times, and after a procession the variable psalms were led from the sanctuary.

In most liturgical traditions where it is found, such a festal vigil reaches a climax in the reading of the resurrection gospel, but here we have the one exception which proves the rule, as for some reason the gospel reading has disappeared (except on Good Friday!). All stand for the litany, and then the morning office begins.

C Morning office

Here is something very remarkable and ancient: all the elements of the ferial office are completely fixed – there is no variation according to the liturgical year or even to the cycle of the week. While the festal office is slightly different, there are even here only exceptional variations in the text. We have in fact a very ancient and pure people's morning office, identical with that described in seventh-century documents.

Astonishingly, the first seven psalms are also in the Sabbath service of the synagogue as it is described to us by the oldest Jewish prayer-book in existence, which comes from the ninth century[27] (17e). Psalms 93, 100 and 148–150 were also said at Sunday Lauds in the old Roman breviary (33b). The service is called the dawn service (synagogue: 'dawn prayers'), and the theme is *light*. Psalm 100 has the refrain: 'Lord and source of light, to you we give glory', and is followed by a prayer on the same theme. Psalm 113 has a similar refrain, and at this point on Sundays the lamps are lit and the bishop or celebrant, who has been seated in the sanctuary, comes to the sanctuary door accompanied by the clergy and proclaims a collect on the themes of light and darkness:

O Lord, the creator of light in your loving kindness, you have ordered the darkness in your wisdom, and you illumine creation with your glorious light. To you, O Lord, belongs continual praise without ceasing, and to your name confession and worship in heaven and earth, Lord of all, Father, Son and Holy Spirit for ever.

He then solemnly intones Psalm 93: 'The Lord reigns, robed in majesty', which is linked with the resurrection of Christ. Psalms 148–150 and 117 which follow used to be sung from the *bema*, to which the clergy went in procession.

The various elements of this first part of the morning office are remarkable for the beauty and joy of their meditation on the theme of light. During the subsequent censing the veil before the altar is opened, and on ferial days all sing Psalm 51 – a strange damper at this point in such joyful proceedings.[28]

The rest of the service is as for evening prayer, except that there is no litany and no procession to the martyr's tomb. It is very rare to find an ancient people's office ending without intercession and petition, though Egeria reported that, in Jerusalem, rather than a full-blown litany there was merely 'prayer for all' at the morning office.

A liturgical tap-root

The east Syrian daily office is in the mainstream of the Church's daily prayer, taking us back to those early centuries when people gathered day by day for the 'morning and evening hymns'. Juan Mateos, the Jesuit oriental scholar, goes so far as to say that 'the Chaldean and Armenian rites have preserved the purest structures of the divine office'.[29] This rite's primitive nature is demonstrated by the surprising fact that there is no Scripture-reading in any of the offices. In the Eastern rites as a whole, if readings do appear in the office they are late local developments. The only exception is the resurrection gospel at the festal vigil, and even that is missing here.

We find in this rite considerable use of poetry and liturgical compositions, which have the advantage of concentrating the attention more directly on the central Christian mysteries than is possible in the West, where the office is very much Old Testament-dominated. The east Syrian offices are particularly impressive for the quality of much of this material. There is, too, abundant use of collects and short prayers, often preparing for the next item in the service or summing up other aspects of its content.[30] A striking characteristic of the east Syrian Church is the apparent inheritance from Israel. The scattered remnants of Jewish practice found in all oriental rites are here found in abundance. Clergy, for instance, are addressed as Rabbi, the table of the cross before the royal door is the Shekinah, Maundy Thursday is Pascha (i.e. Passover, not Easter), and so the list could go on, almost without end. It is difficult to know how enduring was the connection with Judaism, and to what extent one might have affected the other. Discussing a similar phenomenon in the Armenian Church, P. Sigal writes:

Armenian Christianity contains interesting remainders of Christian Jewish liturgy and ritual that passed through the Adoptionist Church which, under the name of 'Pauliani' from Paul of Samosata, was excommunicated at Nicaea. The Church's theological mainstay, *The Key of the Truth*, translated by Conybeare in 1898, repeats Ebionite doctrine, and is another of the many items that lead to the inference that there were many avenues through which Judaism penetrated even second- and third-century Christianity.[31]

The Jewish connection is clearly complicated, and we should beware of trying to see in it a direct inheritance from the first-century synagogue, or the primitive Church.

In the east Syrian daily office the level of the people's participation is impressive, and so are the tenacity with which they have continued to attend daily, the imaginative use of space, movement, music, light and smell when circumstances have favoured it, and the general air of exuberant celebration. This contrasts strongly with our Western understanding of the daily office as quiet, muted meditation on Scripture.

Though certainly not without its problems, east Syrian Christianity is very much alive today in the Middle East and India, and in its Western diaspora. There has been some revival in the use of the *bema*, and the tradition continues to flourish among the laity of daily attendance at mattins and vespers. The very strength of this tradition has probably helped to ensure their survival in what has at times been a very hostile world.

At the end of the nineteenth century two Englishmen, A. J. MacLean and W. H. Browne, published moving accounts of east Syrian church life, in their book *The Catholicos of the East*. There they describe the daily people's worship, putting some flesh on the bare bones we have been analysing:

Every morning and evening before sunrise and sunset, all Syrians who are alive to their religious duties assemble at the church for their daily prayers. They certainly put our apathetic and respectable Westerners to shame in this respect ... We proceed to describe the evening service ... On entering the church the people often kiss the cross on the doorpost; and then proceed to the quasi-altar in the nave, or in the summer chapel, as the case may be, where the cross is lying, and devoutly kiss it, crossing themselves and bowing. The bishop, or senior priest present, first advances, crosses himself, and kisses the cross, saying, 'Glory be to God in the highest (thrice), and on earth peace and a good hope to men, at all times and for ever'. He then stands on the north side of the nave near the cross, and all the people advance in order, kiss the cross and then the priest's hand, and pass down in line, touching the hands of those who have already kissed the cross, and raising their own hands to their lips ...

As the services are all in the classical Syriac, they cannot be generally followed, except at well-known points, by the laity, especially by the old men and women. But all who can read the old books now press forward to the books, of which there are seldom more than two, and often only one, and stand round them. It is a matter of indifference whether the letters are upside down or sideways on, or what we should call right side up; they can be read with almost equal facility in any case. Thus ten or a dozen men may read from one book of large type, some peeping over the shoulders of others ... the singers divide themselves into two choirs ..: As the churches are nearly always dark, rude tapers of beeswax are held in the hand over the books. As these grow dim every few minutes, they are snuffed by the hand, and the greasy condition of the manuscripts testifies to the zeal of the holder to sing rather than to his care to prevent the wax falling.

Certainly the Syrians have a thorough notion of congregational worship. All their services are sung; but all who can read join in at the top of their voice, whether they are musical or not; often not to the same tune, and generally not in the same key as their neighbours ... But all is very hearty and earnest, and one would not exchange the

Syrian evensong for a most beautiful musical rendering in many of our cathedrals. The Syrians would consider a read service as unworthy of the time and place ... [The anthems after the *Shurayas*] are divided into paragraphs; each choir sings one to its proper tune, and the other choir takes up the next to the same tune, and so on to the end. They are sung rather slowly, and take up much more time than a corresponding amount of the psalms. Each paragraph is prefaced by a clause from the Psalter which gives it its keynote. These anthems are a special feature of all east Syrian services, and give an opportunity to all who can read of joining heartily in the worship.[32]

This worship still lives up to the name 'morning and evening hymns', and the way it fosters the corporate spirit in a minority group is perhaps relevant to some of the difficulties of being a Christian in today's world. This at any rate is a phenomenon we shall find again in the history of daily prayer.

The daily offices of the east Syrian Church provide us with a good example of people's daily worship as it was conceived in the period immediately following the peace of the Church in the fourth century. It may be difficult for Westerners to grasp the significance of the Eastern rites, foreign as they are to our experience, and, we might be tempted to feel, irrelevant to our needs, yet nothing could be further from the truth. The Church is one, and all its parts have much to learn from each other which is of vital importance. There are centuries of mutual ignorance to overcome, and anyone who claims to believe in the catholicity of the Church will have to come to terms with the fact that East and West have been ignorant of each other for far too long. Any attempt to understand the divine office without knowledge of the Eastern rites is a sheer impossibility.

I make no apologies, therefore, for staying with the East for the time being before moving on to consider the history of daily prayer in the West.

12

Crowd Scenes

The history of the Byzantine people's office has traced two distinct paths. One resulted in the Byzantine office which we know today; the other was a people's office of a quite different character, which has now disappeared.

The old 'chanted office'

In its earliest form this now-defunct office probably derived from Antioch some time between the fourth and sixth centuries, and from then on continued to evolve and expand. It was this which remained in use in the church of the Holy Wisdom in Constantinople until the disastrous Latin sack of the city in 1204. When the Greeks eventually returned to power fifty-seven years later, they did not restore it, but put in its place the very different St Sabas office. The old rite continued in use in Thessalonica, however, until the fifteenth century, stubbornly defended by its bishop Symeon against considerable opposition from his clergy, who obliged him here and there to simplify it. With the Turkish conquest of the city in 1430 it was finally swept away, never to be seen again. (In Russia too it disappeared in the fifteenth century as a result of the Tatar invasion.)[33] Our information on it is now mainly limited to a few documents, the earliest of which come from the ninth or the tenth century, an account from a Russian monk, Antony of Novgorod, who visited Constantinople hardly a moment too soon in 1200, and the writings of Bishop Symeon himself.

In essence this old rite was a straightforward people's office consisting of mattins and vespers. Symeon called it the *akolouthia asmatikē*, the 'chanted office', and this musical emphasis shows its popular rather than monastic roots. It was the office of all the secular churches of the empire, as well as the Orthodox churches of southern Italy, Sicily and Russia, all of whom had their own local forms of it. The daily office introduced into Kiev in the tenth century seems to have followed it very closely.

The most surprising feature for us in this office is the movement it involved for all concerned. First, psalmody in the narthex, then the dramatic opening of the doors and the entry of the clergy and people singing; the central part of the service was then held in the midst of the church at the ambo, which looked something like a bandstand and was big enough to contain a choir. Then for the last part of the service all were on the move again to the sanctuary, before which the final prayers were offered and the blessing was given. It was imaginative worship for the people. The visual effect of a service was said to have been spectacular, involving in cathedrals large numbers of singers and robed clergy, and for the participants it was a vivid daily pilgrimage from outer darkness to the gates of paradise.

Mattins

The morning office (18) began with introductory psalmody, which was all performed in the narthex, the doors to the church being shut. It normally consisted of eight selections from the Psalter, of equal length, known, as was common in the East, as antiphons, each antiphon having its own refrain. When the seventh antiphon had ended, the doors were opened, the lamps were lit, and all poured into the church singing the Benedicite, the clergy through the central doors, the laity through the side ones. We have already had one traditional morning Psalm, number 63. Now when all are at the ambo in the nave the others are sung. Psalm 51, as usual, comes at the beginning, and then Psalms 148–150, and the canticles.

After the Trisagion everyone had to be on the move once again, towards the sanctuary, where the final part of the service was held standing before the altar.

Vespers

The evening office is similar in form to mattins – introductory psalmody in the narthex followed by vespers proper in the nave, and ending at the sanctuary. There was no lucernarium, except on certain days,[35] despite abundant reference to light and the illumination of darkness – at Thessalonica 'Hail, gladdening light' (*Phōs hilaron*) was sung as participants moved from narthex to nave, where all the lamps had been lit. There was apparently no use of incense either in the earlier centuries. By the time of our earliest service-books, however, there is very elaborate use of the thurible.

(There was originally only one Psalm at vespers, Psalm 141 – as in Antioch in Chrysostom's time. The primitive evening office in Syria was extremely simple: Psalm 141 followed by intercessions (13).[36] So it seems also to have been in Constantinople in the same period.[37])

In parish churches

At the present state of research, we know hardly anything about how this old office was celebrated in ordinary parishes, though one would like to think that its most distinctive traits, especially the movement from narthex to nave and

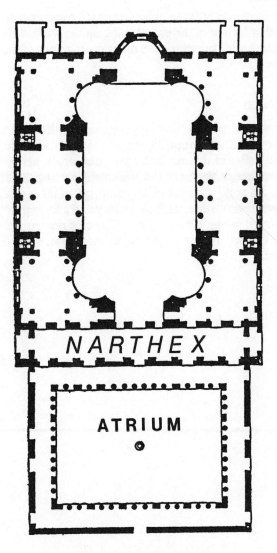

Plan of the church of Hagia Sophia in
Constantinople in the time of Justinian.

sanctuary, will have caught the popular imagination and endeared it to ordinary people. It has that feeling of the crowd bringing the ways of the street into the church which seems to characterize so many descriptions of the public office in the times of the Fathers.

Music and action

The old Constantinopolitan rite helps to dispel the impression that the Byzantine is a monolithic liturgical system: it also provides a splendid example of how the daily office of the secular Church has sometimes been able to make very imaginative use of the body and the crowd, casting doubt on any claims that the divine office is by nature simply a liturgy of the written Word. These services required teamwork, artistic sensibility and a feeling for drama, and far from being a freak in the history of the Church's prayer, they animated the daily prayer of Christians over large areas of the known world for the best part of a millennium.

13

The Byzantine Office

The form of office which replaced the 'chanted office', and which is now in universal use, was no new creation. It had evolved over many centuries in the monasteries of Jerusalem, Sinai and Syria, and on the Greek mainland, in a steady ferment of borrowing and adaptation. Even after it had passed into general use by the end of the Middle Ages, it continued to develop until around the seventeenth century, when the increased availability of printing made possible a static, codified liturgy. (There was widespread variety until the first printed edition of liturgical books went into universal use: this had been based on a very limited choice of one or two manuscripts.[38])

This daily office is in a league of its own (19). The sheer volume of material makes it difficult to discern any clear form to the services, and the amount of variety and possible changes means that anyone innocently trying to follow them with a book will quickly flounder. Its creators over many generations have fused together material from many different sources, giving the impression of an attempt to preserve, at least in token form, as much relevant liturgical matter as they knew of. Some parts of it are impossible to perform fully (for example, the priest's secret prayers at the beginning of mattins); and some have shrunk to a mere shadow (such as brief versicles from once-entire psalms). Scattered fragments of old forms lie embedded in it, making it rather like a battered celestial body.

For the Westerner, Byzantine worship raises puzzling questions. In particular: how could anyone ever arrive at such a form of daily office? How was it allowed to replace the popular 'chanted office'? Political events certainly played their part, and the prestige and influence of monasticism, especially after the Turkish conquest, were partly responsible for the changes which came about. To judge from the problems Symeon of Thessalonica had with his clergy, the old office with all its ceremonies and drama was too demanding for them. A crucial role in the liturgical changeover, however, was played by the rise of hesychasm.

Before the fourteenth century two forms of daily office were in use in the Byzantine Church: the 'chanted office' in cathedrals and parish churches, and the office of the Studite monastery in monasteries (this had many 'people's office' characteristics). Both of these were set to disappear with the introduction of this third form, the Palestinian office of St Sabas. Its use spread out from fourteenth-century Mount Athos, coinciding with the spread of hesychasm. In content it was not something entirely new. The old monastic office had also had deep roots in the Palestinian monastery of St Sabas. This second 'invasion' from Palestine represented not so much a new form of office as 'a return to the more austere sources of the monasteries of the countryside or the desert'.[39]

Remnants of the older office are found in this St Sabas rite, as we shall see, all its contents having come together through a complicated setting of layer upon layer and through successive expansion or contraction of particular elements. We are speaking, in fact, not of three separate forms of office in the history of Byzantine worship, but of three currents within a tradition rooted in antiquity.

The subject is clearly vast and intractable, and all we need concern ourselves with here is to see how it can help us detect, in very simple terms, the survival and progress of the ancient people's office of the early Church.

The character of the services

The daily services are in theory the same in essentials whether used in monasteries, cathedrals or parish churches. There are no separate people's and monks' offices, but a single form which is a balanced combination of both, though weighted in favour of the monastic mentality. In practice, however, the services are adapted and shortened in parishes to make them more suitable.

There are fourteen services in all. Prime, terce, sext, none, and the four 'inter-hours' which are sometimes inserted between them in particularly fervent monasteries, consist essentially of psalms read through aloud by one reader at a lectern, followed by prayers. 'Typica' is in origin an ancient Palestinian office for daily communion from the reserved sacrament, from which the communion has since disappeared. The 'table office' is celebrated at table in association with either the midday or the evening meal. Compline ('little compline') is a shorter version of the 'grand compline' which is celebrated on the eve of certain feasts. This latter appears to combine elements of compline, a night vigil, and the morning office, a survival of another layer of Byzantine history, as is also the night office, which came late into the scheme, and fits in only with difficulty. The day's prayer, finally, is dominated by mattins and vespers, which have a character all their own, and are the only services used in parishes.

Vespers

The use of Psalm 104 at the beginning of monastic vespers is first mentioned in the eighth century (19). During it the priest reads seven prayers secretly. These prayers were certainly in the service-books by the eighth century and

A service in an Orthodox monastery. At the front is the iconostasis; in the alcove to the left a small group of monks sing round a lectern. A similar group sings in the opposite alcove (out of the picture). The monk at the lectern in the foreground may be reading the *kathismata* of the Psalter. Monks and laity freely mix – there is little of the neat precision of Western worship.

probably earlier, and there is good evidence to show that they were originally among the collects to the opening eight antiphons of 'chanted' vespers, each designed to follow a psalm or a group of psalms and relate to them.[40] The *kathisma* ('sitting') of weekdays is the 'monastic' preliminary psalmody which we have found in other rites. In parishes this is normally reduced or omitted altogether.

All of this material constitutes an introduction, and after it comes what is in origin people's vespers. It starts with a group of fixed psalms known as the 'Lucernarium Psalms', beginning with the evening Psalm 141. They are often reduced to a few verses. Then comes the lucernarium proper. The priest puts on his *felonion* (chasuble), all the lamps are lit, the incense is offered, and the choir sings 'Hail, gladdening light' (*Phōs hilaron*), which is regarded as the high point of the service. We have reached the people's office. On Sundays and feast-days the connection with primitive people's vespers is even more apparent, with the entrance procession led by candle-bearers from the deacon's door on the left, round to the royal doors. The deacon, while he censes, cries, 'Wisdom! Let us attend!', and then the choir sings the *Phōs hilaron*. (This, like the east Syrian Great Entrance, may derive from the entrance of the bishop in Egeria's Jerusalem.)

There is no Scripture-reading in the Byzantine office, except for certain great feasts, and every day during Lent, when there are readings at vespers from the Old Testament. Since early times Lent has been a period for communal study of the Scriptures, especially the Pentateuch. This study took place during the afternoon in Lent in fourth-century Jerusalem.[41] In Constantinople and Antioch such instruction went on throughout Lent before vespers.[42] The actual readings eventually made their way into the service they had preceded.

The litany completes the ancient pattern by ending with petition and intercession. The Prayer of Inclination, as in the east Syrian office, was the final blessing, showing once again how the service has expanded (the actual prayer is not now said aloud).

Then outside this kernel come the Aposticha and Nunc Dimittis. The lamps are extinguished, the priest removes his *felonion*, and the rest of the service is conducted in the subdued monastic manner of the first part.

Mattins

The morning office is more complicated than vespers, a fusing of at least four services:

> Office for the Emperor
> Monastic night office

People's Sunday vigil
People's morning office

The opening doxology and two psalms are a relatively recent addition. An office for those in authority follows, probably originating in an office for the Emperor celebrated in monasteries of imperial foundation.

The next part of the service is in origin a monastic vigil, and opens, as does the same service in the Rule of St Benedict, with a versicle from Psalm 51, 'O Lord, open our lips ...'.[43] The main elements in this vigil are the six invitatory psalms (*hexapsalmos*), and the variable blocks of psalmody (*kathismas*). The *hexapsalmos* as a whole is regarded as a solemn moment, during which all should stand, no one moving from their place. During the second three of these psalms the priest reads twelve secret prayers. Like the similar prayers in vespers, they are a relic of former psalm-collects, etc, and are found in the oldest Byzantine service-books known to us (ninth century).[44] The variable psalms (*kathismas*) are recited by one reader while all sit to listen, as Cassian's monks did in fourth-century Egypt. This psalmody is omitted in parishes – when parish churches choose to abbreviate a service, it is significant that monastic elements such as this psalmody tend to be the first to go. We can now see why grand compline and the night office do not fit easily into the total scheme. The Byzantine rite contains in fact three forms of night office, of which this one in mattins is the most naturally at home.

Now the atmosphere changes as the people's office takes over, in the form of a people's festal vigil: this is included in the service only on Sundays and feast-days. The lamps are lit, the royal doors are opened, and the church is censed, while the choir sing the Polieley, Psalms 135 and 136. The name, which means 'much mercy', refers to the refrain in Psalm 136. The high point of this people's vigil, following the classic pattern, is the reading of one of the eleven resurrection pericopes from the Gospels (at feasts on weekdays a proper Gospel is read). Then the resurrection is hymned.

Psalm 51 heralds the start of the morning office proper.[45] The *canon* which follows is an element of great importance, even though it has in fact grown like mistletoe out of an oak tree. Originally there was canticle-singing here,[46] but apart from the Magnificat the canticles have all disappeared (except in Lent); their antiphons have remained, however, and blossomed into a set of full-length poems. In very simple terms, their structure is as follows: a *troparion* is a stanza; three, four, five or more troparia make an *ode*; there are nine odes in a *canon*.

According to Symeon of Thessalonica the *Exapostilarion* ('sending-forth') is named thus because in it Christ is bidden to send forth his light. It introduces Psalms 148–150, which occur perhaps more than anything else in rites monastic and popular, right across the board, at this point in mattins.[47] The Gloria in Excelsis too is a traditional canticle for mattins.[48] As we will by now be coming to expect, this people's mattins ends with a litany. The Prayer of Inclination remains to all intents and purposes the final blessing, and the service ends, as at vespers, with hymns and prayers.

Living prayer

Many problems in the interpretation of the Byzantine office remain to be studied and clarified. It is nevertheless possible to learn enough about it to find our bearings, and to gain some understanding of the particular way in which it has preserved ancient tradition. The most exciting thing about even such a simple investigation as this is the vivid picture it gives of how Christian worship lives and grows, ever innovating, always creative, yet retaining, like some huge tangled old bush, trunk and roots which go down to the vital origins. All it has been possible to do here is examine the skeleton of the Byzantine office. We have more to learn from the actual celebration of worship than can ever be gained from inventories of its contents, and it should be borne in mind that this very sketchy account, which has hardly looked at the theology and meaning of the services, is in no way adequate on its own to form an introduction to the Orthodox prayer of the Hours. Yet hopefully it serves our purpose here, which is to see how the characteristic features of the patristic people's office were preserved and developed in subsequent centuries.

Orthodox worship is so different from what Westerners are used to that some major differences ought to be mentioned.

The Western morning and evening offices have a simple structure, rising to a climax at the canticle and then gently subsiding again. Orthodox worship, however, simply flows on and on. It does have its climactic moments, but there is a dominating sense of a great swell rolling inexorably forward under its own momentum. Subjective, 'personal' religion is firmly put in its place. Anyone who attempted to squeeze the juice out of everything said and sung would soon give up exhausted. It all rolls on objectively, and if we abandon ourselves to it without over-concern about intellectual attention, it will still, like some great river, deposit its rich silt.

Very refreshing for the Westerner is the relaxed unselfconsciousness of clergy and people's behaviour in church, also reflected in the priest's wide liberty to adapt the service, and an unworried acceptance that in such a complicated undertaking some things will go wrong.

Orthodox laity are used to attending the daily office in monasteries and cathedrals, and they feel at home with it, although it may be truer to say that all Orthodox worship has much the same quality, appearance as one stream of worship, whether it be eucharist, daily office or other services of prayer, and people are used to staying for a while, whatever is going on, and can recognize the moments when they have their own part to play. The office is offered for its own sake as a whole liturgical offering. The vestments, ceremonies and music, far from being optional extras, are necessities. There are parishes where the office is celebrated daily, but in others it takes place only on Saturdays, Sundays and feast-days. There is an accepted understanding that although it may sometimes be offered by few, it is always offered for all, in the indivisible oneness of Christ's Body.

14

The Middle Ages in the West

We have little information on liturgical prayer in the West until the fourth century, when the people's office emerges into daylight more or less simultaneously in all parts of the Church. Our first glimpses of it in the West come from the age of Jerome, Ambrose, Augustine and the post-Nicene Fathers **(22 to 29)**. From here on into the 'Dark Ages' we hear of the 'morning and evening hymns' which people and clergy offered together in the churches day by day. They sang 'antiphons', 'hymns' and 'psalms', all rather interchangeable terms for psalmody, canticles, and sometimes newly-composed hymns as well. When they had done that they prayed, for the Church, for the authorities, for those in need and for all members of the community. The same terminology comes from all the then-known world, and anyone who reads the sources cannot but be impressed at the way these two daily services are assumed to be universal. At the evening hymns there was burning of incense and a thanksgiving at the lighting of the lamps. In Spain the poet Prudentius (348–c. 410) wrote of the lucernarium:

... The lamps gleam out, that hang by swaying cords from every panel of the roof, and the flame, fed by the oil on which it floats lazily, casts its light through the clear glass. One would think the starry space stood over us, decked with the twin Bears, and that bright evening stars were everywhere scattered, where the Wain directs its team of oxen. How worthy a thing, O God, for thy flock to offer thee at dewy night's beginning – light, thy most precious gift, light, by which we perceive all thy other blessings![50]

At the morning hymns psalms and canticles were sung, and both services ended with litanies of intercession. People seem to have attended in numbers. Hilary of Poitiers (c. 315–67) was able to say: 'The progress of the Church in the delights of the morning and evening hymns is a great sign of the mercy of God. The day begins with God's prayers, and closes with his hymns.'[51]

It is not easy to imagine what it must have been like to be present at a service. Caesarius of Arles (c. 470–542) makes reference in various places to the people's office **(29c)**. It was performed liturgically, with a special part for the deacon – it was he who bade people kneel for prayers and announced the Prayer of Inclination.[52] People joined in the singing of the psalms.[53] Psalm 104 was sung everywhere in his diocese at evensong, and was clearly a well-known favourite.[54] He makes frequent reference to a problem which seems to have been universal in these centuries, the noise that people made in church, either praying aloud during the psalms and prayers, or simply gossiping.[55] People were expected to stand for most of the service, and Caesarius is much dismayed by some ladies in the congregation who are given to sprawling on the ground during readings (these were at the Eucharist and at an early vigil which he tried with difficulty to 'sell' to his flock).[56] A little later, Venantius Fortunatus (c. 530–610) describes how festal mattins was performed by the bishop of Paris in his cathedral, surrounded by the clergy and people who all sang with gusto to the accompaniment of wind, string and percussion instruments.[57] That may perhaps owe more to his vivid imagination, however, than to any actual events.

City churches

In this initial phase Christian worship was centred on the towns; so when we speak of the people's office we think of large city churches. In Rome there were various types of urban and suburban church, some served by quasi-monastic communities, but most of them depending on the diocesan clergy. Here, and also in Gaul, where our information is particularly plentiful, the bishop and his presbyterium all lived in the city, clergy being sent to hold services outside according to the bishop's discretion.

This was the formative period of the secular office, when the bishop decided on details of its content and presided over its celebration. The offices would be quite different from anything we know today, and of a strongly local flavour. We have little information on these old forms of service which were later superseded by the Roman office in the Middle Ages, but there is sufficient to demonstrate their affinity with the East.

Two survivors, the Ambrosian and Mozarabic daily offices, and surviving fragments of other old rites, contain many elements characteristic of the worship of the Byzantine and other Eastern churches (30, 31). The psalmody would be limited to certain fixed psalms, especially 51, 63 and 148–150 at mattins, together with one or more canticles, the principal being the Benedicite and Gloria in Excelsis.[58] Vespers would start with the lucernarium (lighting of the lamps) and an evening psalm, with perhaps other psalms. There would not be any readings, and both services would end with a litany. There was room for some hearty singing by all, liturgical ceremonies, processions, and a general appeal to the senses. The Ambrosian and Mozarabic offices seem, in their primitive forms, to have been so similar that they may well have typified what was normal in the West.

In the sixth and seventh centuries churches began to be established in the countryside. It would be difficult to expect their clergy to come to town even occasionally for the offices, but this was tried for a while, clergy being required to serve their turns in the cathedral. They still had to perform the offices in their own church as well, or provide someone to do it.

฿ The minster

When churches began to be founded outside the towns it was not according to any parish system – that had not yet been thought of. They were often large churches staffed by a number of clergy and serving a wide, indeterminate area. In England these were known as 'minsters'. They were a replica of the system evolved in the towns. An archpriest or 'abbot' (who was not, however, a monk) would preside, and the other clergy would live with or near him, celebrating the offices together day by day. This arrangement began to arise in Europe in the fifth century and remained paramount until the ninth. In England it only got under way about the seventh century, lasting until the tenth. In some places vestiges of this system have remained until the present day, especially in central and northern regions of Italy, where such a church is known as a *pieve* (from the Latin *plebs*).

The main functions of the minster's staff were to offer the Eucharist and the daily office, to exercise a pastoral ministry to those who came for help, and to administer the church's property. In addition each church had to run a school to train boys in the arts of singing and psalmody, and prepare suitable ones among them for the ministry. As candidates had to pass through the various lesser orders by stages, the staff at any one time would include, say, three priests, two deacons and six clerks in minor orders. These would all take part in staging the offices. From an inscription on the altar-canopy of the church of S. Giorgio Valpolicelli in northern Italy we know that the church's staff in 712 were the following:

> Vidaliano, priest
> Tancol, priest
> Gundelme, deacon
>
> Ursus, teacher
> Juvintino, pupil
> Juviano, pupil
> Vergondus, gravedigger
> Teodoal, gravedigger[59]

All these people will have been involved in singing the daily offices, so that the people of S. Giorgio Valpolicelli must have had (by eighth-century rural standards at least) something worth coming to twice a day in their local church.

The services, of course, will have been performed partly by heart and partly with the use of a collection of books, such as we can still see in an Orthodox church today. There was no one book containing everything. A well-to-do minster could expect to have a mass-book, a lectionary, a gospel-book, a sanctoral, an antiphoner and a psalter, and it would need at least three of those books for the divine office.

In general, continental minsters continued as collegiate churches until Napoleon brought them to an end. In England one church at least, what is now Southwell Cathedral, never entirely lost its status as a minster, and even retained the name. There is another interesting survival at Easby, near Richmond in Yorkshire. There are also still a number of parishes in England whose incumbents retain the title of archpriest.

The parish

We have so far followed two stages, that of the city churches and that of rural minsters. The third phase, the establishing of smaller 'parish' churches, was modelled in turn on the minster as the minster had been modelled on the cathedral. It followed a gradual and muddled process which is difficult to give dates to, but can be traced back as early as the fifth or the sixth century. Often a landowner would build himself a private church and find a priest to look after it. Bishops limited these 'oratories' with stringent regulations, and it was only by a gradual process as churches came to be founded in villages either by the local landowner, by a monastery, or by the Church authorities, that what we know as the parish system took shape, really getting under way with Charlemagne, and coming to its fullest development about the twelfth century. Bishops in the earlier period were extremely nervous about letting priests live on their own, and these parish churches had to be minsters in miniature. The Gallican and Spanish councils of the sixth and seventh centuries tell us that the priest was under obligation to gather round him a team (29d, f, 1). He ran a school, from which he trained suitable candidates for ordination, and therefore had plenty of help in staging the people's office. Knowledge of the Psalter by heart was the principal qualification for ordination, and this obligation seems to have been extended to the priest's assistants too to some extent (29k).

There was a significant difference between town and country. Before the eleventh century the word 'parish' was understood in contrast to 'city'. It was a country phenomenon – the towns had no parishes, but were administered as single units based on the cathedral or basilica. One of the first to be divided into parishes was the German town of Worms, which was split up into four areas in 1016. The position of such parishes remained equivocal for several centuries. The decretals of Gregory IX in 1234 give no impression that the institution of urban parishes was either general or obligatory,[60] and the daily office may well have remained centred on the cathedral until quite late in some places.

If that, very roughly, was how the medieval parish system came into being, our natural response is to ask how this system, at its various stages of development, actually worked in everyday life. In particular, how was the office celebrated? Who attended it? What did it mean to people? The problems in discovering answers are formidable. A whole millennium between the sixth and sixteenth centuries has left behind it little in the way of eye-witness reports, and hardly any research has yet been done on the subject by historians or liturgical scholars. Because of this, we can only treat with the greatest caution any pieces of information which might tempt us to make deductions – no reliable conclusions can possibly be reached on the basis of present knowledge.

Having sounded this cautionary note, we must also add, however, that the evidence at present available is not absolutely nil; and it is just possible, on the basis of it, to venture some hypotheses which will throw light on our attempt to see how daily prayer was offered in the public churches in the Middle Ages.

First of all, we must bear in mind the enormous length of time under discussion, the whole span of a thousand years. To attempt any generalizations about that is equivalent to doing so for the period from 985 to 1985, an almost impossible undertaking, and certainly impossible in the space of a few pages.

Not allowing timidity to get the better of us, we can still gain some insights by taking a small number of particular subjects and roughly sketching in their history through the medieval period. There seem to be three areas which immediately invite this treatment, and in following them through we can perhaps see them as exploratory probes into a gigantic bulk, seeking to yield a preliminary idea of what more thorough and professional tunnellers might expect to find. Our main question in conducting this exercise will be this: how was the daily office celebrated in parish churches on ordinary weekdays?

1　The parish team

We have seen that in the early beginnings of the parish system the priest was not allowed to work alone but had to gather round him a team, part of whose task was to help sing the offices in church.

This practice still seems to have been in vigour in the ninth century, as various sources refer to it. In Gaul, for instance, there are several examples of disputes between two parishes which share one priest, the solution being that for six months the priest should reside with his clerks in one village, all travelling every day to the other village for the offices, and vice versa in the other six months.[61] According to Bishop Hincmar of Reims, if the priest was prevented from getting to church for the lesser hours, the clerks were to sing them without him.[62] A regulation issued at Aachen in 809 likewise says that priests must have disciples who can sing with them and celebrate the lesser hours and vespers when the priest is hindered.[63]

It is at present difficult to say how the Carolingian team of priest-plus-clerks survived in subsequent centuries. The training of candidates for the priesthood continued normally to be done in the parish, and through the Middle Ages it would be common for parish churches to have a variety of clergy on the staff –

the singing of High Mass on Sundays required at least the help of a deacon and subdeacon. But the matter is subject to some controversy, and little can at present be said on the subject other than that many parishes (we have no idea what proportion) will have had more than one cleric on the staff in the later Middle Ages, and that these would be required to sing the offices together in church.

We are on more certain ground with the figure who came to be known in England as the 'parish clerk'. If the priest of Carolingian times was unable to gather round him a team, he was obliged to have at least one 'clerk' to assist him.[64] We hear of such solitary clerks from at least the ninth century onwards. In England the 'Canons of Edgar' (? second half of the tenth century) assume that every priest will be able to bring one clerk to a yearly synod.[65] Not so long after this we see the clerk emerging as one of the standard parish officials. Hugh Grosseteste, Bishop of Lincoln (1235–53) laid down regulations concerning the parish clerk,[66] and from that period onwards information becomes more plentiful.

The duties of a medieval parish clerk were very varied.[67] He had to prepare the church for services, assist at the altar and read the epistle where necessary, put the books out for the daily offices, ringing the bell at the proper times, and sing the offices with the priest, especially the psalmody. He was also expected to visit the homes of the parish, both for matters of parish business and in accompanying the priest to the homes of the sick and infirm. He went about the parish with holy water, sprinkling it on who- or whatever wanted blessing, and he was often responsible for teaching children of the parish and keeping the church choir in good trim. Frequently tonsured and dressed like a clergyman, he was nevertheless normally allowed to marry. A good example of the clerk's job-description comes in a document of Holy Trinity church, Coventry, of 1462, where he is described as a general factotum, verger, sacristan and assistant at services; most interesting for us is the stipulation that he had to be in church daily for the divine office, and sing the psalms antiphonally with his assistant.[68]

The English parish clerk was so necessary to church life that he survived the changes of the Reformation, remaining an institution in the Anglican Church until the present century. In the seventeenth, eighteenth and nineteenth centuries his multifarious duties continued: care of the church, general administration, involvement in education, and leading the psalmody and responses in the services, which often continued to be daily, as we shall see shortly.

The parish clerk was sometimes known by other names. The verger at the church of my childhood fitted his description – a full-time paid officer of the church fulfilling many of the roles typical of the eighteenth-century parish clerk, including making the responses at weddings in a peremptory, nasal voice. P. H. Ditchfield could in this way tell the story of a traveller who asked an old countryman who he was. 'I hardly know what I be,' he replied. 'First vicar called me clerk; then another came, and he called me virgin [verger]; the last vicar said I were the christian [sacristan], and now I be clerk again.'[69]

Although the parish clerk of the Middle Ages included among his duties the singing of the daily office with the priest, we are not able to say how far it was indeed sung. The mere fact of his presence, however, at least made this more of a possibility.

There is one more aspect of parish teamwork that may be important to us in our search, and that is the system of chantry priests, particularly as it developed after the thirteenth century. The boom in the foundation of chantries in the later Middle Ages must have given a shot in the arm to the daily office in many places, for extra clergy were on hand to make its public performance more substantial. So, for example, 'The people of Doncaster told the Church commissioners in Edward VI's reign that by reason of the chantry priests 'there is at daily mattins, mass and evensong [singing] by note'.[70] At St Michael's, Cornhill, in London we are told that mattins, High Mass and evensong were sung daily from 1375 until the Reformation, in compliance with the terms of a bequest.[71]

Lest it be thought that only large towns could afford such things, small villages are known to have maintained similar daily programmes. 'At the little village of Cotterstock a fourteenth-century foundation provided for two clerks with competent skill in reading and singing, and "mattins and vespers and the other hours" were to be "solemnly sung in choir daily, with mass of the day and mass of Our Lady at the high altar, and this distinctly and audibly with good psalmody and suitable pauses in the middle of each verse of the psalms".'[72] Clive Burgess has provided a particularly interesting array of information from fifteenth-century Bristol:

The canonical regulations stipulate that chantry priests were to participate in the day-to-day liturgy of the parish church in which they served. The specific requirements made of the chantry priests' time were as follows. In addition to celebrating their mass, they were to be present in the choir, and not elsewhere, at matins, evensong and other Divine Service, wearing surplices. They were also obliged to assist at matins, mass and the other hours by singing invitatories, hymns, anthems, responds, grails and the like, reading lessons, epistles, gospels and also singing psalms.[73]

He concludes:

There can be no doubt that a parish church's daily liturgy would have been rendered a much more imposing ceremonial if, in addition to the clergy, several chantry priests participated in the parish mass and the canonical offices. Moreover, the scope for variation and innovation in practice that their presence facilitated may well have resulted in a higher standard of observance – to the spiritual benefit of the parish concerned. Conversely, their presence may well have enabled the parish clergy better to fulfil other obligations, confident of the liturgy's full observance in their absence.[74]

An example of such a church comes in the records of All Saints', Bristol, where a legal report describes a brawl during evensong on a Sunday evening in September 1457, from which we learn that several chantry priests were singing in choir with the vicar, assisted by at least one layman, and that a congregation was present in the nave.[75]

The subject of chantries is a matter of considerable debate among scholars, and we must remember that these few local examples cannot, in the present state of our knowledge, be held in any way to be typical of Britain, not to mention the rest of the West. But they show what was possible.

2   The emergence of a clerical caste

The long period during which the Church extended itself from the cities into the countryside could hardly have come in worse times. Any brief glance at histories of the period will show that the Church was forced to evolve its new structures and new self-understanding in the most difficult of circumstances. In this situation the growing prestige of monasticism after the fifth century led to results which were both understandable and regrettable. Bishops came often to be recruited from monasteries, and tended to have clear ideas about what in monastic life would be good treatment for the failings of their flocks. A typical example was Caesarius, Bishop of Arles (470–542). Under him and his successor Aurelian (546–53) the monastic and people's offices were carefully legislated for, and a drive was launched to introduce some of the virtues of monasticism into ordinary church life (29c, 44).

Caesarius' regulations on the people's office were monastic but non-Roman in character. There is no provision for Scripture-reading, typical, as we have seen already, of the people's office. A vigil service in Lent was to have readings and a sermon, but Caesarius had difficulty persuading people to sit this out – in fact we begin to see in this period an increase in the demands made upon people and clergy which often went against the grain, and clergy in East and West were frequently protesting at being forced to attend daily night vigils, complaining that they were being turned into monks. The clergy of the West were eventually put under an obligation to recite a sevenfold office of monastic origin, and ordered to lead celibate lives and devote their time to study and to digging the garden. Behind this perhaps too slavish imitation of the admirable monks, there was, however, a real need which had to be met: the evolution of an appropriate 'life' for parish clergy, an integrated approach to all the dimensions of their daily life and work which fitted the needs of their calling.

Until at least the ninth century there was great diversity in liturgical use, varying from place to place, and subject to the control of the local bishop. This situation was transformed as the old rites came to be replaced by that of Rome. In Rome there had been no uniform rite, but the various forms in use were probably similar in nature and semi-monastic (the 'monastic' churches of Rome were probably served by communities of *devoti*). It was a local rite, out of step with the general picture in the West or even the rest of Italy, as far as we can see (32). It was also in essence a monastic rite which included the lesser hours of prime, terce, sext, none, the night office and compline. Bishops outside the Roman liturgical sphere were already making attempts to monasticize the people's office, Caesarius of Arles being just one example. However, it was the spread of this Roman rite which finally established everywhere a monastic form of daily office for the secular Church, so that in medieval Europe the daily office of parish churches consisted no longer of just mattins and vespers, but of a round of seven or eight services. From about the seventh century a form of the Roman office began to spread in the West. In seventh-century Britain the struggle between the old Celtic rite and the newly introduced Roman rite was fierce. Such a struggle went on all over Western Europe, until in one place after another the opposition lost the battle, eventually leaving the Ambrosian rite of Milan and the Mozarabic of Toledo as the sole survivors. This changeover was achieved earliest in Britain (in the eighth century), but not until the eleventh century did it even begin in Spain.

At the forefront of this Romanizing process was Charlemagne (742–814) who, in seeking to civilize and unify his dominions, saw the Church as an obvious instrument for the purpose. So he attempted to impose the Benedictine Rule on monasteries, and a version of the Roman liturgy on all secular clergy. This met with resistance in many quarters, however, and the supremacy of the Roman rite was not in fact finally established until about the twelfth century. In Ireland, for example, the Celtic rite did not finally disappear until then.[76] Although Charlemagne's reform was easier said than done, it marked a decisive turning-point in the history of the daily office. There was widespread fatigue at centuries of political and cultural disorder, and growing admiration for Rome as a constant point of reference in a turbulent and uncertain world. Thinking people wanted a greater sense of the Church, and higher standards than those of the parish pump.

The spread of the Roman liturgy was largely achieved by secular authority. Forms of it had already been in use in some parts for many years since, but many of the people of France and Germany showed a conspicuous lack of enthusiasm for what they saw as newfangled rites, and even Rome itself was reluctant to let its treasured liturgy pass into barbarian hands. Charlemagne fought more or less alone for its imposition, by all the means at his disposal. One of his approaches, for instance, was to press for its use on feast-days; so candidates for ordination were asked: 'Can you sing the divine office according to the Roman rite on solemn days?'[77] Continuing disenchantment comes out clearly in Lyon, where 'it was Bishop Leidrad, about 813–14, who was finally forced to complete the ruination, and substitute for the rites of Pothinus and Irenaeus those known under the title of *Sacri Palatii*, i.e. of the emperor's choir at Aachen'.[78] In the middle of the ninth century Pope Leo IV sent an acid letter

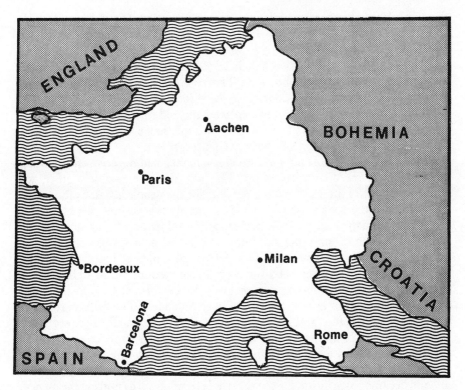

Charlemagne's dream was of a Western Empire equal to that of Byzantium in the East. It was therefore natural that he should want the usages of old Rome, which was now under his dominion, to become the liturgy of the Empire.

to a local abbot, threatening him with excommunication if he did not adopt the Roman rite and the Gregorian chant – the battle had to be fought even on the Pope's own doorstep.[79]

The Franks were selective in their Romanization, however, retaining favourite parts of their old liturgies. The result was a hybrid liturgy which developed in turn into a bewildering series of local uses. Then in the end it all went back the way it came, and replaced the old rite used in the Roman churches themselves. So it has come to be said that everything in Western liturgical study eventually leads back to Charlemagne.

The Carolingian reform, for all its achievements, had negative effects which were to prove peculiarly enduring. The old Western people's office was transformed into a monastic round. Services for the people became offices after the fashion of the monks, at which laity could attend, but not speak much or sing. 'The layman', said one of Charlemagne's ordinances, 'must not read the lesson in church or sing alleluia, but just the psalm or responsory, without alleluia.'[80] Clearly people still did participate, but a highly sacerdotal understanding of the priesthood was now being encouraged, as well as a new emphasis on the sacral nature of worship, now performed by the clergy at a distance, reducing the laity to the role of awed onlookers. The drift was towards greater discipline, too, and a sharper eye on the clergy. There were many experiments in communal living, of which the rule of Chrodegang of Metz (d. 766) is a famous example. This idea of parish priests living together and celebrating the daily office under a partly monastic rule was very much in the air, and became a significant part of the whole trend towards putting the clergy's house in order, leading to the various forms of canons regular. These aims were admirable in themselves, but in their pursuit Charlemagne and his successors imposed on the clergy a form of daily office which was far too elaborate and complicated for them. From the tenth century onwards, as if this were not enough, the office also had added to it supplementary offices such as the Little Office of Our Lady (of ninth-century origin), the Office of the Dead (probably deriving from the eighth century), the Gradual and Penitential Psalms, and an ever more complicated calendar.

Problems inevitably followed. There were increasing complaints about offices being said at the wrong times or bunched together to have them out of the way. The idea began to appear that a monk or cleric should recite an entire office privately if unable to be present at the public celebration. These developments led to at least three consequences, each of which in virtue of the long time which it endured had tragic consequences for church life: (a) priests became a celibate caste set apart from the laity; (b) the laity were reduced to the role of silent onlookers in church; and (c) the office itself became a long and complex 'debt', a quantity of words which had to be paid out in full by each cleric – a clerical exercise mostly incomprehensible to layfolk, and increasingly so even for clergy.

3   Official ideal and imperfect reality

We have abundant information on the ideals held officially by the Church on the daily office at various periods, but it is not always easy to see how they compared with actual practice. What were these ideals? The Spanish and Gallican councils of the sixth and seventh centuries (29) reveal a time of transition from the days of the antique people's office centred on cathedrals to a mixed situation where clergy were to maintain a daily office in their church as well as being asked in some places to take turns in supporting the offices in their cathedral. Two centuries later we see the parish churches becoming entirely independent, and the clergy being required to ensure the singing of the full sevenfold Roman office there every day.

It was assumed that people would attend. Charlemagne's regulations (?802) state that 'all priests must ring the bells of their churches at the proper hours of day and night, and celebrate the sacred offices to God, and teach the people how and at what hours God is to be worshipped'.[81] Two centuries later, Peter Damian wrote that attendance every day was obligatory for all Christian believers.[82]

The country in which this sevenfold office first became universal was England. The synod of Cloveshoe in 747 required all clergy to sing the seven canonical hours daily in church. The Canons of Aelfric (c. 955–1022) repeat this requirement, and go on to enumerate the liturgical books which each church must possess, those for the offices being a Psalter, a canticle-book, and a lectionary for the Bible-readings. The Canons of Edgar, of the same period, add that the bell must be rung for each of the seven daily services. These provisions are thenceforward repeated with very little change over the next five or six hundred years, in the canons issued by synods, in visitation articles and charges, and episcopal regulations. The ringing of the bell seven times a day became so much a part of life that the names of services were used as a normal means of indicating the time. It was universally accepted, and entrenched in canon law, that the canonical hours had to be sung in the church by the clergy of the parish except when there were exceptional impediments. Speaking of the twelfth century Père Salmon says that 'the great canonical collections . . . always testify to the duty of all clerics to participate in the office in their church'.[83] He lists dozens of councils up to the sixteenth century which continue to take the choral office as the norm.[84] It might be said that these councils would have had no cause to repeat the requirement had there not been a need to remind people of it. But it is not usually proposed in any emphatic way, and is regularly accompanied by similar paragraphs on Sunday services which seem on the whole to have been well observed. Père Salmon concludes finally that 'on the eve of the Council of Trent the situation was as follows: every church possessed either a beneficied clergy or a community of canons, they were obliged to ensure the solemn choral office, and there was for each cleric a grave obligation to participate in it at the regular hours'.[85] This obligation addressed itself purely to the public singing of the office. It was simply that. There was no obligation to private saying of the office – that was merely an example of late medieval piety and to some extent superstition, the making up of what was lost if an office had been missed. Like a schoolboy catching up on missed lessons, it was never seen as a normal way of carrying on. The obligation to the office was exactly the same as the obligation to hold Sunday services. A priest could not decide not to hold Sunday mass in church, but celebrate it privately instead: nor was he supposed to do so with the office. It was simply his public job. His *obligation* to it was only of the same nature as his obligation to provide Sunday services, baptize, teach, and all the rest.

This standard of a daily public office is reflected in the domain of liturgical books. Inventories throughout the medieval period show that parish churches continued to keep the full range of books for singing the daily services. In the earlier centuries it was normal for clergy to know most of the office by heart, so it did not matter so much if they could not afford the books. As the office became more elaborate, however, the help of books became necessary. It is important to realize that liturgical books were used quite differently from the way we use them today. There would have been no individual copies. The weighty tomes needed in the performance of a service were placed on a large revolving lectern, and those who could sing gathered round, the rest staying at a distance and singing what they could from memory. The lectern was at the centre of things, frequently being turned to bring different books into play. In the psalmody, for instance, the antiphon would be sung from the antiphoner, then the top of the lectern would spin round to present the Psalter before the eyes of the singers in order that they might sing the psalm. The people tended simply to listen at a distance. In monasteries there were no serried ranks of choir-stalls. The lectern stood in the midst and the brethren stood round, senior brethren in front, the younger ones behind, and they propped themselves on portable 'forms', or often on crutches, while the more elderly sat on a simple wall-seat. The Gothic choirstalls of our cathedrals and abbeys were a new development in liturgical furnishing, and standing in serried ranks facing each other reflected a new feeling for system. Such changes seem to have coincided with the development of smaller liturgical books. The Cistercians preserved a transitional stage, it still being their traditional custom today to share one large book between two or three brethren in choir.[86]

The ancient practice of performing the daily offices entirely from memory without the use of any books at all continued in many cathedrals. At Lincoln in the fifteenth century no one was allowed in choir with a book, save for the dean, precentor, chancellor and treasurer.[87] In France, the council of Narbonne in 1551 forbade the canons to have any book in choir with them, even a personal breviary.[88] At Rouen (and several other French cathedrals) the clergy were forbidden to have any book with them in choir right up until the French

The sixteenth-century choir of Auch cathedral in southern France. There is a large four-sided lectern in the midst, with a revolving top and a cupboard below, which also provides a further shelf for books. As is often the case in French churches, the choirstalls have no bookrests.

Revolution. All the psalmody and chanting had to be done by heart, a book being used only for lessons and collects, when a choirboy would appear with a lantern and hold it over the page for the reader. Procter and Frere pointed out long ago that in such circumstances no one can feel he possesses the whole liturgy in his hands.[89] He has his own part to play, but for other parts he is totally dependent on others. Liturgy then lives up to its name by being shared out among the Body.

The medieval book-situation began to change with the invention of the *breviary*. The breviary was the creation, not of the secular clergy, but of the monks, through a gradual evolution in the monasteries over several centuries, in response to a growing desire to reduce the number of liturgical books needed in the performance of services. Two or three books came to be combined into a single large volume, known – as was any such compendium of information – as a breviary. It was as unwieldy as the other liturgical books, and certainly not suitable for any kind of private use. With the increasing literacy of monks, smaller breviaries then came to be created, enabling them to follow services individually, and to say services in full when travelling. In this way pictures of religious or clerics sitting in choir each with their little book became quite common in the later Middle Ages. The breviary was an inevitable development: it made sense to evolve new ways of making the various parts of the liturgy more accessible and easy to find, and was a product of a world greatly interested in finding ways to do things more systematically.

The moment of take-off for the breviary was provided by the coming of the Friars Minor. They had started as a movement for laymen, who bore no obligation concerning the daily office. They attended the office in parish churches when they could, and otherwise prayed informally on their own. But their imagination was soon caught by the possibility of putting the offices, stripped down to a lean minimum, into a single portable book, with which the services could be said privately as brethren tramped the roads in their vagabond life. The idea caught on after about 1250, slowly gathering momentum too among the clergy. In the thirteenth century a breviary was too expensive an item for most clergy to afford, and tended to cause a sensation if seen in public – books of any sort were rarely encountered by the general public and were considered to be objects of great value. Nevertheless, the Franciscan breviary captured the spirit of the moment, and inevitably was adopted throughout the principal regions of the West. There are two aspects to this spread of the breviary in secular usage which should be made clear: first, the breviary spread to cathedrals and parish churches as a liturgical book, usually a large and unwieldy ledger, used for reference and for easy location of material in the public daily office, and as such it was a supplement to the other liturgical books; secondly, it spread among the parish clergy as a private possession bought at their own expense; here it was small and handy, making it possible to read the office privately on the occasions when those concerned could not get to the

Franciscan friars singing in choir (without books), from a fourteenth-century Psalter.

A group of Minoresses illustrated from the same book (this time with personal breviaries).[90]

church at the right time. So far, that was acceptable. But it quickly came to be abused in that some recited their office privately at the slightest opportunity rather than sing it in choir. Yet while the breviary quite quickly earned recognized status as a requirement for parish churches in episcopal visitation documents and charges, its private use by the clergy never attained official acceptance (except for purposes of travel) until well after the Reformation period. Salmon had been very insistent on this in describing the situation on the eve of the Council of Trent:

... no less than three centuries would still be required before private and individual recitation would become the general practice; all this time it would be looked upon as a substitute for the choral office. It is very difficult to say at what precise time it ceased to be such and became the official form of the priest's prayer. In the sixteenth century it was still justified by virtue of the principle laid down by St Benedict and taken over by St Chrodegang. Just as the monk and the canon of Carolingian times were personally obliged to take part in the office of their community or unite themselves to it in private when they were lawfully hindered, so the cleric attached to the service of the church from which he drew his support was bound in like manner.

One difference, however, is important: for the monk and the canon of St Chrodegang, the hindrances were limited and temporary; whereas for the cleric they lengthened and went on multiplying. For the latter, private recitation, far from remaining an exception, became an habitual thing, a custom sanctioned by authority, on the way to becoming the general rule. It is to be noted that all the texts prior to the Council of Trent which authorized individual recitation issued from private teachers or from particular councils; no Roman pontiff nor any general council – with the exception of that of Basel – as yet expressly permitted it.[91]

The move to privatization was not the only thing sparked off by the Franciscans' breviary: far from being a simple compendium of current liturgical practice, it effected substantial changes in the form of office used, by choosing not the ancient rite of the Roman churches, but that of the Pope's private chapel, which had long been going its own way liturgically. The Pope and his household had become too busy to spend time attending the public offices, and for some centuries had performed their office in private. This evolved in its own way in a hermetically sealed compartment as the centuries passed. Eugenius III had left Rome altogether and for forty-three years took his papal court from one Italian town to another, so that it had even less opportunity for contact with the liturgy of Rome.

The Franciscans' abandonment of so much ancient tradition in choosing this rite for their breviary was not immediately noticed. When it was, some were moved to protest. Radulf de Rivo, a Belgian abbot, is perhaps the best known – he accused the friars of vandalism, and attempted to campaign against their newfangled rites. Radulph had come back from Rome greatly impressed with the offices as they were performed in the great basilicas, especially the Lateran. *This* was the office which should be used. But it was too late. The friars had quickly fanned out all over Europe. In 1227 the Pope ordered the Roman churches to use the Franciscan breviary, and shortly afterwards the Lateran changed over to it too. Part of the resulting loss was in the drastic pruning of the office's richness and range of choice (see, for example, on page 149), and in the institutionalizing of a new invention – rubrics. The divine office was no longer an open-ended affair, as it was when it involved several people manhandling a number of books. Even though many variations on the papal office were now in use, the thing in itself was on the way to becoming a precisely defined system.

The breviary had brought with it a second wave of Romanization, a different version of the Roman rite now replacing that of the first wave, which had by this time fragmented into an array of local uses. But this time we have a new way of pre-packing liturgy in a form which is easily manageable and readily mass-produced, with a consequent drastic loss in the variety and quality of the services. The loss was compounded by the adoption of a version of the liturgy which was a little-known outgrowth from the main bush. This 'take-away' office found its way firstly onto the lectern in the parish church, and by a slightly longer process into the priest's pocket too. Despite these changes, uniformity was still a long way off, however. Variations in the form of the breviary were common, and well-established local rites and uses such as that of Sarum continued, mostly, in their full vigour.

If saying the breviary privately while travelling or otherwise hindered was simply a popular fashion without any legal back-up, the question naturally arises as to what people *were* expected to do if they were absent from offices. It was still felt that one should pray. On a journey a cleric (or, indeed, lay person) might call in at services in churches along the road, or would mark his participation at a distance by saying those psalms and other parts of the office which he could remember by heart.[92] Otherwise, he might tell his beads, and as these had not yet been converted to purely Marian devotion by popular piety, that meant the recitation of a certain number of Our Fathers or psalm-verses. As Van Dijk and Walker put it, 'In general any kind of prayer would do instead of the hours ... The explanations of contemporary jurists make it quite plain that liability to private recitation did not imply repeating the office as sung or said in church: *secundum formam ecclesiae*. Making up for absence in choir was a private affair, in the true sense of the word, and freedom of choice of prayers was proportionate.'[93] There is a nice story of two priests singing the office together when all of a sudden it started to thunder. Far from carrying on reading their office privately, they abandoned it and said their beads.[94] 'Still, the pious office-saying monk or cleric in holy orders favoured a "liturgical" manner of making up. He liked to imitate what he could have done in choir and to observe most of the ceremonies, such as genuflections, inclinations and pauses.'[95]

In this description of officially-held ideals we have already seen that things were less than perfect in actual practice. It was expected that clerics would normally sing the offices publicly together. Yet in the later Middle Ages it was becoming common for the priest to read the services quietly to himself in a corner of the chancel, perhaps even doing all the offices together at one sitting. The people were disregarded, even if present. 'Should the office be said aloud so that the people can hear,' inquires a manual for priests, 'or quietly so that only God can hear?' The answer is revealing: it is always best to recite the offices aloud and distinctly, though whether this is done every day or only on festal days will depend on custom.[96] We have already found reason to suppose that in a proportion of churches the services would have been sung publicly at the proper times. An English official document of *circa* 1540 seems to confirm this picture, speaking of 'the services used in the church daily in some places, or upon the Sundays and other feasts in all places; that is to say, mattins, prime, hours, evensong and compline'.[97]

This brings us to one area in which information is much more abundant, and that concerns the celebration of the offices on Sundays and feast-days. Right through the medieval period we find ecclesiastical documents insisting on the special importance of Sunday mattins and evensong (the latter name is of Anglo-Saxon origin, and was the common vernacular name for the evening service). References in contemporary literature are plentiful. Sunday worship for the average man and woman consisted of mattins and mass in the morning and evensong in the afternoon at 2.00 or 3.00 p.m. (3.00 p.m. is still a normal time in many English country parishes, as well as cathedrals). By evensong people meant the Roman vespers, or the Sarum version of it, and mattins was the title for a double service which we would call vigils and lauds, the monastic-type night office followed by morning prayer. A considerable diet by modern standards, for it was usual to perform Sunday services with full ceremonies, and special elaborations at festivals. At Christmas and Epiphany, for instance, 'a lesson called the "Genealogy" was sung at the end of mattins from the rood-loft with much solemnity by the deacon, robed in dalmatic, with incense, lights, cross, and subdeacon'.[98] In most parishes laity had to take turns at providing candles for mattins and evensong, and it was a usual practice after a death for the relatives to keep a candle lighted on the tomb during the Sunday offices for one year. Saturday evensong was also regarded as important, for it began the Lord's Day, and only a special convention allowed work to continue after Saturday evensong was done, until the sun went down.

The solemn celebration of Sunday mattins and evensong lasted in England until the Reformation. Sir Thomas More is heard to complain that 'some of us laymen think it a pain once in a week to rise so soon from sleep, and to tarry so long fasting, in order that on Sunday they may come and hear out their Matins. And yet in many parishes matins is nowhere near so early begun nor so long in the doing, as it is in the Charterhouse.'[99]

Conclusion

Having teased out three stands in the history of the medieval Church, we are afforded a tantalizing glimpse into the answer which more thorough research might yield to the question: 'How was the secular office celebrated?' Throughout the period the offices were sung daily in cathedrals and collegiate churches. Before 1250 that would be true of most parishes. After that, practice began to vary: in a proportion of them the services continued to be sung daily, involving more than one person in their performance. In others, the priest may have read in a subdued voice in the chancel with his clerk, and eventually, with the advent of the breviary, some will have read entirely alone in silence, often at other than the proper times. The bell would normally have been rung at the seven canonical times, even if there was no service (it was a not unusual complaint for the bell to be rung but the service to fail to take place), and the people of the parish may well have said a special prayer when they heard the bell ring, or made the sign of the cross (of which, more shortly). In most places, though not in all (as we shall see), the old people's office, with its hearty lay participation, was gone. The Roman liturgy, as its use spread, reduced the laity to silence. It is more than likely, though, that there were at least one or two people in the nave on weekdays, to hear the vicar and his clerk and perhaps other clerics singing the main offices of each day, at least in churches where they kept to their bounden duty as repeatedly insisted upon by church authority. On Sundays and feast-days, on the other hand, the people turned out in force to 'hear out their mattins and evensong'.

Most of our evidence has been taken from England, but for most of Western Europe the picture may well prove to be similar, although we must not underestimate the considerable variety which prevailed in all aspects of the medieval Church. The final note must be the one of caution with which we began: for the reliable facts from which generalizations can justifiably be made we must wait upon the labours of the medieval historian.

The border between private prayer and public liturgy was never so rigid in earlier times as it is with us. For this reason, there is yet one more 'bore-hole' we can make into the medieval mountain, penetrating strata which it might not have occurred to us to consider.

15

Personal Prayer

When we consider the momentous effects the study of history has had upon liturgy, particularly in the last twenty years or so, it is strange indeed to see how content we are to pray our personal prayers with hardly any knowledge of how Christians have done so down the centuries. Very little study has been made of this subject, and this may be reflected in the way we often hold out to people ways of prayer which go far wide of the mark. Our interest in the daily prayer of the people of God therefore leads us to take a closer look at this subject.

Popular prayer

In the period immediately following the peace of the Church in the fourth century the heart of people's prayer was seen to be the Sunday liturgy climaxing in the Eucharist, and the people's office on weekdays. If a priest or layperson failed to attend an office in church, there was no adequate substitute for it. They did the next best thing, praying in their own way either alone or with the family. These prayers will have been based on what went on in the public office, but would not attempt to imitate it slavishly, or even in much detail. And yet we gain the unmistakable impression from reading the Fathers that they assume the hours of prayer to be the same thing whether done publicly in church or privately at home. John Chrysostom advised people unable to attend the daily office to pray where they were, whatever they were doing (12g, h). Gregory of Tours (c. 540–94) describes how his uncle, a bishop, while tramping a country road, said Psalm 51, the Benedicite, Psalms 148–150 and the *preces* at the time of mattins (from memory, naturally). Augustine speaks of singing offices at home as well as in church (28b), and in the East, the *Apostolic Constitutions* advise that morning and evening prayer should take place in the home if persecution made it impossible for people to get to church (13c). We know too that people celebrated the lucernarium in their homes. Jerome advised inquirers to do it, and we are told that St Basil's sister Macrina celebrated it in her last illness (24c and 15). A Council of far-away Toledo in the year 400 was indeed moved to stop people doing it for themselves without a priest being present (29a). There are occasional allusions in later literature to public and private prayer of the hours, implying perhaps that the lesser hours were observed privately, or that the hours of prayer went on simultaneously in public and private. Another Council of Toledo in 633 speaks of 'the daily public *and* private offices'. This would not refer to actual saying of the form of the public office in private, but a simpler form of prayer with which the appropriate hour is marked.[100] Traces of this link between ecclesial and domestic prayer can still be detected in several of the Eastern rites today.

Some doctors of the Ethiopian Church, questioned by Bishop Gwynne of Khartoum in 1916, said on the question of daily prayers that, among other things, the people are taught to use certain portions of the Psalter seven times a day. The psalms should be followed by a doxology, the Creed and the Lord's Prayer.[101]

Further north, A. J. Maclean reported of the east Syrian Christians and their daily office in 1892 that the laity learn psalms and anthems as well as the Lord's Prayer and Trisagion for their prayers, and the 'old men, workmen, shepherds and sailors, when far from a church, if they don't know any psalms, should mark a cross on a wall, and make short ejaculations, for example, "Make me a clean heart, O God", say the Lord's Prayer and Trisagion, and prostrate themselves on the earth, making the sign of the cross.'[102] Here is liturgical prayer in parallel, using very simple formulas, and quite at harmony with what we read in Chrysostom, Augustine and other contemporaries of theirs.

There are also traces of this approach to prayer in the Byzantine tradition. For Orthodox laity all prayer is dominated by liturgical formulas. Particularly interesting for us is the clergy's discipline regarding the daily office. There is no concept of obligation in our Western sense, although daily liturgical celebration is strongly urged. Failing that, clergy (and laity too in theory) should say a selection of prayers for morning and evening which are provided in authorized prayer-books. These prayers vary slightly from book to book, depending, it seems, on who has compiled it, but they all draw in the same way on the psalmody, hymnody, canticles and other material which form the heart of the respective morning and evening offices.

Similar connections between the divine office and private prayer are to be found in the West, and, as in the examples above, the connection was made in two ways, either individually or in combination: by the *content* of prayer, and by marking the *times* of the Church's prayer.

The content of people's prayer

The piety of Christians in the late Roman Empire was firmly based in the Psalter. The vast majority who had no access to any book of psalms will have known by heart those few psalms which were repeated regularly in their liturgy, such as Psalm 51, which Basil tells us was known by all the laity in his country.[103] They will also certainly have known particular psalm-verses by heart for frequent repetition. This is a practice attested in both East and West. They will have known too such liturgical formulas as Kyrie Eleison, the Gloria Patri, and the Lord's Prayer. Even in a modern industrialized country of Orthodox tradition, prayer which turns over these kinds of formula in a series of repetitions is in the lifeblood of the people. The peasantry and artisans of the Christian world seem to have prayed in a remarkably consistent tradition by ringing the changes from a small vocabulary of bits and pieces, turning them over in reflective repetition, and in a way indistinguishable from the way they participate in liturgy.

We have some information on what was recommended to ordinary people in the West. Both Ambrose and Caesarius of Arles tell people to repeat frequently the Creed and the Lord's Prayer. So does Bede. From Theodulf of Orleans (d. 821) we have the earliest example of official guidelines on the matter of personal prayer, in which he instructs all priests to ensure that their people recite daily in the morning and the evening either the Creed or the Lord's Prayer or some other prayers, especially the following: 'Thou who hast created me, have mercy upon me', and 'My God, be merciful to me a sinner'.[104] It is probably no accident that the latter is not very different from the Orthodox 'Jesus Prayer' – this repetition of scripture phrases is rooted in the tradition of the undivided Church. The Jesus Prayer was still in use in the West in the seventeenth century.[105] With books very scarce, such means will naturally have been turned to in supplying the need for material for prayer, just as refrains were imaginatively used to enable public singing during the chanting of a wide selection of texts in public worship. Clergy were required to know the Psalter by heart, but it is most unlikely in the Dark Ages that many laity will have known much of the Psalter from memory. In an eighth-century description of a popular procession at St-Riquier in Belgium a revealing distinction is made between educated and uneducated villagers, with an implication that the latter have only very rudimentary means for joining in prayer and worship. There had been a decline in standards as Christianity was spread fast but thinly. The people's office lost out, and so did prayer and general Christian formation; the chronic neglect of the sacrament of confirmation throughout the Middle Ages is typical of a spiritual situation which often left a great deal to be desired. It was not difficult to find people who could barely be called Christian at all. One fundamental element in worship and prayer that was destined to undergo severe diminishment was the use of the psalms. In the diocese of Arles in the sixth century Bishop Caesarius assumed in his sermons that his ordinary and workaday flock knew some of the psalms by heart.[106] Such standards of Christian formation failed to be maintained in subsequent centuries. Edmund Bishop says in connection with the eighth-century procession referred to above:

It is clear that psalmody still survived as the substantial and primitive devotion of the Rogation days as centuries before ... the times, however, were no longer as in the fifth or sixth century, when Latin was the native tongue of all: the layfolk must be content now with something simpler.[107]

So the boys' school and 'the others who can' sing the Apostles' Creed, etc. There was a continuous process of simplification, culminating at a point where the rosary, the angelus and other devotions become almost the sole substitutes for the prayer of Scripture and people's office.

The *rosary* traces its origins back to the Psalter. For centuries the Book of Psalms had been divided into decades or other divisions, each governed by special prayers or themes. Ways were later found of saying a kind of shadow-Psalter if people were unable to say the actual psalms. An English rule for recluses gives five examples of ways in which this was done. Anyone who did not understand Latin should, during the readings of the psalms, do one of the following things:[108] (1) understand each verse to mean 'Lord, have mercy on me'; (2) take a favourite verse from the psalms, such as 'Show us, Lord, your favour and grant us your salvation', and repeat it 2606 times (equalling the number of verses in the Psalter!); (3) learn *one* psalm by heart and say it 150 times; (4) use a psalm breviary (see below) which gives one verse from each psalm; (5) recite the Lord's Prayer a fixed number of times in place of a corresponding number of psalms. All of these, we should remember, are ways of coping with illiteracy and the non-availability of books. Later, with the burgeoning of Marian devotion, the Angel's greeting came in as another form of *ersatz* psalm, and it was that which eventually won the day. So the person who prays fifteen decades of the rosary is really doing the equivalent of saying the 150 psalms of the Psalter.

The Lord's Prayer was one of the standard formulas for use with the rosary until quite recent times. The word 'patter' derives from the rapid repetition of *Paters*, and the rosary is known by this very name in South Tyrol today.[109] Medieval references often assume that the Lord's Prayer is meant when the beads are mentioned, and still today in Poland there are such devotions as the Rosary of the Holy Trinity, and that of the Name of Jesus. The latter, when sung in church, begins with a hymn of St Bernard, and for each mystery there is a short chant, then one Lord's Prayer, one Hail Mary, and ten times the phrases: 'Jesus, son of David, have mercy on us', then a 'Glory be ...', an antiphon, versicle and response, and a collect. Then the same for each mystery. Each of the three parts of the devotion begins with a hymn and ends with the litany of the Name of Jesus, echoing both in form and content the services of the divine office. Of the general practice of saying the rosary an eighteenth-century Swiss catechesis states that it is 'nothing but a divine office for ordinary people'.[110]

For the vast mass of Christian people the Psalter, which was the heart of the

Church's prayer, was simplified and adapted beyond all recognition. For those, however, who could afford books and were in a position to read them, there remained the possibility of imitating the content of the daily office more directly.

Ever since New Testament times there must have been Christians who had their books of prayers and excerpts from Scripture. Our earliest examples of such books come from the Dark Ages, and they usually contain material directly modelled on the divine office. There are, for example, some treatises attributed to Alcuin (c. 735–804) which aim to help people with their prayers. One of these includes a form of daily office for the devout layperson, which seems to have been evolved in France in the first half of the ninth century.[111] The preface states how the person for whom the book was intended 'asked us to write ... a compendium ("breviarium") ... on how the layman situated in the active life should pray to God at these particular hours'. The day begins as follows:

(sitting up): Lord Jesus Christ, Son of the living God, I lift up my hands in your name.
O God make speed to save me ... (three times)
Psalm 5.1–3
Lord's Prayer
Short *preces*

(rising): O Lord open my lips ...
Gloria
Psalms 3 and 51
Psalm 95 (*Venite*)
'Then as many Psalms as you want'

In essence a selective Psalter arranged according to the days of the week, the book also provides hymns, litanies and other liturgical forms. Included is an abbreviated Psalter attributed to Bede which is typical of other similar collections sometimes known as a psalm breviary or 'Flores Psalmorum': one verse (sometimes two or more) is given from each of the 150 Psalms, for example:

Psalm 1 – verses 1–3
2 – verses 10–12
3 – verses 3, 7a
4 – verse 1b

The greatly admired practice of reciting the whole Psalter, immortalized by the Egyptian monks, could thus be performed by taking representative verses from each psalm, which were thought to sum up what it had to say.[112]

In the age of Charlemagne books such as Alcuin's became common, 'libelli precum', books of prayers, partly liturgical and partly collections of assorted prayers and litanies.[113]

Later on, this type of book would be completely overshadowed by another development which would dominate the daily prayer of literate people in a very remarkable way: the Book of Hours, which provided simple forms of office to be said by the laity at home. In the later Middle Ages these were turned out in such numbers that even after the wholesale destruction of the Reformation and the natural loss of four or five centuries, Europe's libraries can still boast thousands of examples of them. They were so widely mass-produced as to enable the whole of educated Europe to pray liturgically. Their content was generally as follows:

> Calendar
> Office of the Blessed Virgin
> Office of the Dead
> The Seven Penitential Psalms (6, 32, 38, 51, 102, 130, 143)
> The Gradual Psalms (120 to 134)
> Litany of the Saints
> Other prayers and devotions
> Other offices on particular themes (e.g. the cross, the Holy Spirit, John the
>   Baptist, etc.)

Most of these were accretions to the normal divine office, accretions which had originated in the monasteries and had later been taken on board by the clergy too. Popular devotion fastened on to these as forms of prayer laypeople could cope with, and so they ended by being reproduced in small books of hours or *primers* which people could use privately or with others, at home or in church. An Italian reported of England in the fifteenth century that:

All attend mass every day, and say many Pater nosters in public, the women carrying long rosaries in their hands, and any who can read taking the Office of our Lady with them, and with some companion reciting it in the church verse by verse in a low voice after the manner of religious.[114]

It seems to have been a widespread practice for people to say their daily primer offices with others, and it was certainly common for people to read them out aloud even while services were going on. A treatise of 1527 advised the reader that he should, 'rising in the morning, go to church and with devotion say his mattins without jangling, also sweetly hear mass and all the Hours of the day'.[115] Even as late as 1570, well into the new reformed dispensation,

Arthur Chapman of Wolsingham a blacksmith was brought before the court at Durham for reading an English book or Primer in the church of Wolsingham at the time of the morning prayer while the Priest was saying his service not minding what the Priest read, but tending his own book and prayer, the Priest after the first lesson willed him to read more softly; he said that he would make amends for his fault.[116]

By this date he would not have been saying the office of the Blessed Virgin Mary, but something of the habit of reading the primer during mattins had evidently survived the best-laid plans of the reformers.

With the greater availability of books after the thirteenth century we see emerging an expectation that wherever possible everyone, be they clerical or lay, should have their own book from which they could pray a form of the daily office in private, and not all layfolk were content merely with the primer. Psalters and breviaries appear too in many bequests made to laity in the fourteenth and fifteenth centuries. When the priest celebrated the offices on Sundays it would not be unusual, apparently, for there to be some people scattered among the congregation who were able to follow the services with their own full breviary (the primer would not have been of much use for this purpose).

In the later 1300s primers in English began to appear. These tended to be much more simply produced than the Latin books, with little in the way of illumination and illustration, and were obviously intended for the popular market. Later, after the arrival of printing, there appeared a new legion of cheap, printed primers.[117] The whole phenomenon of books of hours is one of the most outstanding success-stories in the history of liturgy and popular devotion. Picking up one of these primers today and fingering through its pages, one is struck by the simplicity of it, but also by the solid wealth of Scripture and forms of prayer which it provides its user with. The Office of the Blessed Virgin, for instance, gives the essential shape of the Church's public daily offices, plus a generous selection from the Psalter, with a light lacing of Marian antiphons and propers to provide a unifying theme. The other offices tend to be simpler, always based on a theme. This development in the history of daily office and Christian prayer was impressive for its simple shape, its thematic structures, and fixed content, in these things signalling a fascinating return to some of the principles of the old people's office. Those who prayed it also attended the public offices on Sundays and feast-days, if not also on other days, and it thus had the potential, given a sound understanding of the Church's daily prayer, to enable the old daily communal prayer of former centuries to adapt to a more complex and mobile society.

Times of prayer

Imitation of the content of the daily office was one way of associating with it at a distance. Another was by praying, wherever one was, at the time the office was offered. There are various ninth-century testimonies to a recommendation that laity should pray in the morning, at the third, sixth and ninth hours, and in the evening. This is mentioned, for example, in a treatise by Jonas, bishop of Orleans, written about 830.[118] A letter by a ninth-century Spanish-German princess named Dodana advises her son to pray at the hours when the divine office is offered.[119] Four centuries later an episcopal document from Coventry dated 1237 mentions a practice of saying the Lord's Prayer seven times a day, adding the Creed in the morning and evening.[120] The canonical times for prayer were broadcast by the sound of the bell. Bells rang out by day and by night for all sorts of purposes: to call people to services, and to mark special occasions and emergencies such as festivals, invasions, storms, the curfew, the closure of town gates, and the beginning and end of work. People were also used to hearing the bell ring at the traditional times of the hours of prayer, as has already been mentioned. Among all these things one daily custom which particularly stands out is the ringing of bells at morning, noon and evening, to call the faithful to simultaneous prayer, and this prayer was to be concerned with the particular mysteries with which the corresponding office was associated. Most usually these were the resurrection in the morning, the cross at midday, and the incarnation at sunset. The practice of saying the Angelus at morning, noon and evening when the church bell rings arose from this tradition – it was originally a prayer said to associate oneself with the office being celebrated in the nearby church.

The connection of the morning office with the resurrection is very ancient, as is that of the middle hours of the day with the stages of the passion, and there is a wide variety of evidence which associates the evening office with the incarnation.[121] So the evening office hymn for Advent could include these words:

> Thou cam'st the Bridegroom of the Bride,
> As drew the world to evening-tide;
> Proceeding from a Virgin shrine,
> The spotless Victim all divine.[122]

As late as 1605 a synod of Prague stated categorically that mattins commemorated the resurrection and vespers the incarnation.[123] Many diverse attributions have been given to the hours in their time, but this is certainly one of the most widespread. A prayer to be said 'when the bell rings in the mornings, in memory of the resurrection', is attested to in various sources in the sixteenth century, and its German form translates as follows:

O Lord Jesus Christ, you are the eternal sun who makes all things live; you renew and fill them with joy; on that day made by God which all men had longed for, you rose from the dead. Grant that I may awake from the death of sin and walk in that new life, wherein I hope to stand with you in eternal glory when you will appear in our flesh. For you live and reign with God the Father in the unity of the Holy Spirit, one true God for ever and ever.

It is accompanied by a collect for the midday bell ('in memory of the Lord's death') and the evening bell ('in memory of the incarnation').[124] Such devotions gradually gained an association with the Angel's greeting and the increasingly popular devotion to the Blessed Virgin Mary; the recollection of the incarnation was also taken over to morning and midday; and so we have what we know today as the Angelus, immortalized in Millet's painting of peasants standing in the fields to pray at the sound of the bell. It is 'nothing other than a special form of office for layfolk. The bell calls clergy and monks to the office . . . and while the clergy now perform the great liturgical form of the prayers of the hours, the faithful join with them through the little office of the Angelus.'[125]

The clergy's prayer

If we have by now gained a glimpse into the ways laypeople, according to their circumstances and ability, said their prayers, there yet remains something to be said about how clergy prayed.

When the clergy's prayer is referred to in our sources, it is seen to be the daily office. Even 'in the Benedictine tradition of the Middle Ages ... while public worship was regulated even in the minutest details, private prayer was not touched on save in passing; it was seen as in the framework of the liturgy, it follows or precedes an office, or is a continuation of one of the Canonical Hours; the liturgy is its nourishment and its life'.[126] The prayer of the clergy through all this period was nothing other than the daily office itself, to which could be added the private recitation of some psalms if desired, or the repetition of a prayer with beads. They were never asked or urged to do anything other than the daily office. Even monks were not expected to 'meditate' or spend time in quiet prayer; they were allowed to stay on a little after an office was over if so moved, but Benedict insisted such prayer must be short and pure.[127] It was only to be given space if it came as a gift – then it was by no means undervalued. For Gregory the Great (c. 540–604) 'the voice of God is heard when, with our minds at ease, we rest from the bustle of this world, and ponder the divine precepts in the deep silence of the mind'.[128]

Otherwise, contemplation as we think of it was not deliberately sought in any systematic way by most people. This very objective approach to private prayer meant by the same token a greater engagement of the whole person in the divine office. The problem with the post-Carolingian office was that once it became acceptable for clergy to 'read' it privately, it came more and more to be seen as a legally prescribed dose (overdose!) of verbiage to be worked off. All such generalizations are caricatures, but it is easy to see how the new fashion for 'mental prayer' which first became of importance with William of St Thierry (c. 1085–1148) and those who followed him, met a need which the liturgy, more and more distorted and misunderstood, was unable to satisfy. The great spiritual masters of personal prayer always uphold the importance of seeing the connection between private and liturgical prayer, but in everyday practice, and in the eye of the man in the street, that connection became too attenuated; its direction too was reversed, so that personal experience was necessary in order to validate liturgy, instead of liturgy providing the ground for personal religion. The two in reality are so indivisible that it is not even possible to give one or the other priority. In the earlier period 'an exact distinction cannot always be made between the writings meant for liturgical worship and those whose object is to nourish personal devotion ... the piety of the age was communal'.[129] Such an understanding is still fully preserved in Orthodoxy today, as George Florovsky makes clear:

> Orthodoxy makes little or no use of that form of spiritual recollection known in the west as 'meditation', when a period of time is set aside each day for systematic thought upon some chosen theme. Its place is taken in the Orthodox Church by corporate liturgical worship. As an Orthodox Christian stands in church, hour by hour, during the vigil of some Great Feast or at the services on an ordinary day, he hears the same necessary and saving truths continually underlined, now in one way and now in another. In this fashion the theological significance of the different mysteries of the faith is deeply and indelibly impressed upon his mind, becoming almost second nature; and if he prays with attention during his time of corporate worship, he has no need for a special period of discursive meditation to emphasize their meaning still more. The words that are read and sung in church are by themselves sufficient to provide him with abundant nourishment for his life in Christ.[130]

C. Butler attributes the development of personal 'meditation' to the increasing complexity of life in recent centuries, where the silence which in previous ages had been all around now has to be deliberately sought and cultivated.[131] According to Adalbert de Vogüé, it was also a compensation for the loss of the frequent silences with which the office in the early centuries was punctuated, particularly after the psalms.[132] Most obviously, perhaps, the human psyche has simply evolved, developing a greater capacity for internalizing mental processes. Mental arithmetic and silent reading were signs of the same thing.

Conclusion

It is within the aura of the liturgy that Christians have prayed 'their prayers' in most of the Church for most of its history. Some recovery of what is positive in this tradition seems to be needed in the Western Church, where since the passing of the Middle Ages distinctions have grown up between private and public prayer which have been too rigid, attributing too much importance to individuals and their 'personal devotion', and leaving both liturgy and spirituality impoverished. Thomas Merton sums it up:

> The early Christian tradition and the spiritual masters of the Middle Ages knew no conflict between 'public' and 'private' prayer, or between the liturgy and contemplation; this is a modern problem, or perhaps it would be more accurate to say it is a pseudo-problem. Liturgy by its very nature tends to prolong itself in individual private prayer, and mental prayer in its turn disposes us for and seeks fulfilment in liturgical worship.

and:

The doctrine of the early Benedictine centuries shows us that the opposition between 'official public prayer' and 'spontaneous personal prayer' is largely a modern fiction.[133]

Similarly, if we assume that Christians down the ages have prayed *fundamentally* in a spontaneous, personal manner, we are probably wrong. All the evidence points to the use of well-loved formulas, often connected in some way with the liturgy. We may perhaps say that those were unenlightened ages; their ways of prayer are no longer suitable in the twentieth century. But human nature does not change as much as that, and while we find it so difficult to pray, they did it with alacrity.

Regular 'interior' prayer in silence and stillness is essential today in a religious community – the life would be inconceivable without it. But many books on prayer for ordinary people have a tendency to assume that this is the real Christian prayer which all must aim at. It may in fact be the vocation of many, but not of all.

16

After the Great Upheaval

The Reformation and Counter-reformation of the sixteenth century brought about the disappearance and transformation of many ancient structures and traditions. By no means was this total, however. Many things survived the upheavals, on both sides of the divide.

BRITAIN

In England and Wales the Reformation left intact the ancient scheme: mattins, eucharist and evensong on Sundays, and the two offices on weekdays. While stripped of most of their external richness, they were now intelligible, and couched in superbly beautiful English, and real attempts were made administratively and pastorally to encourage the ideals contained in the Book of Common Prayer. The part of the Elizabethan liturgical settlement which to the Church's great loss failed to be sufficiently sustained was the weekly celebration of the eucharist. There have always been places, especially the cathedrals, where it was celebrated every Sunday, and in London in particular some parish churches had it weekly or fortnightly;[134] but the almost universal norm for Sundays was quite early on established as mattins, litany and ante-communion (the liturgy of the Word from the Eucharist), and evensong in the afternoon. The eucharist itself was added once a month or more intermittently. Anglicans became the people of the office, its anatomy grafted in their very bones.

It has occasionally been pointed out by both Anglican and Roman Catholic observers that some aspects of the Church of England are particularly Benedictine in character, part of an inheritance which stretches back to Augustine of Canterbury in the sixth century, and even before that. In Britain Benedictine monasticism exercised a greater influence over all aspects of church life than in probably any other country in Europe. The peculiar Anglican tradition of daily liturgical prayer is deeply indebted to this inheritance.[135]

The Book of Common Prayer provides for mattins and evensong on every day of the year, and requires them wherever possible to be celebrated publicly, the bell first being rung. This was never lost sight of in episcopal and other injunctions, and crops up regularly in attempts at reform. (32h)

If this was the ideal, what has been the reality? There is a vague assumption that in ordinary parishes the daily office was neglected until the Oxford Movement in the nineteenth century, but the truth is very different. Daily celebration has always been widespread, sometimes with music, and we have particularly full documentation on this from the late seventeenth century onwards.

We shall look first at the non-parochial structures of the Church. A remarkable feature of the Anglican daily office is how medieval liturgical practice continued to permeate civil and ecclesiastical institutions at many levels: collegiate establishments, the universities, the Chapels Royal and private chapels of the gentry, almshouses and charitable foundations, schools and other corporate bodies. In all of these the daily office could be found, and can still be found even today. But the major buttress to the credibility of celebrating the office has always been the daily worship of the cathedrals, maintained through a variety of vicissitudes, and building up over the centuries a unique musical tradition. In some places in the eighteenth century the quality of these services was poor, but in others high standards were kept up. One witness to this wrote sometime after the middle of the eighteenth century:

In my return through York I strayed into the Minster. The evening service was then performed by candlelight. I had never before been in the Minster but in the middle of a summer's day. The gloom of the evening, the rows of candles fixed upon the pillars in the nave and transept, the lighting of the chancel, the two distant candles glimmering like stars at a distance upon the altar, the sound of the organ, the voices of the choir raised up with the pealing organ in the chaunts, service, and anthem had an amazing effect upon my spirits as I walked to and fro in the nave. The varied tones, sometimes low, sometimes swelling into a great volume of harmonious sound, seemed to anticipate the songs of the blessed and the chorus of praise round the Throne of God and the Lamb. I was greatly affected.[136]

The choral daily office of English cathedrals still thrives in our own day, with organists who are at the height of their profession, and resident choirs with their own school. The visitor to any of our ancient cathedrals can look on the noticeboard on any day of the week and see that evensong will be sung to music taken from any period between the Middle Ages and the present day, drawing on an extraordinarily rich and still-growing repertoire. Nowadays, unfortunately, mattins is normally said, but it is not so long ago that mattins too was choral every day.

At evensong on a weekday, those who attend are encouraged to sit in the choir. At the appointed hour, the robed choir of men and boys process in and move to their places with a gentle clockwork precision, and behind them follow the canons. After the opening responses, the psalmody of the day is sung, normally to Anglican chant. After an Old Testament lesson comes the Magnificat, and a second lesson from the New Testament precedes the singing of the Nunc Dimittis. Creed, Kyries, the Lord's Prayer and *preces* follow, and the service ends with collects and an anthem sung by the choir, after which the procession quietly departs as it came. There may be a large congregation, or only two or three. On some winter evenings there may be no one. But the daily round of restrained and fastidious beauty is maintained, because this is what the cathedral is there for.

Such a tradition as this has proved to be crucial for the parishes. For the strength of the people's office of Anglican cathedrals has provided a backbone to the wider discipline, which is all too evidently absent today in most other countries of Europe.

The daily office in the parish

In the period between the accession of Elizabeth I (1558) and the Commonwealth (1649–60) evidence on church services of any sort is scant. St Edmund's church in Salisbury is known to have had mattins daily at 6 a.m. from the mid-sixteenth century until well into the seventeenth. Two separate bequests in 1624 provide between them for the offices to be said daily in St Botolph's, Aldgate and St Christopher's in London, and in churches in Reading, Newbury and Leicester.[137] It is interesting to find that still in the seventeenth and eighteenth centuries bequests which in former times may have supported mass-priests are now used to maintain the daily office. Systematic research into this early period would therefore need to examine bequests and charities as well as the standard ecclesiastical records.

The period which followed the reinstatement of the Anglican Church in 1660 presents a marked increase in information. It is well to start with London, where information is particularly plentiful. The table overleaf gives relevant figures for four sample years over a century and a half.

The figures produce some surprises. In the first half of the eighteenth century the ferial offices thrived in the majority of London churches, some of these even having to repeat one or both of the services each day. So St Anne's, Westminster had morning prayer at 6.00 for the working people, merchants and traders, and again at 11.00 for people in top jobs and the 'quality'. Evensong was at 4.00 and again at 6.00. In 1708 an observer commented that there are

few of the 100 Churches contained in this City, as aforesaid (unless where they stand very thick, as in the Heart of the City) but where there is Divine Service once, twice, or more in a Day and these at different Hours, some in the Hours of Business, which seem to be intended for Masters and those that have Estates; and others in the Evening when Shops are shut, or very early in the Morning, most proper for Servants of all sorts, and labouring Persons.[142]

CELEBRATION OF MATTINS AND EVENSONG IN LONDON ON WEEKDAYS

	1 service daily	M. and E. daily	3 services daily	4 services daily	Wednesdays, Fridays and Holy Days	1 day per week	TOTAL
1714[138] (total: 158 churches)	19	53	7	6	65	–	150
1746[139] (total: 133 churches)	16	39	2	3	72	–	132
1824[140] (total: 111 churches)	5	2	2	–	24	1	34
1866[141] (total: 365 churches)	33	39	–	–	79	38	189

A writer to the *Guardian* in 1713 described how, instead of going to mattins at the usual mid-morning time, he went for a change to the earlier service:

I go sometimes to a particular place in the city, far distant from mine own home, to hear a gentleman, whose manner I admire, read the liturgy. I am persuaded devotion is the greatest pleasure of the soul, and there is none hear him without the utmost reverence... the other morning I happened to rise earlier than ordinary, and thought I could not pass my time better than to go upon the admonition of the morning bell to the Church Prayers at six of the clock. I was there the first of any in the congregation ... there was none at the confession but a set of poor scrubs of us, who could sin only in our wills, whose persons could be no temptation to one another, and might have, without interruption from anybody else, humble, lowly hearts, in frightful looks and dirty dresses, at our leisure. When we poor souls had presented ourselves with a contrition suitable to our worthlessness, some pretty young ladies in mobbs popped in here and there about the church, clattering the pew door after them, and squatting into a whisper behind their fans... [presently] there was a great deal of good company now come in. There was a good number of very janty slatterns... Besides these, there were also by this time arrived two or three sets of whisperers.... There were indeed a few, in whose looks there appeared an heavenly joy and gladness upon the entrance of a new day, as if they had gone to sleep with expectation of it. For the sake of these it is worth while that the Church keeps up such early mattins throughout the cities of London and Westminster; but the generality of those who observe that hour perform it with so tasteless a behaviour, that it appears a task rather than a voluntary act... [particularly] those familiar ducks, who are, as it were, at home at the church, and by frequent meeting there, throw the time of prayer very negligently into their common life, and make their coming together in that place as ordinary as any other action... But were this morning solemnity as much in vogue, even as it is now at more advanced hours of the day, it would necessarily have so good an effect upon us, as to make us more disengaged and cheerful in conversation, and less artful and insincere in business...[143]

This passage has been worth quoting at length for the vivid picture it gives us of weekday mattins in an eighteenth-century London church. It was very different, our gently snobbish author assures us, from the more prim and proper later service at ten or eleven o'clock. Making allowances for period and setting, we could almost be listening to one of the sermons of Caesarius of Arles, except that there his sixth-century congregation would be talking and shouting instead of whispering behind fans.

Those few churches which had no regular weekday offices commonly had evensong on Saturdays in the best medieval tradition, so that it is possible to make the conclusion that to all intents and purposes all the churches of London in this period had weekday offices of some sort. It is therefore not surprising to find references to them in contemporary literature.

Samuel Pepys tells us in an account which could have come from Basil or Gregory of Tours that as he was passing St Dunstan's in Fleet Street he heard psalms being sung, and went in to take part in the 6 o'clock mattins which was offered daily.[144] Not far away, at St Clement Danes, Dr Johnson was given to going to church in the week: 'Whenever I miss church on a Sunday, I resolve to go another day.'[145]

Church attendance on such a scale could be lucrative for vergers, who might be tipped for showing people to their seats. For high society and its imitators 'daily prayers' were a fashionable social event, whose entertainment-value was not immune from competition. In 1711 the following plaintive letter appeared in the *Spectator*, from one claiming to be a verger of St Paul's, Covent Garden, where the congregation was being enticed away by other attractions:

I have been for twenty years under-sexton of this parish . . . and have not missed tolling in to prayers six times in all those years; which office I have performed to my great satisfaction till this fortnight last past, during which time I find my congregation take the warning of my bell, morning and evening, to go to a puppet-show set forth by one Powell under the Piazzas. By this means, I have not only lost my two customers, whom I used to place for sixpence apiece over against Mrs Rachel Eyebright, but Mrs Rachel herself is gone thither also. There now appear among us none but a few ordinary people, who come to church only to say their prayers, so that I have no work worth speaking of but on Sundays. I have placed my son at the Piazzas, to acquaint the ladies that the bell rings for church, and that it stands on the other side of the garden; but they only laugh at the child.

I desire you would lay this before all the world, that I may not be made such a tool for the future, and that Punchinello may choose hours less canonical. As things are now, Mr Powell has a full congregation, while we have a very thin house; which if you can remedy, you will very much oblige . . .[146]

One peculiarity which emerges in the table on page 118 is the celebration of the offices on the ancient 'station days', Wednesday and Friday, and on the Holy Days of the Book of Common Prayer. These outnumbered any other single category in 1714, and still in 1866 made up a significant proportion of the total. The canon law of the Church of England (of 1604) directs that the litany be recited in every church and chapel on all Wednesdays and Fridays at the usual times of service (except if they are feast-days), and that households within half a mile of the church send at least one member to be present – an interesting example of delegation, the few praying in the name of the many.[147] It was probably as a result of this that special importance was attached to these days when it came to weekday liturgy. Where the offices were celebrated only on Wednesdays and Fridays, it seems to have been common for the clergy to say the offices on the other days at home with the family.

Another striking fact which emerges is the continuity between the eighteenth century and 1866. I have not discovered figures for the end of the eighteenth century, but the statistics suggest that practice in parishes continued independently of the new impetus provided by the Oxford Movement after 1833. A writer on St Anne's, Soho in 1898 claims that the daily celebration of the offices had never been interrupted in the history of the parish, and presumably there are other churches in London and elsewhere which could reasonably make the same claim.[148]

In the provinces, daily celebration of the divine office was normal in town churches. At Bath it was considered *de rigueur* for those who came to take the waters. William Best invites us to 'witness Bath and Tunbridge ... where a non-attendance on the daily service has been, and I trust still is, accounted a disreputable thing, a scandalous and offensive irregularity'.[149] At Manchester parish church not only were the offices performed daily, but they were kept up also in the daughter church of St Anne's, which meant that the parish always had to have two curates. An old lady who attended the parish church almost daily, and who died in 1790, was brought in a sedan chair, in her latter years, by two footmen in livery.[150]

Newcastle upon Tyne had only four ancient churches, but all of them had weekday services. We are told by a visitor in 1769 that they were as follows:

St Nicholas': mattins and evensong daily;
catechetical lecture once a week;
sermon on Wednesdays and Fridays in Lent and Advent.
All Saints': mattins and evensong daily.
St Andrew's: mattins every Wednesday and Friday.
St John's: mattins and evensong every Wednesday, Friday and Saturday.[151]

When St Nicholas' was refurnished in 1785, a special chapel was created for the weekday offices in the south transept. In the rebuilding of All Saints' too, in 1789, a similar chapel was included in the new design. Such chapels were common, often being known as morning-prayer chapels.[152]

Outside the towns, it is clear that the daily liturgy was not unusual in country parishes, although, given the usual problems of rural ministry, services were not always likely to be well maintained. Izaak Walton tells us in his life of George Herbert (1593–1633) that he

brought most of his parishioners, and many gentlemen in the neighbourhood, constantly to make a part of his congregation twice a day; and some of the meaner sort of his parish did so love and reverence Mr Herbert, that they would let their plough rest when Mr Herbert's saint's-bell rung to prayers, that they might also offer their devotions to God with him; and would then return back to their plough.[153]

In Leicestershire in 1718, according to diocesan returns, daily service was to be found in almost 10 per cent of parish churches, while a further 20 per cent offered mattins and evensong on the 'station days', Wednesday and Friday, and on holy days. Another 20 per cent celebrated them on holy days only. That leaves a further 50 per cent where nothing seems to have been done outside Sundays.[154]

Perhaps the highest figures outside London come from the north-west of England, where more than 60 per cent of the churches in the West Riding, Staffordshire and southern Lancashire had some form of weekday worship in the eighteenth century.[155] Examples of the regular celebration of the offices in rural parishes can be found in contemporary literature. The poet William Cowper wrote in 1765 of a local clergyman:

Another acquaintance I have lately made is with a Mr Nicholson, a north-country divine, very poor, but very good and very happy. He reads prayers here twice a day, all the year round...

Of his own daily habits Cowper writes:

We breakfast commonly between eight and nine; till eleven we read either the Scriptures, or the sermons of some faithful preacher of those holy mysteries; at eleven we attend divine service, which is performed here twice every day...[156]

Eliza Berkeley, who grew up in White Waltham in the Windsor Forest, 'read Hickes's Preparatory Office for Death every Thursday, and attended prayers at church every afternoon'. Later, after she had married George Berkeley, son of the famous bishop, she wrote that in the 1760s, when he became a country vicar, 'he found weekday prayers at both Bray and Cookham', but attendance was so poor that in one of these churches it had to be abandoned.

Later, in 1799, she was moved to comment that

... one great cause of the ignorance of the lower ranks of the people, and of course the lamentable decay of Christian piety, is the almost universal abolition of weekday prayers in the country, either that the pious parson may hunt or shoot, etc., neither of these sports recommended by St Paul to Timothy or Titus.[157]

Decline

The latter years of the eighteenth century saw unbecoming habits creeping into the lives of the clergy, and the fact that many no longer wore their cassocks and felt free to hunt and dance caused frequent comment. But in the market towns, at least, a thriving daily service could still be found. In 1799 Eliza Berkeley was able to express pleasure at seeing

what numbers of traders high and low attend the weekday prayers at Henley upon Thames, and some few of the gentry, who are not too fine; several of the aged poor, very nearly blind, some totally blind, what a blessing are weekday prayers to such poor souls! Very early and late prayers in London are still attended, as about thirty years ago they were at Canterbury. [I have] . . . frequently counted twenty ladies, gentlemen, traders, and servants, in the sermon-house, where they were read at Canterbury on a morning at six o'clock.[158]

Towards the end of the eighteenth century church life began to experience a serious decline, so that by the 1830s 'daily prayers', while still continuing in some ordinary parishes, had completely disappeared in most. This was reflected in an unparalleled decadence, and a new atmosphere of exaggerated Protestantism. The figures given in the table on page 117 tell their own story. A biographer of Joshua Watson wrote that at the turn of the century 'daily prayers in some London churches was not yet discontinued', and that Watson was a constant attender at St Vedast, Foster Lane. Thirty years later, in 1832, the *British Magazine* assumes their general disappearance, asking, "Is it nothing that cathedrals are the only Protestant churches in England which preserve the daily offering of supplication and thanksgiving?"[159] This was a little too sweeping. Beresford Hope, recalling childhood memories from the time of George IV, wrote in 1874:

In cathedrals, in College Chapels, and in a few old-fashioned town churches, the good tradition of daily prayers had still survived.[160]

Until this period, evangelicals had been in the forefront of the protagonists of daily public prayer. Daniel Wilson, for example, became vicar of Islington in 1824, and by 1828 had established 'three full services in the church on Sundays and great festival days, and one in the week, besides morning prayers on Wednesdays and Fridays, and on saints' days'.[161] That was very late, and swimming against the tide. In the hiatus around this period when the daily office was at its lowest point, the ball slipped into the court of another party, and the public daily office became one of the hallmarks of Tractarianism. It is often thought that the Tractarian insistence on the daily office was an attempt to introduce revolutionary practices, when in reality it was a living memory for many. 'Our daily service', wrote Dr Pusey, 'has been nearly lost.'[162] It is as a result of the Oxford Movement which began in 1833 that mattins and evensong are a well-established part of the daily programme in many parish churches today. But the preceding tradition must be given its due. When Tractarian vicars said the office in church they were doing what they were used to from school (sometimes) and university, and perfectly aware that it used to be normal practice in parishes and had gone on from time immemorial in their cathedral. The importance of the cathedral in maintaining the main trunk of the tree can hardly be overestimated, and it is sad by comparison to see how the office has been neglected in the vast majority of Roman Catholic cathedrals in most parts of the world since the withering away of the choral tradition in modern times.

Private prayer

As a result of what has been briefly sketched above, we shall not be surprised to find that the personal prayer of Anglicans has shown close connections with the liturgy. A popular devotional manual entitled *A Companion to the Altar*, which went through many editions in the eighteenth century, has this to say on public prayer:

It is certain that the Turks, whom we call infidels, go to their public devotions five times every day; and shall not they rise in judgement against us Christians who cannot afford to go once or twice a day to God's house, when we have both leisure and opportunity?[163]

Many of the Anglican classics on prayer repeat similar sentiments. These books often provide forms of freely composed prayer for morning and evening which have little connection with the liturgical offices, but urge attendance at those in addition. But the offices spilled over into private practice anyway. It was common for families, particularly those of clergy, to say them together. Wickham Legg tells us that:

The domestic practice of reading the pith and marrow of the divine service, the daily psalms and lessons, persisted in many families till after the middle of the nineteenth century. At the end of the eighteenth century Mary Lamb had to read to her elders 'the psalms and the chapters, which was my daily task': and the same was the practice of Mrs Temple with her son Frederick, afterwards Archbishop of Canterbury.[164]

Dr Pusey wrote in Tract 18:

... many pious individuals, it is well known, have habitually read just that portion which the Church has allotted.[165]

This also happened in schools; one author remembers how around the 1830s

we used to be in the schoolroom at eight, and then we read round, by turns, the psalms and lessons for the day.[166]

In addition to private or domestic use of the Book of Common Prayer, the production of books of hours or primers continued uninterrupted after the Reformation. Henry Bull's book of 1566 was typical of over eighty such publications which appeared in the second half of the sixteenth century, and continued to be published through the succeeding centuries.[167] John Cosin in 1627 issued a book, with the Bishop of London's licence, which became particularly well known, and went through many editions. In it all the lesser hours are provided, in addition to Prayer-Book mattins with the *Laudate* Psalms added, and a vespers which included Psalm 141; also the seven penitential Psalms, and several collections of prayers and devotions. Some of these books were very Catholic in tone. The non-juror George Hickes published in 1701 a book of hours which bears his name but was in fact the work of Susanna Hopton[168]. It went through at least nine editions in the first half of the eighteenth century, and included:

Office for each day of the week; Office of our Blessed Saviour; Office of the Holy Ghost; Office for the commemoration of saints;	vigils, lauds, vespers and compline
Preparatory office for death by way of commemoration of the faithful departed	vigils, lauds, vespers

Short offices for special occasions and festivals

One of the regular users of this book was Eliza Berkeley who, as we have seen, said the Office of the Dead from it every Thursday. If she used the ordinary daily offices from it, they would not have duplicated the offices she was also attending in her parish church, for these offices consist almost entirely of free compositions. The forms follow those of the Roman office – vigils had its invitatory, psalms, readings and responsories, for instance; but the material is a very free Christian paraphrase and pastiche based on the Old Testament texts. It is an interesting parallel to the Orthodox treatment of the hours, where Christian theological reflection tends to supplant the psalms and canticles on which it is based, and seems to meet the need which the offices in the Book of Common Prayer particularly fail to meet, in making the words of the office relate directly to Christian belief. Here is the opening of Sunday vigils:

℣. O Lord, open Thou our lips.
℟. And our mouth shall shew forth Thy praise.
℣. O God, make speed to save us.
℟. O Lord, make haste to help us.
℣. Glory be to the Father, and to the Son, and to the Holy Ghost.
℟. As it was in the beginning, is now, and ever shall be: world without end.   Amen.

THE INVITATORY.

Come, let us adore our glorified Jesus.
Come, let us adore our glorified Jesus.

PSALM I.

Behold the Angels assembled in their choirs, and the blessed Saints ready with their hymns; behold, the Church prepares her solemn offices, and summons all her children to bring in their praises.

Come, let us adore our glorified Jesus.

The King of heaven Himself invites us, and graciously calls us into His own presence; He bids us suspend our mean employments in the world, to receive the honour of treating with Him.

Come, let us adore our glorified Jesus.

(etc.)

Other books appeared throughout the eighteenth century. To take another example, the Company of Stationers published a primer with royal approval which went through eight editorial editions between 1758 and 1783. It included the alphabet, the catechism, various graces and prayers, mattins and evensong based on the Prayer Book, but including litanies, the seven penitential psalms, and a large collection of prayers. Such books as these were produced steadily by a variety of authors until the early nineteenth century, and witness to a persistent inclination in the Anglican Church for private prayer to have a liturgical form.[169]

These practices of liturgical devotion are unlikely, however, to have found much place among ordinary working people. How they prayed, as always, is a difficult thing to discover. They will have known their Our Father and Creed, and they will probably have learnt the collects for every Sunday of the year, a very common discipline in schools until this century. They would be likely also to know some Psalms by heart. Those who attended church regularly will have known most of the liturgy by heart too, but whether they would have thought to recite the Magnificat or the Te Deum, for instance, in their private prayers, it is impossible to say. They certainly had their funny folk-prayers and poems, which no doubt filled a gap which the Church, if it had been doing its job, would have been better able to fill.

Roman Catholics

A survey of English liturgical piety would be incomplete without mention of Roman Catholic ('recusant') practice after the Reformation. A wide variety of devotional books quickly emerged to help people cope with the difficulties of being in a diaspora. Most important among these were the primer and the manual.[170] The primer gained an official character after its definitive reform at the behest of the Council of Trent, coming to be very widely used in English. The manual, on the other hand, was simpler and less directly related to the breviary, and proved to be the most widely used, being specifically designed for ordinary and unlettered people.[171] The provision of daily liturgical prayer in a variety of related forms was evidently high on the agenda, and J. D. Crichton comments:

Both the Primer and the Manual, I believe, witness to the desire of the laity to have a form of devotion that was comparable to the Divine Office of the priest and was parallel to it.[172]

It is interesting to see how the evening office continued to be known by Roman Catholics as evensong until the nineteenth century, and how these books showed an ability to transcend the post-Reformation divisions. John Austin's *Devotions in the ancient way of offices* (first edition: Paris 1668) became the basis of several Anglican books of devotion, including that published under the name of George Hickes which has been mentioned above; and it had other Anglican imitators throughout the eighteenth century.[173] With regard to the public offices, when churches began to be more numerous in the nineteenth century, more widespread participation in the offices became possible, and in many churches Sunday vespers was, surprisingly, sung in English until the end of the nineteenth century.[174]

FRANCE

Our picture of Roman Catholic liturgy as it was before the Second Vatican Council, typified by baroque altars with six candles and tabernacle, and text and ceremonial standardized in all their detail, is a misleading one if we assume it to be older than the second half of the nineteenth century. Before that time liturgical usage on the continent of Europe, and the layout of the churches, presented a surprising variety and richness. France, for example, possessed an array of local traditions inherited from the Middle Ages which were still flourishing in the eighteenth century. We have a good description of some of these from one Jean-Baptiste Lebrun, who in 1718 published a report on his liturgical tours of the country, describing in detail the peculiar ceremonies, vestments, church furnishings and variations on the Roman liturgy which most dioceses possessed. He shows how cathedrals maintained proud traditions of a choral office (such as that of Rouen described above on page 96), which were to last until the Revolution. In more than one cathedral the canons had to know the entire office by heart, and it was strictly forbidden to take any books into choir. There are frequent references in these local rites to ceremonies with light. For instance, in Orleans Cathedral, Lebrun tells us that:

Every day, at the verse: 'to lighten those in darkness' of the Benedictus at Lauds, and at the verse: 'to be a light' of the Nunc Dimittis at compline, the sacristan carries a lighted candle to the middle of the choir in relation to these words...[175]

Parish churches

The survey reveals a surprising number of churches served by colleges of priests, most of them parochial, in which the offices were sung every day. Here we find splendid examples of that superabundance of clergy which was a peculiarity of pre-Revolutionary France. Most sizeable towns had several collegiate churches. Lebrun does not comment on the divine office in every case, but in Rouen, for instance, he makes passing reference to it in the following churches: the Cathedral, St-Ouen, St-Lô, Notre Dame de la Ronde, St-Georges, St-Étienne, and St-Caude-le-vieil.[176] We must presume that the offices were also sung in at least some of the other churches he mentions: for instance, St-Godard and St-Maclou each boasted over 100 clergy! St-Etienne was a simple parish church, and the author selects it for comment because it 'is one of the best-kept in the town ... and they perform the divine office there very well'.[177] In the collegiate church of St-Georges 'there are only four canons, who pay four chaplains for the singing of the office ...'[178]

In Paris, a memorable example of parish practice can be found in the life of the mystic Mme Barbe Acarie (1566–1618), who was in the curious position of having to give up the daily office in order to become a nun:

... although, in all humility, she appreciated the lowliness of the position as a lay-sister, she felt a certain repugnance to it because it would deprive her of the Divine Office. She was greatly attached to singing the praises of God and to be barred from the choir was to take away from the religious life, in her view, one of its essential elements...

Her reaction ... is revealing for it shows that Barbe, the leader of the mystical movement in seventeenth-century France, was fully aware of the importance of the corporate worship of the Church of which the Divine Office is the expression. She owed that attitude to her schooldays at Longchamp, though she developed it in after years by her assiduity in going to her parish church or eleswhere...

Still in Paris we can visit the churches that she frequented – Saint-Méry, Saint-Gervais, Saint-Étienne-du-Mont. Yet much of the life has now gone from them and it is sad to see the choir stalls at Saint Méry no longer occupied by seven canons to sing the Office there, or to look at the great lectern standing in Saint-Étienne-du-Mont still with its eighteenth-century folio antiphoner open on it, gathering the dust and never used. Barbe lived in a different age with different standards, at a time when those standards were moving slowly towards a change.[179]

Sundays and feast-days

By far the most common reference to the canonical offices in France at this period is in connection with Sundays and feast-days, and it seems to be to this deeply-ingrained tradition that Francis de Sales refers in his *Introduction to the Devout Life*, where, typical of the usual attitude, he accords the office highest praise while dismissing it in a few words:

Besides hearing Mass on Sundays and holidays, you ought also, Philothea, to be present at Vespers and the other public offices of the Church as far as your convenience will permit. For, as these days are dedicated to God, we ought to perform more acts to his honour and glory on them than on other days. By this means you will experience the sweetness of devotion, as St Austin did, who testifies in his confessions, that hearing the divine office in the beginning of his conversion, his heart melted into tenderness, and his eyes into tears of piety. And, indeed, to speak once for all, there is always more benefit and comfort to be derived from the public offices of the Church than from private devotions, God having ordained that communion of prayers should always have the preference.[180]

Until recent times the public singing of the morning and evening offices in parish churches at weekends and on festivals was a strong element in French religious observance. It was normal for parishes to possess the large liturgical books containing the material for the festal offices and their chant, and these were frequently reissued in fresh editions up to the present century. However, it also seems to have been usual for them to include the material for the ferial offices of the daily round too, and we must conclude from that that the choral office was always seen as the ideal, and the private recitation of the breviary as a substitute for it. As we shall see, it was normal for laity to have their own copies in small format too, sometimes complete with plainchant.

The 'Gallican' liturgies of the seventeenth to nineteenth centuries

In addition to this, France has a special interest for the daily office in the local rites which flourished from the seventeenth to the nineteenth centuries, the so-called 'Gallican breviaries'.

The seventeenth century saw a gentle, measured campaign to bring the local rites inherited from the Middle Ages more into line with Roman usage. Towards the end of the century, however, there came a marked change in attitude. Growing nationalism combined with an infatuation with classical literature and an increasingly scholarly and critical approach to religious matters produced a new zest for liturgical reform, and reform which would be specifically French.

From the last two decades of the seventeenth century local diocesan forms

Opposite. Title page of a folio antiphoner of the 'Gallican' office of Rouen, newly constituted in 1728, and issued to all parishes. When this new office was introduced into the cathedral in 1729, books were permitted for one year to give the canons time to learn everything. In the winter of that year lanterns were allowed at the hebdomadaries' stalls on each side, and one by each of the two antiphoners, one on the eagle and one on the lectern in the middle of choir. To help the choir struggle with the chant, two serpent-players were hired to play the plainsong with each side. When the year was up, book and lanterns were once more forbidden (on singing by heart, see p. 96).[182]

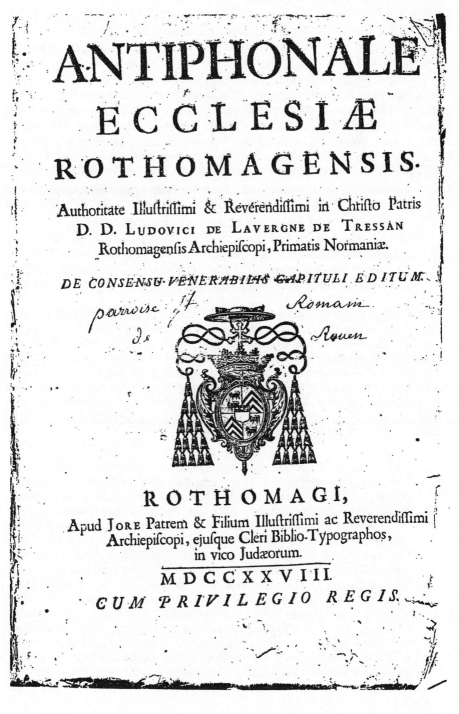

ANTIPHONALE
ECCLESIÆ
ROTHOMAGENSIS.

Authoritate Illuſtriſſimi & Reverendiſſimi in Chriſto Patris
D. D. LUDOVICI DE LAVERGNE DE TRESSAN
Rothomagenſis Archiepiſcopi, Primatis Normaniæ.

DE CONSENSU VENERABILIS CAPITULI EDITUM.

parroise de   Romain   Rouen

ROTHOMAGI,
Apud JORE Patrem & Filium Illuſtriſſimi ac Reverendiſſimi
Archiepiſcopi, ejuſque Cleri Biblio-Typographos,
in vico Judæorum.

M D C C X X V I I I.
CUM PRIVILEGIO REGIS.

of daily office began to appear which not only made a point of emphasizing local peculiarities, but became increasingly more radical in their revision and transformation of the basic content of the services. In particular, responses, antiphons and other components which were original compositions were replaced on principle by texts from Scripture. Lives of the saints and patristic readings were drastically pruned or replaced, calendars simplified, and the overall content of the office greatly reduced. In many diocesan rites so much had been completely rewritten or replaced that they bore little resemblance to the Roman rite. By the time of the Revolution nearly all French dioceses – eighty of them, to be precise – had produced rites of this kind for the daily office.

It was not until the middle of the nineteenth century that circumstances had changed sufficiently for a return to the Roman rite to begin, and there were still clergy at the end of the nineteenth century who stuck to the old forms.

These Gallican offices were for a time held in bad odour in official circles, but in this century it has been increasingly recognized that they made a valuable contribution to the development of liturgical prayer. The Roman Catholic scholar Edmund Bishop was one who thought particularly highly of them:

Soon after his return to London from his 'pilgrimage' of 1871, he promised the Abbé Malais that he would daily recite some part of the breviary office according to the moribund local use of Rouen. This use of Rouen and the other 'Gallican' books, though less than two centuries old, conformed more nearly to the most ancient liturgical practices than the contemporary method of reciting the immemorial Roman breviary, which Abbé Guéranger (who did not use it) was responsible for reintroducing into one French diocese after another during Bishop's own boyhood. Various other considerations told in favour of the diocesan books, such as these, enumerated for Dr (afterwards Cardinal) Mercati in 1903:

Their excellence is not to my mind merely theoretical but was justified by results. I remember the old type of French priest, who when the 'Roman' was adopted in France in the 50ies and 60ies of the last century were, as having been ordained many years before, permitted to make their choice between continuing to use the 'local' breviary to which they had been accustomed and the newly introduced 'Roman'. And I remember what the breviary was to some of these latter [sic] who had 'opted' for the old 'Gallican' ones which they had hitherto used: I remember that the Breviary was to these men I knew, just what one would desire it should be to a priest, but what the Roman as now used is not. Also I remember the *solid* type of piety of these men – not showy but deep, in a word what I have called 'the piety inspired by the Psalms and the Gospels' ... Of course I think that this appeals to some of us in England more than it would in Italy; for you must know that here in England the memory and tradition of what that great body of 8,000 to 10,000 French clergy who took refuge in England during the French Revolution really *was*, the memory of *what sort of men* they *were*, has not yet died out.[183]

With no little help from Bishop, these breviaries had their discreet influence upon the 1911 reform of the Roman breviary, and have more direct heirs in that which resulted from the Second Vatican Council. Some prayers from these Gallican liturgies were also included in the new Roman missal.[184]

The reforms of the office which were carried out in seventeenth- and eighteenth-century France were part of a wider movement for liturgical reform and proper participation by all, which amounted to a full-blown liturgical movement very similar to that which we have seen in this century, and which is yet to be properly researched and given its due appreciation.

Great efforts were made to encourage the laity's participation, and one instrument for this was the *paroissien*, an abbreviated breviary and mass-book for laypeople. This contained a selection of private prayers for various occasions, the offices complete with chant, and often with a parallel text in French, the Mass and its propers for the year, and various additional material. Some *paroissiens* contain the full *cursus* of the daily office for every day of the year – were they for private prayer, or for following the services in church?[185] Initially provided for the 'Gallican' rites, the *paroissiens* later became an important instrument in the return to the Roman use, and have continued to be produced ever since. They bear witness to a strong tradition of popular participation in the daily office, borne out by the following reflections on the eighteenth-century Gallican rite of Rouen:

... the plainchant of our Rouen service-books rapidly became extremely popular. The use of *paroissiens* with music soon spread and helped to make it familiar to church-goers, and the people, above all in the country, gradually became used to joining their voices with those of the clergy, and considered it an honour to sing at the lectern. They were keen to have their "Complete Offices", and proud to have "their eight tomes" [*sic*], as they used to say, and they used it to sing Mattins on great feasts, and all the Hours on Sundays. This plainchant was doubtless badly sung, but it was sung with all the heart by the people all together.[186]

Little offices

Private prayer in France showed an enduring liturgical bent. The lesser offices which had been popular among the laity in the Middle Ages continued in favour in subsequent centuries. The seventeenth and eighteenth centuries saw the publication of many simple forms of daily liturgy for the laity. Henri Brémond, speaking of this period, says:

The prayer of the time tended to ... crystallize into forms of office ...[187]

offices on an endless array of themes, 'Office of the Holy Family', 'Office of the Good Shepherd', 'Office of Penitence', 'of Providence', 'of Eternal Wisdom', and so on. A composer of one such office wrote in 1758:

This prayer has been put in the form of an office because this manner of praying is consecrated by the usage of the Church, which would see with joy all the faithful not only opening their hearts, but joining their voices, seven times each day, to that of her ministers.[188]

Often in rhyme, these continued in general use until the nineteenth century, both in Latin and French.

GERMANY

In post-Reformation Germany daily celebration of the offices seems to have been common in the towns of Roman Catholic areas. In Cologne, for instance, all the offices were sung daily in the larger parishes in the seventeenth and eighteenth centuries.[190] It is not with this, however, but with two other aspects of the daily office that Germany has attracted the interest of historians: the clergy's breviary, and Sunday vespers in parish churches.

The breviary

In the Enlightenment, the era of what was supposed to be reason, science and common sense, the breviary inherited from the Middle Ages appeared to many to be barbaric. A Roman Catholic writer was thus able to write in 1792 that 'in the breviary there is no order, no cohesion, no understanding of humanity, and I would guard against the sin of wasting time in such a way'. Such 'prayer without involvement of the heart and without feelings of devotion in the soul is not prayer, but a mockery of the Almighty'.[191]

By that time reform was more than in the air – it was very much in print. The eighteenth century saw the appearance of several outstanding local reforms in the same spirit as those undertaken in France, the most influential being those of the dioceses of Aachen, Cologne, Münster and Trier. Such forms of the daily office came to be widely used in German-speaking lands, despite considerable opposition from Rome.

In these books antiphons, *preces*, prayers, hymns, readings, propers of saints, including those of St Peter and the Blessed Virgin Mary, were shortened, rewritten, replaced or abolished in a thoroughgoing effort to make the breviary accord with the spirit of the age. There was a tendency to put instruction, edification and 'utility' high on the list of priorities, to the extent that some protagonists of such reforms held a vision of the breviary more as a private book for the edification of the clergy than as anything suitable for public worship. Even these reforms were not radical enough for some, however, who sought more drastic measures. In 1789 the Archbishop of Mainz set up a commission to prepare a breviary containing just mattins (three psalms and one lesson), a 'day-office' (five psalms and one non-Scripture reading) and

Office of the Eternal Wisdom by le Jeune de Franqueville, 1693.[189]

compline.[192] The plan was never carried out, but the public discussion continued, one proposal being that very busy priests be dispensed from the breviary, at least in winter, or have it commuted into Scripture-reading and other spiritual exercises suited to the circumstances.

Thaddäus-Anton Dereser, who made a name for himself through outspoken support of the more radical currents for reform, produced in 1792 a 'German breviary for sisters, nuns and all good Christians', subtitled a 'Book of edification for the use of Catholic Christians for every day of the year'. It provided three hours of prayer :[193]

Mattins	*Vespers*	*Compline*
morning prayer	versicles	confession
versicles	three psalms	versicle
Gloria	Magnificat	absolution
three psalms	prayer	prayers
prayer before hearing Scripture		long thanksgiving
NT lesson (usually from the Gospels)		Salve Regina
2 non-scripture readings reflecting on		prayers
the lesson		Lord's Prayer
prayer		Ave
		Creed

This breviary was approved by the diocesans of Augsburg, Cologne, Worms, Constance and Würzburg. The bishop of Würzburg used it himself instead of the Latin breviary and recommended it to his clergy too. Although its official approval did not last long, it had gone through sixteen editions by 1847, and continued in use in many parts for most of the nineteenth century. Nor was it alone. Other books of a similar type were produced and enjoyed comparable success, some of them in German, some staying in Latin.

Parish vespers

The second area of public worship which is of interest here is German parish vespers. After the upheavals of the wars which came in the wake of the Reformation, the Roman Catholic Church in Germany found itself in considerable disarray, and in the following centuries great efforts were made by church leaders to restore church traditions to something like their former richness. The office came in for attention, and by the mid-eighteenth century its public celebration on Sundays had become the norm. It was always in Latin, and was often limited to vespers, but it became extremely popular.

Towards the end of the eighteenth century, however, dissatisfaction began to creep in among the 'experts'. One cause for unease was the quality of the music in many small parishes. In the 1780s gradually the whole of Austria came under an order by means of which vespers were not to be performed at all if it could not be sung well! The Latin vespers was 'to be sung only where there is an orderly choir, and on feast-days with the addition of the organ . . .'[194] Similar orders were made in various parts of Germany. The second principal objection was the use of Latin. There grew up a strong feeling that it was nonsense for the people to sing words they did not understand. Both objections appear in this Hogarthesque outburst in a sober learned journal: 'It is something when the people aren't completely anaesthetized through the frightful bellowing of the Latin Mass and Vespers. But it is raving nonsense when a few selected choir-singers . . . loudly thunder out the Dixit Dominus etc., without either tune or dignity, so that one is near to going deaf, while the other Christians, greatly distracted, silently perform their habitual daily prayers in dryness, empty of feeling.'[195]

At first the inclination was to discourage vespers altogether. So a parish in Cologne archdiocese was allowed in 1765 to replace Sunday vespers with an hour's catechesis, except on important feasts. In the diocese of Linz in Austria, in places where there was no choir, vespers was to be replaced by a service consisting of a litany, a prayer for the authorities, a general prayer, five Paters and one Ave.[196]

After the 1780s we begin to see two types of reform emerging, concerned either with replacing vespers with freely composed forms of service, or with creating German forms of vespers more or less faithful to the ancient model.

(1) Vesper-devotion ('Vesperandacht')

In 1788 the diocese of Mainz published a diocesan songbook something after the manner of the French *paroissien*. These *Gesangbücher*, produced usually by dioceses, but sometimes privately, became an extremely important factor in German church life, and have remained so until today. The Mainz songbook contained, among other things, a form of service in German which was intended to replace the parish vespers. It had the following form:[197]

entrance hymn
opening prayer
two verses of hymn
three psalms
Bible-reading
people's prayer in response to the reading
two verses of hymn
two psalms
Te Deum
one verse of hymn
Lord's Prayer with solemn extended introduction
final hymn

This was the first of a wide variety of forms produced by dioceses and others in subsequent years, all of which come under the generic title of *Vesperandacht*, which we would probably translate as 'evening service'. They varied from forms which approximated to traditional vespers, to hymn-sandwiches, simple litanies, and free forms of service, but they stand out clearly from those other services which were more or less straight translations of the breviary office. The liturgical plurality which emerged, and the freedom given to the parish priest, were remarkable, and inevitably there was an unevenness in the quality, aesthetic, liturgical and theological, of these homemade services. The most serious criticism is that they were too subject to the passing fancies and misjudgements of the age. There was often an intention more to edify and instruct than to give glory to God and to pray. The psalms received strong criticism, and their various translators all rewrote and 'improved' them. This rationalist, anthropocentric approach to worship did reflect the spirit of the age, but the outright condemnation it later earned from Rome went too far. Some of the forms of worship which arose expressely aimed to help the people to pray and adore, and proved their worth by their continuing popularity.

(2) German vespers

More conservative reformers were content to keep to the main shape of traditional vespers, and the most famous of them all was I. H. von Wessenberg, Vicar-general of the diocese of Constance (now Freiburg). His German vespers, published in the Constance diocesan songbook of 1812, was an unqualified success, and is the only form of German vespers to have enjoyed continuous use up to the present day.[198]

From 1815 onwards the various forms of German vespers gradually spread over Roman Catholic Germany, and gained increasing official recognition. The criticism of Latin vespers was everywhere too strong for this to have been otherwise, and when after 1830 pressure began to be applied by a more conservative leadership to abandon these German services and return to Latin, this was shown to be impractical, and gained only a limited success. German Sunday evening services had come to be expected.

The geographical extent and the thoroughgoing nature of these eighteenth- and nineteenth-century reforms come as a surprise to those of us who assume obedience to have been strong doctrine in the Church of the Counter-reformation. While inevitably suffering from the limitations of the age, they can be appreciated more coolly today than perhaps the contemporary Vatican was much in a position to do, as honest attempts to make common-sense reforms which would enable both clergy and laity to pray the Church's office, and their success speaks for itself.

Little offices

The forms assumed by the 'evening devotion' often seem to be indebted to a type of little office in the vernacular which became popular in the Counter-reformation period, but can be traced back at least to the medieval books of hours.[199] They contain no psalms, but simply the following:

> O God make speed...
> Gloria
> Hymn
> Antiphon
> ℣ and ℟
> Collect

These little offices were widely used in the fraternities dedicated to particular saints or ideals. The members would pray the office (usually five or sevenfold) privately every day, and once a month or so would come to church on Sunday evening to sing it together. This naturally ended by replacing the official vespers in many places, and so was fed into that variegated blossoming of Sunday evening services which are so characteristic of Catholic Germany.

German Protestantism

In German Protestantism the story is very different. Luther had attempted to institute a German daily office, but the project was ill thought out, and due to the lack of both uniformity and books it quickly shrank down to those places which had a school where Latin was taught, and finally disappeared altogether. In Germany, that is. There is a German-speaking area in a quite unexpected part of the world where the story was very different.

TRANSYLVANIA

Transylvania, in what is now Romania, is home to a large German minority who had been invited into this eastern part of Europe not far from the Black Sea in the twelfth century, to farm the fertile valleys neglected by the mountain peasants. In future centuries it was to be a place where Catholics, Orthodox, and, later, Protestants, were to live amicably side by side. Romania is a meeting-place for many cultures, and this produces some unexpected results. The medieval churches of Moldavia, long and dark with Gothic windows, were built by the Orthodox, whose liturgy, still more confusingly, is in a Latin language. Of particular interest to us is the Transylvanian region known to the German-speakers as Siebenbürgen. About 200 km. square, it centres, as its name implies, on seven principal towns. In this region in the mid-sixteenth century mattins and evensong were still celebrated daily everywhere with full churches and hearty singing led by parish choirs. The services were not contained in any one book, but seem to have been largely performed from memory, use still being made of the old antiphoners, psalters and other liturgical tomes where necessary. Private recitation of the office was unheard of, and while the breviary was known, the few copies were kept in libraries for reference.

In the middle of the sixteenth century the Siebenbürgen Saxons came to be affected by the Lutheran reform, but their restrained implementation of it left the old ways inherited from the Middle Ages largely untouched. Much of the office and the eucharist continued to be performed in Latin with full ceremonies. The eucharist was celebrated solemnly every Sunday and Thursday, the offices every day. There was fierce resistance to any further change, so that through the seventeenth and eighteenth centuries a remarkable continuity was maintained.

In the towns mattins and evensong were celebrated daily. In the villages the situation was different – there the daily service was mattins only, to the first part of which all the schoolchildren came (with a resultant 'dismissal of catechumens'!). Evensong in such rural parishes, however, was celebrated too on Saturdays, Sundays and feast-days.

An attempted tidying-up of the propers in 1653 shows that at that date little had changed.[200] However, after the 1547 documents it is not until the eighteenth century that we have any clear idea again about the actual content of services. In 1764 reports were invited from all parishes in an attempt to obtain an overview of the liturgical situation. These reveal that a surprising degree of uniformity was still being maintained. Evensong took the following basic form:

> Introit
> Collect
> Deus in adjutorium (O God make speed . . .)
> Hymn
> Psalms
> Prayer
> Music
> (Sermon or reading on Sundays and feast-days)
> Magnificat or hymn
> Collect
> Benedicamus (Let us bless the Lord . . .)[201]

Kinship with the Roman office was heightened by the rich heritage of proper material (in Latin) which continued to be used in relation to the traditional Church calendar of seasons and saints' days. In Lent, for instance, compline was sung daily, when 'bread of heaven' was distributed to the children – round wafers the size of a hand, bearing the image of the crucified. There is sufficient evidence to show that all these usages continued in vigour well into the nineteenth century.[202]

There are frequent references in the liturgical directions to the church choir, and an assumption that it would be in church every day to play its part in the office. Besides the choir, we see that the parish priest was surrounded by a team of helpers of all kinds, something which has continued into modern times. Vergers, elders, servers, deacons, 'neighbourhood fathers', 'maiden-mothers' and 'youth-fathers': all had their role in mustering their troops and in performing different parts of the services.[203] In addition, most parishes seem to have had their assistant preachers.[204] There is a tremendous sense of common participation. An eighteenth-century writer describes how it was amazing to hear the whole church resound with Latin hymns sung by literate and illiterate alike, men, women and children together.[205] On certain occasions the entire congregation became involved in the ceremonies. Still today, on the vespers of Christmas Eve, the young men and women divide into four groupings round lamps decorated with greenery, some in the galleries, the rest in the chancel, in the form of an illuminated cross. They sing the hymns, psalms and canticles antiphonally between themselves and the congregation.[206]

Erich Roth comments that the preservation of such traditions in this isolated part of Eastern Europe can be compared with the insular traditions of the English.[207] Something which springs even more to mind is that extraordinary *ancien régime* which persisted in the Isle of Man until the end of the eighteenth century, in its last flowering under Bishop Wilson. There all was destroyed through the forcing of a rational Protestantism on an unwilling people. The same was to happen in Siebenbürgen.

Since the mid-eighteenth century voices had been raised against the area's liturgical traditions, but in the nineteenth century the campaign was begun in earnest. In Braşov (Kronstadt) in 1805 the daily mattins and vespers were abolished, against the general will. In the surrounding villages people were having none of this. The ordinary folk showed great obstinacy in the face of the onslaught from on high on their liturgy, and it took a whole century to break them. What was left when the work was done was a church life demoralized and impoverished, a rich and colourful liturgical tradition replaced by contemporary creations from Germany, over which no one could agree, so that uniformity and sense of unity were lost. By the century's end, church attendance had greatly fallen off.[208] The last known indication of a parish where the offices were still celebrated is in 1911, although no survey has been done to discover whether the tradition still survives anywhere.[209]

This story presents striking parallels with what we have heard about the east Syrian daily office. Here in Siebenbürgen was a substantial but scattered ethnic grouping with fiercely strong customs centred very much on their religion. Their sense of community and need for mutual protection required strong shoring-up, and this is dramatically illustrated in the local walled churches, where living quarters rise in several storeys round the inside of the defensive wall, basic accommodation for the population of the parish during times of invasion. These citadels are a strange and moving sight, rising almost to the

Interior of the Black Church in Brașov (Kronstadt) in Transylvania, looking east. It is a magnificent example of central European Gothic of the thirteenth and fourteenth centuries, indicative of the prosperity and civic pride of the town's German citizens. Here the daily sung mattins and evensong were well attended until they were abolished in the nineteenth century.

height of the church steeple itself, and even today the parishioners may have to pass through portcullises and dark passages to get to church.

POLAND

Little do we realize how diverse and rich have been the popular liturgical customs of Europe. Every nation seems to have a heritage of fast-disappearing or already forgotten customs of popular prayer which may have much to tell our age which finds it so difficult to pray. Often they have been discouraged by more 'educated' church leaders, forcibly depriving the man and woman in the street of forms of prayer which are most natural to them.

Any investigation of such traditions could hardly overlook Poland, where a particularly rich heritage has flourished until recent times, and in some respects continues still. There are many Polish usages which have connections in one way or another with the divine office. The *Gorzkie Żale* (Bitter Sufferings), which are sung in churches in Lent both in Poland and in the Western diaspora, follow the form of vigils, divided into three nocturns, each consisting of three *ersatz* psalms.[210] Another example would be the 'Great O' antiphons to the Magnificat for the week preceding Christmas, sung with the addition of verses in Polish, partly to plainchant, partly to a Polish folk tune.[211]

Popular prayer

Shortly before the tragic outbreak of the Second World War a German admirer of Poland, Josef Gülden, made a diary of a liturgical tour of the country. He gives a particularly vivid description of people at prayer in the church at Mszana-Dolna:

The people sing a curious prayer which is known also in the Eastern church as 'The Rule of Prayer of the Holy Pachomius' ... Educated people (even some of the clergy) are involuntarily ashamed that the country people still sing in this primitive way. You often have to wait a long time, until there is no priest or educated person left in the church ... On the Sunday in the octave of Corpus Christi at 6.30 a.m. we heard the people sing the mattins of Our Lady, after which came the High Mass with procession of the Eucharist round the church. Then the parish priest and some of the people went home. But some country men and women gathered again in the church. Now it had to come. But they all stayed silent – because of us. We got up, went into the vestry and waited to see if they would begin. And indeed after a little while some of the old people began to sing ... 'In the name of the Father'. ... (several times), the Trisagion, the Lord's Prayer, Ave Maria, Credo, Gloria Patri. It was almost the same as the beginning of the divine office. Then came the actual Jesus Prayer, repeated innumerable times: 'Lord Jesus Christ, Son of the living God, have mercy on us!' ... The participants did not tire of their song. Did they sing it 1,000 times? Or more? We lost, like them, any sense of number or time.[212]

Gülden adds: 'Is this primitive? Then so were the great Fathers of the Church primitive, and all the old monks as well, who testify that such verses were repeated whole nights through.'

Polish traditions, however, take us nearer than this to the Church's hours of prayer. Mention is made in the above account of mattins of the Blessed Virgin Mary. Poland has a tradition of popular singing of those little hours which evolved in the Middle Ages, in particular a form of prayer known as *godzinki* (little hours).[213] They usually consist of seven hours: mattins, prime, terce, sext, none, vespers and compline, and in form they closely resemble the little offices we have already discovered in Germany (see page 137). Each office begins with the usual responses in verse, then a hymn, versicles, collect and benediction. They come complete with characteristic music, and in the period Polish into which they were translated in the sixteenth century. They were sung in the home, at work in the fields or workshops, in schools, in the army, or wherever people found themselves.[214] One nineteenth-century short story describes a housewife singing one of the *godzinki* quietly to herself while she does the cooking,[215] and in an old folktale the wizard Twardowski, kidnapped by the devil, is saved by beginning to sing his Godzinki.[216] Josef Gülden gives a delightful picture of them being sung at home, 'alternating between the housewife in the chamber and the farmer in the stable'.[217] The point of these devotions being in rhyme, of course, was that they should be easy to sing from memory. Rhymed offices were popular all over Europe in the Middle Ages, and this is a relative of that tradition.[218] The *godzinki* are short, simple, thematic, easy to learn, easy to sing, and easy to love – people's prayer at its best.

The form of *godzinki* best known today is that of the Immaculate Conception, whose origin is probably medieval (the oldest printed version of the hymn is dated 1476), but it was freshly promoted by the Jesuits in the sixteenth century, particularly through the efforts of the Spaniard Pedro Rodriguez (1531–1617) who recited it every day himself.[219] The promotion of the *godzinki* in the Counter-reformation may deserve further investigation: Charles Borromeo spoke of something similar in his diocese of Milan,[220] and we have seen a close equivalent in Germany, which also turns out to have been given a boost by a Jesuit in the sixteenth century.[221] There were other forms of *godzinki*, such as the little hours of the Holy Cross, which have continued in use into modern times.[222] A visitor to Upper Silesia in the 1930s describes three types of little office in use there on the themes of the Passion of Christ, the Departed, and the Blessed Virgin Mary. The Godzinki of the BVM used to be sung every Sunday in parish churches in Poland, but the liturgical changes of the Second Vatican Council meant their weekly celebration has often come to be moved to Saturdays; in some places they are still sung every day in May.

Polish vespers

As we will by now be coming to expect, another Polish tradition is the singing of a form of vespers (*nieszpory*), which, making allowance for local variations, takes the following form on Sundays: after all have said the Creed, the officiant appears at the altar surrounded by a throng of brightly-dressed servers and clergy. He sings the opening versicles in Latin, to which all the people respond. Then Psalms 110–114 and 117 are sung in archaic Polish, the verses alternating between the men's and women's sides of the church. After the little chapter in Latin comes the hymn, again in Polish. The versicle is in Latin, and the Polish Magnificat is sung by alternating sides as in the psalmody. The service ends with the collect and final formulas in Latin, and the Marian antiphon in Polish. While in recent times *nieszpory* has been confined to Sundays and feasts, it possibly goes back to days when the offices were sung daily.

In the same way as for other countries of Europe the history of the public divine office can be traced through the standard church documents, the usual stipulations being made. A synod of Kalisz in 1357 ordered priests to recite or sing the canonical hours with their assistants 'in order the better ... to excite the devotion of the people'. Synods at Włocław in 1402 and Gniezno in 1512 revealingly urge the priests to recite the hours in church rather than in their house, 'so that the people will in a certain manner be able to take part in these prayers of the Church and be accustomed to them'.[223] By the eighteenth century the general practice seems to have been the singing of mattins and evensong on Sundays and feast-days and their eves. The parish schoolmaster was bound, together with the cantor and organist, to help in the singing of all these offices. Such team leadership of the offices seems to have been an accepted fact from time immemorial. So in one place in the seventeenth century, for instance, we find mention in a visitation return of an endowment intended to ensure the daily singing of the Office of the Holy Cross by a chaplain together with the rector of the local school, the cantor and the bellringer.[224]

The psalms had been widely known in Polish since the sixteenth century, but during the eighteenth at the latest the practice grew up of encouraging the congregation to sing the main prayers, hymns and chants of the mass and offices in the vernacular, and this has continued into modern times.[225] In the office, in the early stages of this movement, the priest said his office *sotto voce* in Latin. The end result was that in Polish vespers all the people's parts of the service are in Polish, and the priest's in Latin. Gülden gives vivid accounts of vespers in his pre-war visit to Poland, when in many places Polish vespers was sung on Sundays all the year round. He happened to be there for the Corpus Christi octave, however, when the service was sung solemnly every day. 'They sing the five psalms with the full participation of all the people, with very beautiful, lively Polish melodies totally unknown to us, always all together. How it rings! The young folk lean their elbows on the altar rail, prop their heads in their hands, and sing with all their strength. Most people know all the Psalms by heart. One or two have a tiny book.'[226] With his companion, Gülden goes from church to church night after night and witnesses the same scene. In Tarnów he is told that people prefer vespers to all the other devotions that go on in church outside the mass, and when vespers is in Polish the church is packed. In many places the clergy were looking down on this as a peasant custom, and replacing Polish vespers with devotions of other sorts, 'so that the people often come earlier of their own accord, in order to be able to sing vespers for themselves'.[227]

Significance for today

It is not easy to say how far Poland's rich array of religious customs are survivals of ancient tradition. Such things come and go: they have their times of popularity and times of neglect, and can be greatly changed in the process. But they are without doubt relevant to our inquiry into the nature and meaning of the hours of prayer: for if these are unbroken traditions, they tell us something about the ancient past and its continuing vitality, and of the importance of our staying in communion with it; but if they are more recent developments, they reveal to us how this type of prayer springs from natural human inclinations.

The search for such survivals could well go further, and it is not improbable that in other areas of Europe, particularly the more remote parts, similar customs may be remembered by older folk, or even still be in vigour.

THE MODERN PERIOD

To return from rich local customs to the mainstream history of the divine office comes as a cold douche. Despite the surviving traditions of public celebration of the offices with music and ceremony which we have found, there can be no doubt that the practice of clergy saying the breviary privately came to dominate the Roman office to such an extent (although never more than in the nineteenth and twentieth centuries) that it was eventually conceived of as a clerical preserve, and 'breviary' became its name. In liturgical works which preceded the Second Vatican Council, the subject was more likely to receive this title than any other. So Cabrol and Leclercq's mammoth encyclopaedia of archaeology and liturgy puts its history of the divine office under the heading: 'Bréviaire'.[228]

Allusion has been made to the muddle that it became. Occasional attempts at reform, such as that by Cardinal Quiñones in the sixteenth century and the Gallican breviaries of the seventeenth and eighteenth centuries all came to nothing. The story has been well told elsewhere and there is no need here to go over the sad tale again.[229] All reforms were quashed or undermined in their turn, and the Roman breviary endured impregnable, a crushing quota of words to be worked through daily by the clergy, some of whom might understand little of what they were saying, or even find it difficult to assent to if they did.

It would be easy to dismiss the triumph of the breviary in the Roman Catholic Church as a total disaster, but that would be an exaggeration. The spirituality associated with it produced enough saints and gifts of spiritual insight to disprove any such claim. Private recitation also had something in common with the early Christian prayer-hours as prayers said by individuals in the knowledge that they were praying with the Church. Many clergy, not least Cardinal Newman by his own admission, set immense store by it. Sitting in church or study or walking up and down in the garden reading the breviary, they recognized that in contradiction to all appearances it had the power to help mould the inner man and conform him to the character of Christ and the saints, in a framework strongly evocative of the Church with which he is praying.

None the less, the fact that the breviary can be associated with personal sanctity is its great flaw as well – while the Church produced some outstanding people, it was weak in the ability to share out its spiritual gifts equally among the whole Body. An office which was the prayer of the Church in theory but a devotion performed by isolated individuals in practice was a shadow of its true self.

The outstanding value of the old breviary without any doubt is that despite all imperfections, and all the waves of change which have smudged the lines of continuity, it is still redolent of centuries and centuries of the Western way of prayer. We only have to look, in the Sources section at the end of this book, at the general lines of development of the Western monastic rites, to see how much it has in common with them. Its genius is monastic and clerical, and as such it is an invaluable heirloom and resource. But as an embodiment of the Church's prayer it lasted far longer than it should have done in the form which it had gained in the Middle Ages.

Modern reforms

The new Roman breviary which appeared in 1971 (34) is an adventurous reform, achieving a good many of the things clergy have been asking for for centuries, and it is very indebted to the scuttled sixteenth-century breviary of Quiñones (32g), simplifying the offices in a drastic and imaginative manner, and coming as springs of refreshing water to many grateful clergy tired of the *pensum* of dry recitation which the old book limited them to. It also gives a wide liberty to adapt services to particular needs. There are in cathedrals and parish churches many encouraging attempts to restore the public celebration of the office, at least on Sunday evenings, and simplified forms have been produced for use by the laity which have had a positive response. The order for compline, and the shorter book containing morning and evening prayer, have proved to be a particular and unexpected success with the laity.

It is to be doubted, however, whether the needs of the Church, complex as they are today, can be met with one book. The amount of material to be recited is still considerable, and many clergy who spend their day among the tensions, noise and endless talk and movement of modern life find this kind of office difficult to sustain daily. What is needed, paradoxically, is a range of material which is much more rich, but much more adaptable.

The same is even more true of the new forms of office in the Church of England's Alternative Service Book (35) and its relatives in other countries, (excellent as one or two of these are). These services are well appreciated by many, and have made the office easier to pray; but they have not yet succeeded in tackling the problems many people have with daily liturgical prayer. In many Anglican parishes the offices continue to be said daily, but there is no doubt that this practice, and indeed the whole prayer-life of the clergy, are in crisis.

While being thankful, therefore, for present mercies, it seems that we must press on in the search for renewal, particularly keeping in view the renewal of the *community*'s prayer, and renewal in our understanding of the divine office as *celebration*.

PART III

The Content of Daily Prayer

17

The Prayer of the Body

The preceding chapters have sketched a narrative history of the *practice* of daily liturgical prayer, paying less attention to details of content. In these next four chapters, we shall turn our attention more closely to the content, and it has seemed best at some points here to add to the historical account a dash of pastorally-oriented comment.

Corporate and corporal

Because Christian prayer has been so damaged by the general assumption that 'external' elements are simply an optional extra, it will help to put first on our agenda those physical gestures and ceremonies which have been so important in the history of the daily office. For some people indeed they will be the most important element in it.

Both in private and public prayer the most common of such signs are kneeling, bowing, standing, sitting, making the sign of the cross. At the words: 'Come, let us bow down and bend the knee' in the Venite it is an old practice for all to bow or kneel. So too is bowing for the first half of the Gloria at the end of each psalm. In its fuller form this was known as an 'imposition', and included a prostration and time for silent prayer such as we hear of in John Cassian or in the people's office of Caesarius of Arles. Pachomius' monks prayed in this silence with their arms outstretched in the form of a cross.[1] The private prayer of Syrian shepherds included something similar (see p. 105).

We have found offices beginning and ending by sharing the peace, and widespread use of the lectern as a focus for people to group together while still leaving the others free to remain more inconspicuous if they want to. We have found daily services which made use of various parts of the church building, sometimes involving processions, or less organized movement of crowds. One such tradition which can be traced through many rites in East and West is a regular procession after the office to a cross, tomb or baptistery, where a further short service took place. Even the Roman office had this – an *ordo* of the Lateran Basilica which dates from the twelfth century prescribed such a procession to the baptisteries. This is one example of those riches which were lost through the coming of the breviary.[2] This procession occurs so often in so many forms that it even deserves to be considered among the first rank of the contents of the divine office, and invites a historical and theological investigation.[3]

Similar claims can be made even more strongly for the so-called Prayer of Inclination, which is found in many places.[4] In it the deacon bids the people bow their heads, and then the officiant pronounces a solemn blessing. On grounds of antiquity and the extent of its diffusion this can claim to be an important constituent of the office.

Enough has also been said to show the part played by music, light-rituals, incense and vestments. Processions, sometimes accompanying the bearing of symbols such as the cross, gospel-book or icon, the participation of servers and ministers of different kinds, and the parish team of singers, are all part of a wider aim to give expression not only to the fact that we need to do things physically, but also to that very Christian belief that worship must be a corporate act, in which different functions are distributed among the various people present.

If the physical is necessary in corporate worship, it is just as important in private prayer: standing, kneeling, sitting; prostrations, sign of the cross, icon corners, music and singing, candles, beads, bells and well-loved books – all have their role in the prayer of the people of God. They may not all come so naturally to us today, but our response has to be to evolve new interpretations of this tradition, rather than simply to abandon it, and claim that the word can do without the flesh.

18

Sacred Poetry

If the text of daily liturgical prayer is dominated by anything it is by poetry: psalms, canticles, hymns and other forms in which the rhythmic word is allowed to roll us forth on an interplay of allusions, evocations, searchings and meanings. Poetry is the office's main substance, and with poetry it usually begins, in the form of the Psalms. It will be best to examine first of all the particular problems we have with them.

The problem of the Psalms

For Western Christians the most important poetical element in the offices is the psalmody, and yet it is this which presents the most problems too. For the Fathers and medieval Christians the Psalms were a compendium of the gospel, the very words of God through the voice of David, encapsulating the mysteries of Christ. The time when such an understanding was possible has probably gone for ever, at least in the simple way in which it used to be held. However, that is not to say that the actual way the Psalms worked for people has necessarily changed much. There are several ways in which our approach to them has changed very little, for example:

(a) There is the fact, mentioned in chapter 4 (pages 21ff.) that we can sometimes seem to use the Psalms simply as verbal confetti, a stream over which prayer can ride like a raft on the waters. It is of course inadequate on its own as a method for making the most of the Psalter. Rather does it simply describe a phenomenon which can happen. But it also helps to explain why attempts to replace the Psalms with good-quality poetry do not work. There is a sameness about them which suits the purpose much better. It is interesting to see that where the Psalms are successfully replaced by other poetry, as is effectively the case in the Byzantine office, this poetry has that very same quality of sameness. Familiar themes come up again and again. The vocabulary and imagery return with a regularity which frustrates all desires for stimulation and 'food for thought', even though there are the times when it 'makes you think'. This is an aspect of the Psalms which will always have been there, particularly when psalmodizing is plentiful and regular. We see through their glass darkly, to the eternal prayer beyond.

(b) Linked with this is another aspect of the Psalms that will not have changed much – the capacity of their rhythm to calm us down and make us receptive. The Psalms can be seen as a preliminary to prayer, or its first slow paces. In the office they seem to lead to the prayers (e.g. the litany) in the same way as a long-winded natter is necessary before two people can get down to a deeper discussion; like a starter at a meal, or scales before a concert. That, at least, is how it can feel sometimes. But lest this should mislead, there are plenty of witnesses to the way the recitation of the Psalms can feel to be the purest prayer in itself.

(c) Another way in which things have not changed much is the response we can make to the Psalms as they stand. They concern themselves with some of the most basic elements of human experience, taking us, in effect, on a tour through our unconscious: the fear of enemies, desire for revenge, depression, concern with material things, jubilation, victory, glory – not always representative perhaps of our ordinary experience of life, but all primary colours of the hidden ground of our nature, which were still close enough to the surface in our childhood for us to remember them. In this way it is possible to see the Psalms as holding before us the real selves we often overlook, and laying them before God. They therefore use the archetypal imagery of our unconscious and of our dreams.

(d) There is still another, related way in which the Psalms will not have changed, and that concerns their very elementary *theological* nature. As they stand, there is no knowledge of Christ; even, in some places, little knowledge of mercy, hope or love. They can thus be seen as bringing us back relentlessly to the simplest and crudest levels of the relationship between human and divine. Often they speak of the meeting between the individual or the community and God, full stop. They circle around an inexorable truth of great simplicity: *God* and *Humanity*. It is just this passionate and stormy relationship with God in all his transcendence which we find so difficult today, and which is probably one of the most important things the Psalms can remind us of; like the pianist who concentrates his practice on just those fingers which are weakest.

(e) The thematic use of the appropriate Psalms can be extremely telling, particularly at festivals. Good examples would be Psalm 24 for Ascension, 116 for Maundy Thursday, and 84 for Dedication. When in Psalm 116 we sing: 'I will lift up the cup of salvation and call upon the name of the Lord' with the Eucharist in mind, this colours the whole Psalm, so that both it and the theme we impose upon it are filled out by their coming together. Some Psalms which were originally written for a very different purpose can seem just right when chosen for special occasions such as this. When we use Psalm 121 at weddings it appears to exalt and be exalted, as if it were written for that very occasion. The Psalms can have the ability to gather up what we hold out to them and make it expand into a larger space. It may be, then, that some will be helped by a use of different Christian themes, selecting suitable ones for the purpose, rather than reciting them in numerical order. Here there is no problem about the more difficult Psalms – they are simply not used.

(f) Listen, at an English harvest evensong, to countryfolk weighing in to Psalm 65. This is not contemplation in the silence of the heart, but Basil and Caesarius of Arles would have recognized it very well. It could be called the *hymnic* use of Psalms – simply singing them like hymns or songs chosen for the occasion. The people's office has been very selective in its use of the Psalter (see pages 80 nn. 45 and 47; and 85 n. 58), with a particular interest in the themes of morning and evening, darkness and light, praise and thanksgiving. To this should be added the use of the penitential Psalm 51 at mattins.[5] The content of individual Psalms has been used selectively too. Often outstanding verses are woven together in responsorial forms, sometimes with the addition of Christian phraseology (e.g. 17b, 19, 30, 31).

Having found six ways in which the understanding of the Psalms will not have changed drastically for modern people, we come finally to a traditional approach which many find truly difficult – the systematic Christian interpretation of the Psalms. In contrast to the thematic use mentioned above, this is specially concerned with the problem of praying the Psalms when they are performed *in course*, or at least when most of the Psalter is put to use in a systematic way. It aims to apply Christian themes in a variety of ways, usually by either understanding the Psalm as speaking *about* Christ (e.g. Psalm 23), or being the *voice* of Christ himself (e.g. Psalm 22), or being the voice of the Church (e.g. Psalm 126). This is precisely the way quotations from the Psalms are used in the NT, and it may even be because of that that we find this approach unsympathetic! We say to ourselves: 'The NT writers believed the psalmists actually knew about Christ and deliberately sought to express God's plan concerning him. We know that can't be so, and therefore any Christian interpretation of the Psalms is phoney for us.' This is a misunderstanding: in no way does it depend on believing that the original author meant a 'Christian' interpretation. Rather is it simply our way of acknowledging the repetitive patterns in God's way of going about things. The Exodus is linked with the resurrection, Israel is equated with the Church, quite legitimately, because they are part of a repeating pattern in the way things work. This is why typology, the matching-up of stories and pictures such as these two examples, is more than merely fanciful and picturesque. It works on the basis that God's methods remain true to type. Circumstances and requirements differ according to the times, but the acts of God are seen often to follow archetypal patterns. That is why some passages of Isaiah resonate so strongly with the story of the crucifixion, or the history of Israel resembles so much that of the Church. It may perhaps be compared with the way Leonardo da Vinci was both a great artist and a consummate scientist. The two fields are as different as the OT and the NT, and yet the same innovative genius emerges in both, showing points at which they both relate. So it is with typology in the Bible. It does not matter that a Hebrew king entering the Temple to celebrate a victory (Psalm 118) knew nothing about the resurrection of Christ. The same God was revealing himself in the same inimitable manner in both events, and both reveal a similar trait in his character, and in the character of his Truth.

Even if this is so, there are still niggling problems for us, probably crystallizing in the fact that the higher criticism of modern times has been keen to rediscover how texts were *originally* used, and *why* they came to be written. We want to understand what was going on when these things came to birth, and are not prepared to accept that God might have been working in hidden ways not open to our scrutiny. It ties in with tastes and preferences of our times. We like to see the grain of bare wood rather than paint it; we want to hear Mozart on authentic instruments; we want unadulterated food; we want plain speaking. We do not take kindly to saying one thing while we mean another, or to drawing conclusions which seem forced or unnatural. All of these attitudes are extremely good, without doubt. But they have their negative side. They can, for example, obscure the importance of *game* as it has been outlined in chapter 5. The typological interpretation of the Psalms has to be understood as serious game, something we find very difficult, because of our deep conviction that the prayer should 'sincerely mean' exactly what it is uttering. In isolation this leaves us prey to all kinds of pride and self-regard. It has to be balanced by game-prayer, and that is exactly the role the daily office often fulfils.

That is one focal-point of our problem. There is another which is close to it. This concerns the way practices or objects can, with the passage of time, undergo a change of use. The alphabet evolved from pictures, chasubles started off as raincoats, the seating arrangement in the House of Commons, so central to the British concept of parliamentary debate, derives directly from the cathedral and monastic choir! It is important to know how things evolved, in order to understand them, but it is not always desirable to return to the authentic original. It is like this with the Psalms as used in the daily office. Even by the time of Christ this was so, and he will have prayed them in a way which was often different from the original intention.

It may therefore be an unpopular lesson which we must learn, and it may take generations for the Church to recover such an approach, but this way of understanding the Psalms and indeed the whole of scripture is essential if the Church is to stay with the deeper springs of her traditions of prayer. That moves are being made in this direction is indicated by the appearance of such books as Andrew Louth's *Discerning the Mystery*,[6] which would be of great help to anyone seeking a more solid introduction to the problem.

In practice the Christian interpretation of the Psalms makes use of a very small range of themes. For example, Israel can equal the Church, the king can stand for Christ, the adversary can be evil in general. Towering above these are the three general principles mentioned above, through which the majority of the Psalms can be referred to Christ. One good way-in to this is by understanding the first person singular, when it occurs, to refer to the Church. The 'I' who speaks, praises, fears, laments, hopes, is then the Body of Christ, and our voices embody 'the voice of the Bride calling to the Bridegroom'.[7] The Psalm now becomes not the self-preoccupied moanings of an individual, but our prayer with and for the Church, reflecting on her trials and testings, the opposition and misunderstanding she faces, both from without and within, the faith and hope in which she is grounded, and the love and praise which endlessly go forth in the round of worship and prayer. As the subject is plural, concern for the Church's 'self' leaves self-concern behind and becomes a part of love of the brethren, both those people of which she is composed, and those who need yet to receive her message. The divine office then becomes in a vivid way what it is, 'the prayer of the Church'. Many of the Psalms can suddenly be revealed in this way as the prayer of Christ in his Body. 'When the Body of the Son prays, the head is not separated from the body. It is the one saviour of his body, our Lord Jesus Christ, who prays for us, prays in us, and is prayed to by us' (see page 40).

Such an interpretation is not an act of make-believe. It is an act of the will grounded in theology and in faith, a *willing* of this meaning, given weight by being shared in space and in time by all those Christians who have brought it to be accepted as a tested way of prayer, emerging at the life-giving behest, they would affirm, of the Holy Spirit.

Different Psalms can be referred to Christ in different ways, and sometimes even within one Psalm this can oscillate every few verses. First Christ is speaking in his Church, then the earthly Christ speaks, and so on. This comes with practice, but we need assistance. In the past this has been given in three ways:

(a) In commentaries on the Psalter, especially the great commentaries of the Fathers, such as Augustine's *Enarrationes in Psalmos*. The ancient propensity for imaginative flights of fancy is not always sympathetic to the modern mind, however. It is a question of learning, with a certain amount of patience, to enter into this way of thinking. The effort is abundantly worth it and needs to be persevered with – it is certainly no more demanding than the same exercise we often have to do with Scripture. But there is also a need for contemporary material for the Church's front-line troops, which can show the Christian sense of the Psalms without putting cultural hurdles in the way.

(b) The use of titles or introductory paragraphs written before each Psalm. These were usually distillations from the commentaries of the Fathers, and came to be known by heart. The new Roman 'Liturgy of the Hours' provides two such titles for each Psalm. Their quality varies, and we really need to have a wide choice of collections of such psalm titles.

(c) The use of Psalm-collects. At least until the time of Benedict each Psalm was normally followed by a silence and then a collect which elaborated on some part of its content. There are several ancient collections of these prayers, and more than one modern collection is in print.[8] The ancients considered the silence and prayer after the Psalms to be very important. Caesarius says:

> What good does it do you to sing the Psalms faithfully if, when you stop singing, you do not want to entreat God? Let each one who has ceased chanting pray and entreat the Lord with all humility, so that what he utters with the lips he may deserve with God's help to fulfil in deed. Just as singing the Psalms, brethren, is like sowing a field, praying is like the sower who cultivates it by burying and covering the ground ... So whenever a person stops chanting, let him not stop praying if he wants a harvest of divine mercy to grow in the field of his heart.[9]

Are the Psalms suitable for all?

It is probably legitimate to say that difficulties in praying the Psalms will usually be different for the nun or monk than they will be for the busy person set in the world (which is not to say that monastics are not busy people – there is no room for a life of leisure in a monastery). The more we are involved in the *inner* journey, the more the Psalms will function as work, *askesis*. The more we are caught up in the *outer* struggle of 'the world', the more they will need to be carefully chosen according to their ability to refresh and feed.[10] Many of the NT passages which are now being used as canticles are just the thing for the people's office – they can not only swell the list of favoured Psalms, but also enable Scripture to be prayed. Whether these or more recent forms of Christian poetry could actually replace the Psalms is a difficult question. It would not be easy to use the Byzantine ecclesiastical poetry shorn of the context in which it is understood. It is not theoretically impossible that we might find a way of using our own Western poetic heritage, or even creating anew, but no one has yet succeeded in such a venture, and the prospect seems unlikely.

This has of necessity been a very sketchy treatment of an important and difficult subject. The reader wishing to pursue it further may gain considerable help from one or other of the works listed in a separate section in the Bibliography (page 234).

Canticles

The origin of the use of biblical canticles is not clear. Quite early on, the Song of Moses (Exodus 15) and the Benedicite found their way into the morning office as part of the psalmody. The number of OT canticles used in this way gradually increased. After them use began to be made of canticles from the NT too, again as part of the morning psalmody. Niceta of Remesiana (d. *c.* 414) is first to mention the use of the Magnificat. In the Orthodox Church the Magnificat and Benedictus have remained among the canticles of the morning office (even though the Benedictus is usually omitted in practice). This was once the common practice of the universal Church. The use of the canticles, if mentioned at all, was in the psalmody of the morning office.

The list of canticles had more or less reached completion by the fifth century. There have been many versions of the list, but the Greek and Roman canticle schemes listed below are typical:

Greek	Roman
Exodus 15.1–19	Benedicite
Deuteronomy 32.1–43	Isaiah 12.1–6
1 Samuel 2.1–10	Isaiah 38.10–20
Habakkuk 3.2–19	1 Samuel 2.1–10
Isaiah 26.9–20	Exodus 15.1–19
Jonah 2.3–10	Habakkuk 3.2–19
Daniel 3.26–56	Deuteronomy 32.1–43
Daniel 3.57–88 (Benedicite)	Benedictus
Magnificat and Benedictus	Magnificat (in evening office)

Benedict introduced many new ones for alternative use on feast-days, and in the Mozarabic office the list runs to over seventy.[11]

Before Charlemagne's reforms various forms of the Greek scheme seem to have been in use in the West wherever the Roman rite was not followed. Old French Psalters of the mid-8th century couple the Magnificat and the Benedictus, in that order, in company with the OT canticles of mattins, and an old Psalter written about 705 in the south of France gives the Magnificat in a list of OT canticles where the Benedictus is missing altogether.[12] In Gaul and Spain the Benedictus was frequently used as a canticle in the eucharist, a role later taken over by the Gloria in Excelsis. The rule of Caesarius of Arles puts the Magnificat in morning prayer, and it was probably so used in the Celtic rites (44).

In the West, therefore, the canticles underwent a further development. The Roman office brought with it, as it spread, a practice which remained unique and whose origin is obscure: the transference of the Magnificat from mattins to vespers, and the elevation of it and the Benedictus to isolated positions of honour as the high-points of their respective services. When or how this happened we cannot say, but it was almost certainly from the Roman rite that Benedict took this model for the two services, although he nowhere stipulates the Magnificat and Benedictus by name, and our earliest information on the Roman daily office is later than his time.[13]

No mention has yet been made of what are probably the oldest Christian canticles. Some scholars believe that hymns and other original compositions played an important part in the earliest Christian liturgy, and examples of this type of composition have been identified in the NT in recent years. As a result of these findings, modern reforms such as those of the Roman breviary and the Anglican daily office have made use of some of these texts, and the hunt is on, particularly among religious communities, for biblical passages of any sort which can serve as canticles.

Non-biblical canticles

A third-century writer (Hippolytus?) refers to 'psalms and odes such as from the beginning were written by believers, hymns to the Christ, the Word of God, calling him God'.[14] As with most aspects of the daily office, the early centuries give us little information on the development of such a tradition, but from the fourth century onwards we can begin to map the course of two types of composition, the non-biblical canticle and the metrical hymn.

Outstanding among the former is the Gloria in excelsis: it is first quoted in the *Apostolic Constitutions* (13), and its typical use in the undivided Church was as a canticle at mattins, especially on Sundays. In the early centuries its association with the morning office was deeply ingrained, and something of this association seems to have survived in private devotion, where it is sometimes cited as a prayer for Sunday mornings. A ninth-century prayer book gives it for mattins,[15] and a tenth-century rule for private prayer from Hyde Abbey, a Benedictine house at Winchester, says: 'Every Sunday take care that you call upon the name of the Trinity ... and sing the Benedicite, the Gloria in excelsis Deo and the Credo in Deum, and the Pater Noster, for Christ's sake'.[16] It has become so closely associated with the Eucharist in the West as to feel odd in the office, but there is no doubt that that is its original home.

The Te Deum, probably composed by Niceta of Remesiana in the late 4th century, begins to be heard of early on in the West, and in the Benedictine and Roman offices it is used after the last lesson of vigils on Sundays and feasts.

Metrical hymns

There are probably more Greek and Latin hymns in existence than could ever be made use of, and their history has been a rich and chequered one. At first popular, from the fourth century onwards they came to be associated with heresy and controversy. In Constantinople the Arians sang their hymns through the streets while Chrysostom organized a counter-demonstration of orthodox hymn-singing. Particularly in the West these associations led to the feeling that only biblical texts should be used in worship. In the early sixth century Caesarius of Arles was one of the first to restore hymns to the daily office, and Benedict seems to have followed his lead, but as late as 563 the Council of Braga forbade the use of poetical compositions in church, this Council being both strongly pro-Roman and also politically opposed to any influence from Visigothic Spain (29.i). By then hymns were generally coming to be accepted in monasticism, but not until the twelfth century did the Roman Church permit them in the secular office.

Other local uses were even more conservative. No hymns were ever allowed in the rites of Lyon and Vienne (except at compline) until the French Revolution.[17]

The history of hymnody is a vast subject, too little known. In the West enormous numbers of hymns were composed in the Middle Ages, not to mention the abundant flowering of tropes and kindred forms whose place in the medieval office bears many similarities with that of hymns and poetry in Orthodoxy.[18] Their history in the Eastern office is an equally vast subject. They play a major part in the worship, and the Byzantine office itself is made up very considerably of such material – Alexander Schmemann estimates that as much as 80 per cent. of all printed liturgical material is hymnody. J. M. Neale criticized the poor quality of much of it as poetry, but confessed himself struck at 'the marvellous ignorance in which English ecclesiastical scholars are content to remain of this huge treasure of divinity – the gradual completion of nine centuries at least ... What a glorious mass of theology do these offices present!'[19]

The vocal choreography of the office

The poetry of the divine office is performed either by soloists or as choral song or choral speech. This mainly concerns the psalmody, where at least five different ways were evolved of deploying choirs and cantors in its performance: direct (solo and choral), responsorial, antiphon-psalmody, and alternating groups.

(a) Direct (solo)

This denotes reading or singing of a Psalm straight through, normally by one person (but sometimes by a small group) while the majority sit and listen. The Egyptian monasteries give our earliest evidence of the practice (36, 37). In the two daily services of vespers and dawn office, the Psalms were read in groups of twelve. After each Psalm all rose for a period of silent prayer, the middle of which was marked by a prostration on the ground, and this was rounded off by an improvised collect summing up the particular Psalm. Early writers regularly refer to Psalms as readings. The eastern Orthodox often still do.[20] St Benedict mentions the direct method (RB 17); he mentions no silences or prostrations, but it is possible he may have assumed them.[21]

Such direct reading of Psalms is capable of many permutations which can be particularly helpful in the worship of a small group.

For example:

> one person reads all;
> two people say alternate verses;
> several people read a section each

(b) Direct (choral)

The most characteristic way of performing the Psalms in Anglican parishes is the singing of the entire Psalm, by all present, to Anglican chant. This mode of singing evolved after the Reformation from the familiar plainsong, but employing four-part harmony.

Choral direct singing of the Psalms has an ancient history. We hear from Basil that his congregation used to sing Psalm 51 straight through all together.[22] At various periods from early times, through the Middle Ages to today, the Psalms have been sung in metrical verse, a practice more ancient and respectable than we might think. A good number of the Psalms are the basis of well-known hymns, and these provide a possible alternative to the usual ways of using the Psalter.

(c) Responsorial

In responsorial psalmody the Psalm is sung by a soloist or a choir, but after each verse or group of verses all present sing a refrain. For many centuries this was one of the principal ways of executing the Psalms in the people's office, and it had an important place in the monastic office too.

This type of psalmody disappeared from everyday usage for reasons which will shortly become clear, but a truncated form of it survives, which is known in the West as a responsory or *respond*, and in the east as a *prokeimenon*. Here is a typical example from compline:

℣   Into your hands, Lord, I commend my spirit.
℟   Into your hands, Lord, I commend my spirit.
℣   For you have redeemed me, Lord God of truth.
℟   I commend my spirit.
℣   Glory be to the Father, and to the Son, and to the Holy Spirit.
℟   Into your hands, Lord, I commend my spirit.

This short form of the Gloria pre-dates the Arian crisis of the fourth century (see 29f). Originally a whole Psalm was used, the first versicle being its refrain, but this shrank, and later still other parts of Scripture came to be used instead, especially the text of a preceding reading. It has a curious form, but the respond turns short texts over in a way which helps us 'chew the cud' of Scripture, and the principle of repetition of the same phrases more than once is important. The way it is done in the respond is complex enough to be engaging without losing simplicity. It is more suitable for group than individual use, but good responds can be particularly effective when they take up themes from a lection.

(d) Antiphonal
The Greek *antiphonon* may best be translated as 'countertone', and seems to refer to two choirs singing an octave apart. It is really a more elaborate form of responsorial psalmody, and Joseph Gelineau gives it the following characteristics:

(i) The *verses* are sung by a soloist; *or* they are sung alternately by two soloists or small groups.
(ii) Two choirs alternate in singing the *refrain*, one of men's voices, the other of women and children, an octave higher. These would correspond to the normal division of the church into two halves for men and women.
(iii) The refrain is often an original composition.
(iv) Its melody tends to be elaborate.[23]

It is just like responsorial psalmody in *shape*, but differs *musically* in that the refrain in responsorial psalmody is normally a phrase from the psalm sung to the same or similar chant, while in antiphonal psalmody the refrain is a free musical composition, perhaps with freely composed words too, and its elaborateness contrasts with the simplicity of the chant to which the verses are sung. In addition, the division of those present into two choirs, male and female, meant that the refrain was now alternately sung in different octaves:[24]

Cantor(s)	Choir 1 (men)	Choir 2 (women)
	Antiphon	
Verse 1		
		Antiphon
Verse 2		
	Antiphon	
Verse 3		
		Antiphon
etc.		

This kind of antiphonal psalmody is first mentioned in the fourth century, and became extremely popular as the Catholic answer to the Arians' rousing hymns.[25] In the early centuries the word antiphon refers not to the refrain alone but to the Psalm itself, or even a group of Psalms. The old Byzantine office began with eight antiphons in the narthex (18). They were of roughly equal length, containing from one to six Psalms each, and were split into two groups, the odd-numbered antiphons having *Alleluia* as the refrain, the even-numbered a series of ten refrains, all very similar:

> Hear me, O Lord.
> Have mercy on me, O Lord.
> Save me, O Lord.
> etc.

Perhaps this type of thing is meant when in the West the Council of Agde (506), for instance, speaks of antiphons, although later sources seem to mean one Psalm performed in this way (29c, 43, 44).

Monasticism introduced something new into the Church – the male voice choir. In their churches the singing in octaves would inevitably be lost. There were often children in monastic communities, but they would have sung together with the men, if at all. The term *antiphonal* thus came to refer to the alternating of a refrain between two equal choirs.

(e) Alternating

In Western monasticism a still more radical change took place in the method of performing antiphonal psalmody. From about the ninth century onwards, as far as we can see, the singing of the antiphon after each verse began to disappear, in favour of a simple alternating of the verses of the Psalm, the antiphon surviving solely at its beginning and end.[26] Thus when we speak about *antiphonal* performance today we usually mean the alternating of verses between two sides of the choir, or between congregation and minister. This practice would be better known as 'alternating psalmody'.[27] It is unknown either to the Eastern churches or the early Christian writers.

Gregorian chant is still deeply marked by the original antiphonal usage, in that the endings to the chants are made variable not simply in order to provide a choice of tunes, but also to lead into the recurring antiphon which is no longer there, except after the Gloria Patri.

19

Holy Reading

The practice of public reading of the Scriptures passed from the synagogue into the Christian eucharist but not into the daily office, except later in the night prayer of the monks. The two services of the monks of Scete in Egypt were each followed by two readings from the Bible (36). Attendance at this was voluntary, and brethren were expected to bring some work with them while they listened. They had to work while they listened in Caesarius' monasteries and convents too.[28] According to John Cassian the lessons were 'an extraordinary element on a voluntary basis, for those who wished by assiduous meditation to retain the memory of the divine Scriptures'.[29] This practice in Egypt is not mentioned, however, in any other contemporary source. Again according to Cassian, the monasteries of Palestine and Syria had a special vigil on Friday nights which included three readings (38). Egeria describes it as taking place in Jerusalem on every Friday in Lent (16). By the time of the *Ordo Monasterii* (43) we see emerging a daily night office at which the Bible was read. When we come to the people's office Egeria tells us that at the church of the Holy Sepulchre there were normally no readings in the offices of the day (except the gospel at the Sunday vigil).

These examples show us the two classic usages in the daily office regarding Scripture-reading. The *monastic* office came to attach great importance to prayer during the night, made up of psalms and readings; the *people's* office conversely normally contained no readings.

Where the two usages are unanimous is that neither has systematic Bible-reading at mattins or evensong. Instances of such readings are suprisingly rare, and even where evidence can be found in the early centuries, it usually cannot be relied on, due to the frequent interchangeability of terms. 'Reading' sometimes means a psalm, 'gospel' can mean a canticle, 'prophecy' sometimes refers to the Benedictus, and the office was frequently described as 'meditation on Scripture', which indeed it is. The information in the Sources section at the end of this book shows up very clearly the curious avoidance of lections at the two main offices.[30] These offices are so often described as 'praises', 'psalmody', 'hymns', that it is possible with justice to conclude that there was here what might be called a 'doxology imperative'. Robert Taft has shown the extent to which the morning and evening services were dominated by the themes of praise, light, celebration and prayer.[31] They were *hymns* with a vengeance, and have managed to retain much of this character throughout their history in the main rites. The experience of singing the Laudate Psalms (148–150) daily at mattins can bring home very clearly this spirit of thanksgiving and blessing (*berakah*) which is surely indebted in some way to the synagogue.

The absence of readings is referred to explicitly by at least one source. An abbot of Montecassino pointed out in a letter to Charlemagne that:

If anyone wonders why blessed Benedict prescribed only one lesson from the Old Testament to be read at the night office on weekdays in summer, let him understand that it was not yet the custom at that time for Holy Scripture to be read in the Roman Church, as it is now, but this was instituted some time later, either by blessed Pope Gregory [*c.* 540–604] or, as is claimed by some, by Honorius [d. 638; Pope from 625].[32]

As the Scriptures began to find a place in the monastic office, this took two forms in the West, both of which later spilled over into the people's office: (a) a brief reading said from memory, which came to be known as a *little chapter*; (b) systematic reading *in course* from the book.[33] The first, whose content tends to vary little, can be likened to other snippets of Scripture such as antiphons, responsories and versicles, different kinds of liturgical 'lego-brick', small components which in related ways dip briefly into the Scriptures. The history of the little chapter is obscure, and as far as I know has not undergone thorough investigation. It is not clear whether in early usage it was always so small as it is in the Roman and Benedictine offices, or whether or not it included any element of reading *in course.*

The second type of reading was a different matter altogether, a systematic scheme for reading through the whole of the Bible over the year, and it found its place in the vigils office (or 'night office' – the terminology, and the various types of service it can refer to, as well as the question of which part of the night or early dawn is its proper home, are complicated questions scholars have yet to resolve).[34] This office contained a number of 'nocturns', each of which included a single passage divided into three parts, separated by responsories:

Nocturn 1: Scripture lesson in three parts

Sundays and feast-days only { Nocturn 2: patristic lesson in three parts
Nocturn 3: homily on a gospel passage in three parts

(Benedictine only: reading of gospel from the day's Eucharist)

The readings of nocturn 1 from the eighth century onwards (until 1911 in the Roman breviary) worked through the Bible as follows:

Septuagesima to Passion Sunday   Pentateuch, Joshua, Judges, (Ruth)
Passion Sunday onwards   Jeremiah

Easter to Trinity	Acts, Canonical Epistles, Apocalypse
Trinity to First Sunday in August	Samuel, Kings, Chronicles
August	Wisdom books
September	Job, Tobit, Judith, Esther, Esdras
October	Maccabees
November	Ezekiel, Daniel, Minor Prophets
December	Isaiah
Christmas to Septuagesima	Paul

For most of the year the ferial reading is taken from the OT alone. Nothing is thought to be wrong in this. The Gospels on the other hand are not read in the office at all. On Sundays and feast-days non-biblical readings predominate. Astonishingly, Benedict directs that the lessons be not read in the summer months, and replaces them with one memory-reading. What a conundrum – where were these books read, then? In the refectory during meals.[35]

Just to confuse us, each of the three divisions of the readings is called a lesson, and is numbered accordingly. A 'feast of nine lessons' in the Roman office is one way of talking about an important feast; but these nine lessons are in fact three, each one cut up into thirds which are separated from each other by responsories. The passages are not very long, and sometimes very short, so there is no question of wading through uninterrupted tracts of Scripture. This reading is very definitely oriented to *prayer*, and moments of prayer regularly interrupt it.

Originally there would have been no lectionary: the reader picked up where he had left off previously, and carried on reading until the superior intervened to stop him at a moment that seemed fit. Later the places came to be marked in the Bible, and later still, higher authority co-ordinated the exercise by producing standard schemes.

Benedict follows his third nocturn on Sundays and feast-days with a reading of the eucharistic gospel of the day. This must be an adaptation of the resurrection vigil which is dimly reflected too in the gospel homily of the Roman office.

This monastic vigil crept into the people's office. We find widespread references from the sixth century to the attempt to bring people to daily vigil-services at which the Bible was read (see 25, 29c, g, h, i). People did not respond favourably to adding all this to the mattins they were already committed to attending, and it had no lasting success: perhaps an example of a recurrent problem in the Church, the failure of the intellectuals and ordinary people to understand each other. The people's attendance at this service may well have been better on Sundays, however, for they certainly attended it (as part of the Sunday morning office) in the later Middle Ages.

The point of having such a readings-office seems to be that systematic reading of the whole Bible is hived off into a section of its own in the day's programme, and the offices of the day are devoted to prayer, reflection and praise, grounded in the psalms and canticles. This tradition could well be re-created today by introducing an independent unit into the daily scheme devoted to Bible-reading. Rolf Zerfass has concluded from his study of the subject that services of praise and Bible services are two separate types which express two central aspects of the community's life: adoration on the one hand and hearing God's Word on the other, and that they should not be confused.[36] For we are not dealing here with an undervaluing of Scripture by our ancestors. In the early centuries the people's office was balanced with meetings for Bible-reading and instruction, and Lent in addition has always retained a particular association with such building-up in the Scriptures. To that must be added the proclamation of the Scriptures and their exposition each Sunday during the eucharist.[37]

In monasticism Scripture blows in at the sacred and secular moments of the day regardless. Books that were not finished in the night office were read in refectory during meals, and Scripture was read prayerfully outside the office as *lectio divina* (divine reading), and in communal reading-sessions before compline.

Non-scriptural readings

This seems a misnomer, so drenched are the writings of the Fathers in the Word of God. In sixth century Gaul we find Bishop Caesarius keen to preach to those he has badgered along to his Lent and Advent pre-dawn vigils. If a bishop was for some reason unable to be present to preach, he would sometimes send the script of his sermon to be read out. From there it was a small step to collecting sermons in books which became in time part of the corpus of readings from the 'homiliary' or 'the Fathers' (29f). Sometimes readings would be taken from a recent book too. About 600 Pope Gregory had to object to the bishop of Ravenna, who was having the Pope's latest book read out in church. Gregory pointed out that he was not among the 'honoured writers', and that anyway his book was too difficult for ordinary people to follow.[38] Later on, biographies of saints came to be read as well, and in this way there grew up the readings from the Fathers and the lives of the saints in the night office.

These facts suggest that non-biblical readings should throw light on the passage from the Bible which has been read in the same service, or should relate to the theme of the service on festivals and saints' days.

We have a natural expectation that such readings should be stimulating. But in the office this cannot really be so: we are concerned more with recapitulating the Church's reflection on Scripture as it really is, not with picking out 'purple passages'. The office works on a low-key, routine principle, which involves constant return to the same things, the grand themes, the ever-familiar but constantly forgotten laws, the day-by-day face of God.

The function of Scripture-reading

In the early writers we read either that the Scripture-reading was to aid memorization (see page 163, n. 29), or that it was to be material for prayer.[39] These are complementary facets of the way the readings of the night office lead the participants through salvation-history in a systematic manner. The constant retelling of the saving story is one of the primal functions of liturgy, and one of the ways in which we make *anamnesis*. In the people's office this has not been present. People entered the story rather through the psalms, the calendar and the Sunday eucharist, and in parallel instruction in the Bible.

Experience seems to show that reading of the Scriptures more or less *in course* is very fruitful for many, but is not suitable for all. If it was true in the past, it is certainly true today. In former centuries Scripture was seen very simply as God's Word – when the monks heard the Bible being read, they were hearing the very words of God, rich fruit-cake, full of wholesome nourishment. The modern situation could not be more different. J. D. Crichton has said that 'it would be an illusion to think we can, like medieval or even seventeenth century Christians, read the *nudus textus* with spiritual profit'.[40] Nowadays we need to enter into the text with the help of outside resources. Mere quantity is no longer sufficient. We are interested in the quality. If in less sophisticated times people were content to treat the Bible as a film-strip rolling before their eyes, today we have a greater need to see into the organic substance; we understand the Bible much more as a complex network of interrelated strands. The parts need to be related to the whole. An inexorable reading of Scripture from cover to cover can, in a monastic context, enable the Word of God to shine resplendent as the sun; but shorn of such a context this can render Scripture dim and lifeless, and thereby seriously undermine it. If Scripture is to be the busy Church's sun, we need a more organic approach to it, which may mean more selective use of the Bible, or, preferably, taking much longer to cover all of it, but by the same token a more adequate relation of the parts to the whole, drawing on the immense riches of Christian reflection in past and present.

Our forebears were more aware of this than perhaps we give them credit for. Their approach to Scripture-reading was manifold. Not only was the Bible treated as food for prayer in the night office and proclaimed and expounded at the eucharist and special vigils; it was also treated in a manner exemplified in the monastic practice of *lectio divina*. When Benedict prescribed this for his monks, he intended that each should spend a reasonable time in privacy each day reading through a chapter of the Bible. This was to be done aloud and slowly, the monk chewing over Scripture as a cow chews the cud. It was far from mere study – part of its purpose was to fulfil the role performed today by 'meditation'. Benedict gave guidance for those who felt an impulse to pray in silence, but made no provision for the 'meditation' which modern religious (and clergy) aim to perform regularly for half an hour or more each day. The monks' prayers and relationship with God develop through the liturgy, in their daily work, in moments when moved by the Spirit to pray, and in the faithful practice of *lectio divina*: slow, quiet chewing-over of the Word of God.

In modern times *lectio divina* has refracted into a spectrum of at least three things: Bible study, 'spiritual' reading, and 'meditation'. Bible study covers that done alone with a commentary or Bible-study notes, in preparing sermons, and in study-groups. It is difficult in modern life for this and spiritual reading not to be spasmodic, and one of the claims put forward for the daily office is that it provides a disciplined framework which ensures they are done. This, however, is not without its detrimental effects on the way the office is approached, and it may be better in some circumstances to separate off the two disciplines, as the Roman breviary does in part, providing a system of *lectio divina* parallel to the offices of prayer and praise, which can be observed by individuals as suits them best. In principle the office lections need to be considered together with all the study and teaching in which laity and clergy participate, and if lections have a place in the public office, they must be governed by the dominant motives of prayer and praise.

Spiritual reading and meditation ought in the light of this to have some connection on and off with our reading of Scripture, as they all spring from *lectio divina*, and are ultimately inseparable. This should help us to remember that mere Bible-*study* with a commentary is never enough. Like a psychologist's report on someone we know, all that a textual commentary says can sometimes be true and revealing, and yet in itself a travesty and a belittling. The vast repertoire of Christian reflection on Scripture, in all the forms it has taken, has to be brought to our aid.

20

The Prayers of the Church

The concluding prayers of intercession are both so ubiquitous and so evidently important in the people's office that we can judge it an eccentric office which lacks them.

The form always used was the litany. Litanic prayer was known in the early synagogue and in pagan worship, and in the early period the people's response was not essential: the biddings could be followed simply by silences, as for example in the second litany of east Syrian vespers. Responses and refrains became very popular in public worship, as almost the only means of enabling congregations to participate, in an age when books were not generally available.

Tertullian says that to the Lord's Prayer should be added a 'superstructure of petitions for additional desires', which elsewhere he shows to include prayer 'for the emperors, for their ministers, and for all in authority, for the welfare of the world, for the prevalence of peace, for the delay of the final consummation' (8). In Egeria's description of vespers in Jerusalem we read that 'hymns and antiphons [i.e. Psalms] are recited. When they have finished them according to their custom, the bishop rises and stands in front of the screen (that is, the cave), and one of the deacons makes the commemoration of individuals according to the custom, and when the deacon says the names of individuals, a large group of boys always respond, *Kyrie eleison*, or as we say, 'Lord have mercy'. Their voices are very loud. When the deacon has finished all that he has to say, the bishop first recites a prayer and prays for all . . ., [41] It is in this kind of way that the litanies are performed in the Byzantine office today, and in the early Western people's office too there was a litany at this point in the services.

Benedict says that while at the lesser hours the final Lord's Prayer is preceded by *Kyrie eleison*, at mattins and vespers it is preceded by a litany.[42] Sometime between the sixth and the ninth centuries one of those things then happened which make the Western office so inexplicably different both from the Eastern offices and from the common origins. In the monastic office the litanies simply disappeared, leaving behind them three stranded *Kyries*. In the Roman office on the other hand they were replaced by something else in a process similar to that by which an axe gains first a new head and then a new handle.

The Irish monks were for some reason not content with the response *Kyrie eleison* and supplanted it with pairs of versicles from the psalms, each pair being known as a *capitellum*. These capitella were used, for example, in Caesarius' monastic office at the very end of services, and may bear some relationship to such doublets as 'O God make speed ... etc.', which were ejaculations to be repeated in the silence between the psalm and its collect. They sometimes became attached to canticles – hence those at the end of the Te Deum, which tend to be omitted nowadays. The Celtic monks' usage with such capitella can be seen from the following excerpt from a litany:

> *Let us pray for every condition in the Church:*
> Let your priests be clothed with righteousness,
> And your saints sing with joyfulness ...
> *For our King:*
> Lord, save the King
> and hear us when we call upon you.
> (etc.)[43]

Each petition now has a different versicle and response taken from the Psalms, in place of the original *Kyrie eleison*.

When this usage was taken back to the continent by the missionary monks, it supplanted the old litany where that survived, and lost most of the biddings in the process: merely the versicles and responses remained. These came to be known as the *preces*. There were various forms of *preces* in the Roman rite, for use at different services in different seasons. Here are the *preces* from lauds, which are of particular interest through having preserved some of the original biddings (printed in italics):

> *Verse.* I said: Lord, be merciful unto me.
> *Answer.* Heal my soul, for I have sinned against Thee.
> *Verse.* Return, O Lord, how long?
> *Answer.* And let it repent Thee concerning Thy servants.
> *Verse.* Let Thy mercy, O Lord, be upon us.
> *Answer.* According as we hope in Thee.
> *Verse.* Let Thy priests be clothed with righteousness.
> *Answer.* And let Thy saints shout for joy.
> *Verse.* O Lord, save the King.
> *Answer.* And hear us in the day when we call upon Thee.
> *Verse.* O Lord, save Thy people, and bless Thine inheritance.
> *Answer.* And govern them, and lift them up for ever.
> *Verse.* Remember Thy congregation.
> *Answer.* Which Thou hast purchased of old.
> *Verse.* Peace be within thy walls.
> *Answer.* And prosperity within thy palaces.

Verse. Let us pray for the faithful departed.

Answer. O LORD, grant them eternal rest, and let the everlasting light shine upon them!

Verse. May they rest in peace.

Answer. Amen.

Verse. Let us pray for our absent brethren.

Answer. O Thou my God, save Thy servants that trust in Thee.

Verse. Let us pray for the sorrowful and the captives.

Answer. Redeem them, O God of Israel, out of all their troubles.

Verse. O LORD, send them help from the sanctuary.

Answer. And strengthen them out of Zion.

Verse. Hear my prayer, O LORD.

Answer. And let my cry come unto Thee.

In the later Middle Ages the *preces* came to be thought unsuitable for Sundays and feast-days, and were relegated to ferial days only; hence the common name *preces feriales*. They were finally banished to penitential seasons and special days. In one part of the world they continued to hold their head high, however, and that was in the Anglican daily office. Thomas Cranmer's instinct served him well here. In making all the offices end with solid *prayer*, and in taking a form of the *preces* as its centre, he did something to restore the ancient shape of the services. The Roman Liturgy of the Hours is surely right, however, in returning to the litany form as a principal model.

The Lord's Prayer

The history of the Lord's Prayer in the office is not simple. We gain the unmistakable impression that it was a latecomer. The Didache (5) says it should be recited three times a day, but other references to it in the earliest period are very few. In the West our first mention of it comes with the Council of Gerona in 517, which decreed that the Our Father was to be added to mattins and vespers – this, surprisingly, met with opposition from the clergy, and was evidently an innovation (29e, j). Thence it comes and goes in the various rites. It early disappeared from the Roman people's office, if it had ever been there.[44] Where it was used in places outside Rome, it was apparently as an alternative to the collect, which only the Pope or his deputies could say (in fourth-century Jerusalem we have already seen that only clergy were allowed to recite a collect: see page 60). Only since the Second Vatican Council has it been given a place in the morning and evening offices of the breviary. It is obviously highly suitable for use in the hours of prayer, and its uncertain career there may be attributable to the fact that it was much more closely associated with private prayer and the eucharist.

The function of the prayers

The final prayers are not simply intercession. It is particularly noticeable in Byzantine worship how the frequently recurring litanies are doxological in their effect: they become a vehicle for adoration. The purpose of prayer is the quest for that unity together in Christ which is held before us in the Gospel. The litany of intercession can be a crowning expression of that quest which we have sought to attend to throughout the service. The 'doxology imperative' sometimes emerges very clearly in these intercessions; for example, in the first litany of east Syrian vespers:

...
O you who are rich in mercies and overflowing with compassion we beseech you: LORD, HAVE MERCY ON US.
O you who exist before all ages and whose power abides for ever ...
O you who are by nature good and the giver of all good things ...
O you who wish not the death of a sinner but rather that he repent of his wickedness and live ...
O you who are glorified in heaven and adored on earth ...
O you who ... made the earth to rejoice and the heavens be glad ...
O you who are by nature immortal and dwell in the most resplendent light ...
    (etc.)[45]

There is also another sense in which the prayers in the office involve more than intercession in its simplest sense: if, as history suggests, the office is concerned with the unity of the Church's prayer, then the intercession is not simply a praying-for but also a praying-with. A mere centring of worship on intercession can lead to a functionalism which implies that prayer needs to justify itself by being seen to be useful, by having a practical aim. It is for similar reasons that the practice of announcing before an office starts that it will be offered in aid of some 'intention' is so questionable. To say that the service will be offered *with* others may be better, but the proper place for that is in the intercessions. Our prayer for others is not being done justice to if it is allowed to distract us from that rendezvous with the divine mystery which is the necessary setting for our petitions. Intercession is deepened and transformed the more it is affected by and taken up in that standing in the presence of God which is the prayer of the Church:

If you abide in me, and my words abide in you, ask whatever you will, and it shall be done for you (John 15.7).

The form the intercessions take is a matter of some importance: detailed and particular intercessions can be of one kind in a prayer-group and another in the Sunday eucharist. In some situations similar or freer forms may be appropriate in the office, but it is perhaps more in character here for the prayers to be relatively formal and concerned with general issues, and that the element of doxology be not forgotten.

While in the divine office prayer has a section all to itself, this should not be allowed to hide the fact that the whole of the office is prayer, something particularly borne out by the ancient and widespread practice of associating collects with various parts of the office. Such prayers were used not only after the psalms, but also before or after canticles, anthems, processions and ceremonies, drawing their content together and consolidating it in acts of prayer (see, for example, 17, 19, 30, 31, and also page 156, n. 8). Anyone who has experienced the Ambrosian office in the diocese of Milan will know how tremendously helpful such collects are in enabling the office to be *prayed*.

We have by now ranged over a wide assortment of subjects, and the point has come where we must seek to understand how they relate, and whether we might be able to distil from them any general principles.

PART IV

Interpreting the Facts

21

Definition

Legitimacy

The divine office in the eyes of many modern Christians appears to lack that foundation in the New Testament and the Lord's message which other aspects of Christian faith and practice depend on. It is like one of those political dictatorships which, having supplanted an ancient democracy, suffer from permanent problems of legitimacy, and have to resort to rhetoric in order to fill the gap. Many today can see no reason why such stilted and formal repetitions should be bound on people's backs as if by some divine law. Unless its legitimacy can be founded in the origins of the Christian faith, people can hardly be blamed for finding it unconvincing. This is therefore a problem that needs urgently to be addressed.

The beginnings of an answer can be found by challenging the way we frame our question. We ask, 'can the daily office be justified from Scripture in the same way that the eucharist can, or baptism, or absolution?' The history as we have traced it over the last few chapters suggests that here we are making a fundamental mistake in seeing the office as an independent branch of liturgy. It is incorrigibly liturgical, certainly; but the borderline between it and 'personal' forms of prayer is in no way so clearly defined as we might have thought. We see the divine office as an independent floor in the skyscraper of worship, which must justify itself by how it compares with other floors such as the Eucharist and the others. Such an approach, although apparently obvious, distorts the question. To pigeon-hole it as a distinct and exalted branch of liturgy is to put it into clothes which refuse to fit, and modern Christians can hardly be blamed for judging it to be unconvincing when it is propounded in these terms. The daily office as such springs from no 'do this' uttered by the Jesus of the New Testament. It can only be understood in relation to those 'do this' utterances of the Lord which refer to prayer in general: it is integral to the whole subject of *prayer*, and cannot be understood apart from it.

Let us press the comparison with the eucharist. The Lord gave the command to do what he had done at the Last Supper, but the account given in the Gospels is brief and enigmatic. Paul gives further detail, but it was left to the early Church to evolve the eucharistic liturgy as we know it today. Only the very simplest details of its structure can be found in or deduced from the NT accounts. The rest has all been evolved by the Church, partly on the basis of inherited Jewish traditions. Even the practice of celebration every Sunday was evolved by the post-resurrection Church.

In just the same way there is clear instruction from the Lord on *prayer*; but the Church had to work out the implications for itself, so that the main trunk of the Church's tradition in praying was developed in the first three or four centuries.

Just as we accept the basic shape of the eucharistic liturgy which was forged in the first few centuries after Christ, so therefore, to be consistent, we will have to give due weight to the basic patterns of Christian *praying* which were established in the same period. And the daily office traces its origin unmistakably to those patterns of Christian praying which grew up side-by-side with the eucharist. Our concern will therefore be not merely with what in the English language goes by the name of 'office', but with the all-round response of the Church to the command to *pray*. It is here that the Dominical legitimation of daily liturgical prayer is to be found, and this gives a legitimacy not simply to the 'office' as in isolation, but as an outstanding strand in the wider phenomenon of Christian prayer. If all this is understood in the light of the first seven chapters of this book, which try to show how this kind of prayer is natural to human nature, we can see that the history we have traced has arisen from a natural outworking of the Lord's command to pray.

Definition

Not only are we unsure of the office's legitimacy: we are uncertain of what in fact it *is*. The relationship with private prayer which we have discovered renders it even more confusing to behold. When is an office not an office? Add to this the jumble of prejudices and misconceptions we have inherited from the Middle Ages, and we can see that we need to be clearer in our minds about what exactly it is we are dealing with.

The rest of this chapter is devoted to attempting such a clarification which, inadequate as it probably is, may possibly be conducive to further thought and discussion.

Prayer

Daily liturgical prayer is distinct from the sacraments in being simply prayer, unattached to any special sacramental or other operation. It is not distinct from prayer in general in the way that the eucharist, baptism, confession and the rest are. It is always described above all else as 'prayer'. Neither 'devotion' (whatever that might be), reflection, edification, feeding, worship, cult, nor any other term is used so frequently and consistently as 'prayer'. No other form of Christian liturgy can be so simply described as prayer without further qualification. And when writers of the early centuries talk about prayer, they describe what we would call the daily office: prayer at morning, third, sixth and ninth hours, evening and midnight, as well as prayer at mealtimes and other daily occasions. Until the end of the Middle Ages in the West, and until today in the East, the prayer of Christian individuals and households has had intimate links with the Church's daily liturgy, and has built upon a foundation of liturgical forms and phrases. Even after the sixteenth century the connection between the personal prayer of ordinary people and the daily office persisted in many places, and in some ways through to modern times. It is difficult to evaluate the significance of these facts, and tempting to build on them an impressive picture of a system of co-ordinated prayer in which Christians down the ages have been committed to linking their prayer with the celebration of the divine office in church. This would be to push the evidence further than it can bear. What we can say, however, is that the links between the various types of prayer are sufficiently strong to be significant, and to be valuable evidence in showing the daily office to be an inevitable consequence of the Lord's command to pray.

Prayer in parallel

First, it is clear that the notion of praying in parallel with the liturgical gathering in church is something which arose naturally and persisted because people from widely differing periods and backgrounds found it to be good. There is a natural need to associate prayer with the gathered assembly in a way which evokes it. The Methodist who sings favourite hymns at work will imagine the organ and the assembled voices, as they are evoked by the music which is associated with them. The national anthem immediately makes us aware of the whole nation, reminding us of the bonds through which we and it belong together. The hermit at prayer becomes a microcosm of the Church, and senses the participation of a great cloud of witnesses. Prayer in parallel is in this sense perfectly understandable and natural.

But as we look, secondly, over the whole spectrum of this type of prayer, it is possible to see the daily office as emerging from, and of one flesh with, all that we call Christian prayer. It has a receding penumbra of less markedly liturgical ways which eventually merge into that wordless, more personal way of praying which since the Middle Ages has been so probingly thought and written about, and which for the sake of brevity we could call 'meditative and contemplative prayer'. Perhaps in the way a snail's horns emerge, when it wants, from its even skin, so the daily office in full swing is the Church's prayer emerging into the visible, tangible realm of every day. The tradition of private prayer modelled on the daily office helps us in this way to understand the status of the daily office and its relationship to other forms of praying. It reminds us that formal, liturgical prayer can indeed be an authentic expression of a deep inner relationship with God, while on the other hand personal prayer is always set in the context of the Church. The practices which we have discovered, from the prayers of Syrian shepherds to the *Godzinki* of Polish housewives, from the psalms of Ethiopians to the Angelus of modern Roman Catholics, from the domestic lucernarium of Jerome and Gregory of Nyssa to the late medieval books of hours, not only arose and continued through meeting a natural need, be it for evoking the presence of the Christian gathering or for completing the spectrum of Christian prayer, but their very existence is helpful to us today by being a source of ideas for revival of this tradition in contemporary form, and also by providing perspective and roots for any modern attempt to experiment in that area which comes between the public daily office and free personal prayer.

The core group

Let us now look more closely at that which we call the 'divine office' proper.

Between the fall of the Roman Empire and the high Middle Ages, the office was offered by those who gathered together daily in the local church. In country areas in particular, services were organized by the parish priest with his staff of assistants. These provided a kind of quorum, ensuring that the daily office did not have to depend on whoever happened to turn up. In many cases people will have come in numbers, but it was no doubt not unusual for there to be very few in the congregation sometimes, so that those few who were present constituted a core group offering the services on behalf of all. Here is an understanding of the daily office as something offered for its very own sake, regardless of who is physically present, something we have met with many times in its history. In the Roman Church this later led to a juridical notion of delegation, the priest being nominated by the Church to recite the daily offices on the community's behalf. This was an attempt to hold down in codified form something which is by nature more wayward and ambiguous. History presents us, rather, with the phenomenon of the quorum. In the first-century synagogue, a quorum of ten was required before a service could take place. In Matthew's Gospel this is reduced to 'two or three'. In the early centuries after Constantine something similar appeared. Alexander Schmemann has this to say:

It may be supposed that not all believers had the opportunity to gather twice each day, and that from the beginning it was a minority which participated in these services. Tertullian's distinction between *coetus* and *congregationes* is possibly a reference to this situation; also the exhortations to attend these assemblies which we find, for example, in the *Apostolic Constitutions* and in the *Order*. But this does not alter the ecclesiological, liturgical character of these services. The Church is praying 'in order to surround God with common prayers as with an army, gathered together in a single place.... ' This idea of the praying Church, *ecclesia orans*, clearly corresponds to the whole spirit of early Christian ecclesiology, to the liturgical piety of the pre-Nicene Church.[1]

The quorum approach began to be expressed in a number of ways. Sometimes it was maintained on a rota, or the offices went by turn from church to church. In fifth-century Gaul we find the round of services being shared out among the churches of a town, a kind of pass-the-parcel approach.[2] Later the core group of the early parishes (the priest and his *schola*) provided the quorum, together with those of the parishioners who attended. This was always seen as ensuring a minimum, and never as a deliberate limitation, as later practice saw it. The lone priest saying the daily office is indeed doing it on behalf of all, but it is turning everything on its head to establish this as a principle of action, assuming and legislating for the absence of the community. The Second Vatican Council has recognized this, putting forward the public office as the proper model. Even though the priest counts as a quorum of one, such a quorum is always a regrettable minimum.

The history of the daily office, then, consistently presents us with this notion of a quorum which in celebrating the daily office picks out, highlights, what is going on all the time in more modest ways throughout the one Body. The office is a pulling-together of threads, a summing-up, and private prayers of individual Christians consciously or less consciously link up with public prayer as one offering by the whole Body. The formal daily office is therefore a gathering-up, a *marking*, of something more widely spread, in which the whole Body is involved in different ways.

Content

If it is possible to say something like that about the outward configuration of daily liturgical prayer, what can we say about its inner content?

If we take the Fathers as our cue, the answer is simple: first, it is prayer, and secondly it is prayer offered daily at commonly agreed times. This disarmingly simple formula might seem too meagre, and yet this is what the Fathers say. The priority for them is that certain hours of the day should be consecrated to Christ by the prayer of the Church. All questions of content follow as further development. They may be necessary developments, but the order of priorities cannot be altered. This is important, for instance, in establishing that the verbal content cannot stand in its own right. That is to say, if a monk misses the midday office and reads it through after tea, he is understanding the daily office as a system for providing a quota of Scripture and prayers, the main object being to get through all of it. That is not the way the Fathers see it – for them it is a balanced method for sanctifying the time. If the monk misses the midday office, well, the rest of the Church has said it for him. The daily office is the marking of times before it is the repeating of formulas, and it marks them simply to foster by these regular rhythms that prayer-without-ceasing which is one way of describing a life totally oriented to God.

That said, however, we have next to recognize that it is *also* the repetition of formulas. When medieval clerics spoke about 'paying up their debt of psalmody' they were expressing in a grotesque fashion what is evidently true – the daily office provides us with a balanced scheme of Christian word, story and reflection to get our jaws around, and that balance of jaw-prayer needs to be reasonably well maintained. The more frequently we are absent from the common service the greater this need becomes. However, it should not be a question of being grimly chained to unalterable tablets of stone, but of being content to tick over with little when there are occasional impediments, and of finding balanced ways of keeping up the diet when they are more frequent. And an arrow prayer at the right time is generally preferable to cramming in the legal dose at a very limited wrong time.

Once we reach the detail of the content, what do we make of that? Can these dry historical bones live? That they are bones is something, for it shows that they have lived in their time. Historical study is a way of making anamnesis of the past, seeking to taste something of the flavour of life as it was *lived*. But it is not simply that. It also seeks to understand how things evolved into their present state, and to assess the value of that evolution. In any process of development and evolution the same principles are evident. Our parliamentary system evolved out of dictatorship, the digital wristwatch evolved from the man paid to sit in a tower and ring a bell every hour; and Beethoven's symphonies from knocking bits of bone together round the campfire. In some domains evolution has become constant, travelling so far from the origins that the connection seems improbable without knowledge of the intermediary stages. Such is language, which never stands still. Other things quickly reach their classic form and any further developments are mere refinements. Coinage developed quickly and has not changed since ancient times. The motor-car quickly surmounted its main problems at the beginning of the century, and since then has stayed in all essentials the same. Christian liturgy is familiar with all these things.

And so we study our faith, of which its worship is a central part, in order to rediscover the primordial motives, to return to square one, to imagine what it was like starting from scratch, and trying to understand what moved people to do things as they did. It is based on an assumption that we are basically the same as they, but unable to start from scratch because too conditioned by all that has happened in the intervening centuries. Therefore we feel that they saw more clearly and simply than us, in that first flush, and would have a unique insight into the priorities.

But each subsequent development too is the tidemark left by a once living impulse or insight, which has things to reveal which were unique to those who experienced them. So we have tried to find out how people came to evolve daily liturgical prayer, trying to see at what points it may have reached optimum development, at what points it may have gone wrong, the clarity of the original vision having receded, and in what ways it is still open to further development. All three possibilities have to be weighed. We cannot assume that at some point in the past the Church 'got it right', and from that point the daily offices remain unchangeable. God leads his Church gradually to the truth, sometimes through tortuous paths to surprising conclusions.

The historical dimension in Christian liturgy leads us further. Not only does it help us to understand why certain things are so, but it enables us to affirm our communion with those who were the authors and mediators of what we have inherited. When we do things which were done in the past it is not simply for their face value. They are also links with the past, materials with which the unity of the Church is built. When we sing the psalms at evensong we are recalling the work of Christ in those who first put them there; we are making anamnesis of the work Christ did through St Benedict or through the countless parish priests and people who sang them down the centuries. Whether we use the psalms is therefore not simply a matter of whether we like them or find them helpful. By both enjoying their fruits and bearing that in them which seems barren, we are affirming the historical unity of the Church, and the real presence of Christ in that history. One of the most disorienting features about our times is the way we are out of touch with our history. Like a long trail of thread behind us through the labyrinth, history enables us to know where we have come from, and therefore to understand who we are, and why we are as we are.

Because of all these things, an attempt to identify the principles governing the content of the divine office cannot be easy. The primordial rituals and gestures of the eucharist (the celebratory meal), baptism (washing, immersion), marriage (joining in front of witnesses), and other services with a determined particular in view, find no clear parallel in prayer which is done purely for its own sake, and the verbal content of all these services is determined in a much more absolute way than that of pure prayer can be. To be sure, history presents certain patterns which commend themselves through being widely shared, especially the pattern of psalmody followed by intercessions, i.e. prayerful reflection on a certain type of Scripture, leading to straightforward prayer. But it is not possible, as the General Instruction on the Liturgy of the Hours suggests, that a certain basic order exists which cannot be altered.[3] The new Benedictine guidelines on the daily office take this claim further:

... various parts contribute to its structure. Some are so necessary that they can never be omitted, and these must be arranged in a constant order, namely: hymn, Psalms, reading, prayers.[4]

Both the content and the order of this list are questionable, as must be clear from the history as we have traced it.

The actual content of daily liturgical prayer has varied so much that it is very difficult to lay down any hard and fast principles on the anatomy of services. The most common elements to be found in virtually all uses that we know of are psalmody and prayers. We have no evidence, however, that the early Christian prayer hours used the former, and we know services (e.g. east Syrian mattins) which lack the final intercessions. It seems to be like a table – remove one leg and it will still remain standing. Remove two and it will fall. Yet it does not seem to matter which three legs you use to keep it standing. Any combination will do. The range of 'legs' on which the daily office can stand increased with the passage of time. From what we know of it, which is not very much, Christian prayer in the early years gave great importance to thanskgiving and anamnesis (berakah), petition and intercession.[5] Use of the Lord's Prayer is early but intermittent. Psalms have played an outstanding part, but we cannot be sure about the first two centuries. Canticles came in a little later, and Scripture-reading later still. Soon a very widely acknowledged pattern emerged which became the universal basis for subsequent elaborations. According to this, the lesser hours consist simply of psalmody, and the principal hours of mattins and vespers take the following form: (1) psalmody; (2) prayer and intercession.[6] Until today this has remained the ground-structure of the texts of the two main offices of the day. Further details, such as the immemorial use of the Benedictus and Magnificat in the West, depend on the extent to which the local community identifies a vocation to sustain particular aspects of local tradition.

Authority and uniformity

Who should decide the content of daily liturgical prayer? The local community has had a strong hand in shaping the office it uses, and local initiative is on the whole a very respectable thing to encourage. Even in Orthodoxy, whose worship has been fairly stable over the last 200 years, this vital urge has been difficult to repress. The Russian Church, for instance, has a long tradition of wide freedom in the parish daily office, which may seem surprising to an outsider. There is sometimes considerable difference from monastery to monastery, and the differences between parishes can vary ad infinitum. All of this is based on a recurring phrase in the rubrics, 'if the superior wants', which comes directly from the ancient Palestinian office of St Sabas out of which the Byzantine office has grown.[7]

Sufficient responsibility needs to be given to the local church to enable it to adapt its worship to local circumstances – for it is there that the struggle to relate the faith to daily life is most keenly felt, and there is the place where the Church's prayer will be tested and shown up to be either living prayer or mere escapism. It is surely mistaken to adhere to forms of prayer which pin down the dialogue with the Lord in forms ill-suited to the spirit of the community, and inappropriate to their day-by-day experience. Worship is always on the move. However hard ecclesiastics, councils and emperors in the past have tried to tie it down, it will not sit still. In the days before printing it was never anything other than a cornucopia of local uses normally centred on the local cathedral. As William Durandus put it in the thirteenth century:

... nearly every church has her own observances, and attaches to them a full meaning of her own: neither is it thought blameworthy or absurd to worship with various chants, or modulations of the voice, nor yet with different observances; when the Church Triumphant herself is surrounded, according to the prophet, with the like diversity, and in the administration of the Sacraments themselves a variety of customs is tolerated, and that rightly.[8]

It seems important to spell that out. Yet on the other hand the unity of the Body has to be maintained. It is important to have some general agreement on content, and history points to the local bishop as the guarantor of unity with the Church catholic. It is even possible to say that the more a service sets itself up as *the* public worship of the Church, the more it must have the authority of the bishop behind it.

History tells us that there must be recognizable links which express the spatial unity of the whole contemporary Church on earth in its prayer, and the unity of the Church with its past. No one liturgical ingredient can do this, as there is hardly anything which is shared by all forms of the daily office. But there are many things which are very widely shared, and historically they have expressed the unity of the Church by being interwoven through a multiplicity of local uses. This can be illustrated by the diagram overleaf, in which the letters stand for separate elements such as psalmody, Magnificat, Lord's Prayer, etc. Rites 1, 2, 3 and 4 all share things in common, even though 3 and 4 share nothing directly. Their unity is found through unity with the others. Rite 5, however, is cut off from such moorings. This diagram gives an idea of the way in which it is possible to see the unity behind the diversity of the daily office.

It is not possible to claim on any early authority that uniformity of content is important in giving expression to the unity of the Church's prayer, but in so far as we can do so later, it is in this kind of way that it operates.

The manner in which the office is celebrated

While we need to be reasonably clear on verbal content, the text provides only one facet of the personality of liturgy. Often we think that a renewed liturgy can be created simply by producing a new text, when it may be better achieved by keeping the old text but changing the manner of celebration. The spirit in which services are celebrated, and the ecology of the setting in which they

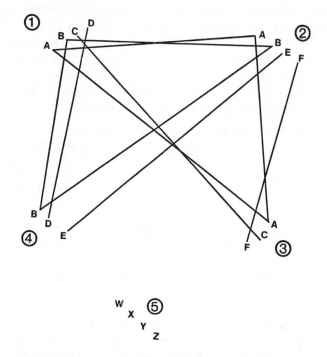

evolve, are things which we totally underestimate. If the offices of the Book of Common Prayer were performed at Taizé as they stand, and if the Taizé offices were staged by an English cathedral in its traditional manner, the distinctive approaches of two such very different communities would be strong enough to predominate over the alien spirit of the texts. Differences in approach to liturgy are as manifold as the varieties of culture, weather, politics, economics and other factors which go to produce unique manifestations of the human spirit. Who could imagine that the people's office of the late Roman empire and the private recitation of the Tridentine breviary were relations? An Italian used to attending Sunday vespers in his parish church would be at a loss to say what was going on at Orthodox vespers. The restrained but exquisite clockwork evensong of English cathedrals touches on very different departments of the spiritual life from the weighty, inexorable and primeval drama of vespers in a Russian cathedral. And yet if all were brought to use a common text, the power of these differences in *celebration* would still be there.

It is impossible to ignore these things when we are trying to say what daily liturgical prayer *is*, and the production of new orders of service such as those in the English Alternative Service Book needs to be accompanied by serious thought on how the worship is to be done. Perhaps even then, little can be achieved simply by discussion and planning. The great liturgies, each with its unique spirit, evolved over long periods, patiently feeling the path, in the midst of living worship and prayer.

Times of transition

While liturgy is ever changing and developing, there are moments when it undergoes more profound transformations: Christian prayer emerged from a background of Jewish and heathen traditions as fixed hours of private prayer for the devout, whose content was only vaguely defined. It went through a metamorphosis in the fourth century to emerge, like an imago from its pupa, in the form of public ceremonies of a popular cult. The succeeding period in the West saw a gradual change in understanding which led to the breviary of the clerics. Parallel to all of this, yet another metamorphosis was effected very early on by the monks for their own purposes, a transformation which in turn imposed itself on the people's office. Such drastic transformations are accepted as part of history, and it is clear therefore that further ones cannot be ruled out. The daily office, in response to major shifts in its environment, is open to changes in outer appearance, while remaining, like a chameleon, the same animal underneath, even when these changes appear to have been detrimental.

People's office and monastic office

The word monastic is very difficult to define, as anyone in the religious life will testify: it is one of the most misunderstood and romanticized terms in the Christian vocabulary. Any assertions about it in the fields of prayer and worship run a great risk of being fallacious and misleading. The simple distinction between monastic and non-monastic forms of worship, useful in making sense of history, is not in fact so helpful in understanding the business of praying today. For a start, monasticism has become so diversified that the borderlines are almost completely smudged. Many religious are more apostolic than some parish priests. There are some Christians 'in the world' whose lives are in many respects monastic.

More to the point may be a comparison, say, between the prayer of a fluctuating group and that of a permanent, committed group, or a comparing of differences of temperament. In particular, it would be helpful to speak of two poles which sum up quite aptly what the secular/monastic distinction seems to stand for: on the one hand there is worship which aims to attract the worshippers, engage their emotions, and use any appropriate means to enable them to transfer from a state of indifference to one of attention to God. It is specially prepared wholesome food, easily digestible, and coming in doses the person can cope with. This kind of worship is needed, for instance, for those who are in their Christian infancy, not yet ready for solid meat. It is for people passing through a difficult time such as bereavement. It is for those who often find themselves far from a state of inner quiet, such as some busy parish clergy. It can be more necessary when praying alone than with others. And there will always be some people for whom it will be the only way of prayer.

The other pole we can discern is worship as a discipline submitted to in loving obedience and self-giving. It is taken as it comes, and is characterized by a certain sobriety and indifference to frills. It presupposes a degree of commitment, continuity, and ability to be attentive. These two poles could be indicated respectively by the words *courtship* and *covenant*. The one courts the worshippers, even to the extent that each act of worship is seen as 'priming the pump', or 'charging the batteries' which in the intervening times are rapidly depleted. The spirit of covenant, however, is more concerned with sustaining that 'prayer-without-ceasing', that constancy in recollection of God in and out of church which was so important to the early Fathers. Courtship and covenant are never alternatives, always partners. While one often predominates in the worship of a particular community, it is impossible to have one without at least something of the other.

The spirit of courtship and that of covenant, however, are never equal: the dynamic thrust of the spiritual life is from the one to the other, from courtship to covenant, from wooing towards the mutual surrender of bride and bridegroom, from dependence on frequent encouragement to a committed constancy. They are points on the forward-moving journey of the Spirit within us. So there is in the divine office not simply a resting on what we are content with: there is that reaching-forward mentioned earlier, known among the Fathers by the word *epektasis*.[9]

So long as we continue to bear in mind this drawing-forward, it may well be more helpful to talk of the daily office in this kind of way, than to distinguish and set apart a so-called 'monastic' office, and make assertions about who it is suitable for. We have seen in fact that throughout history the secular and monastic daily offices have refused to remain in neat compartments, but overflow into and fertilize each other. Yet it can be said that on the whole the people's office has been more in the spirit of courtship, and the daily office of religious communities more in the spirit of loving obedience and self-giving. But wherever the daily office is celebrated, it has to be such that 'the strong have something to strive after and the weak are not driven away' (Rule of St Benedict 64.18). It is in essence a covenanting of disciplined prayer, but it is content to meet us where we are and work from there. It can never be said that Christian liturgical prayer is a fixed discipline which must be submitted to as it stands. It is more gentle and encouraging than that, though the truth about discipline cannot be hidden from us for ever. Without discipline we have to keep up a search for fresh stimuli; with it, we grow through struggle.[10]

That the spirit of submission and covenant is a real goal which can attract Christians in all walks of life is shown by those Anglicans who respond to the very 'monastic' saying of the daily offices in their parish church.

The medieval vision of the office as a static rather than a forward-straining discipline has in the subsequent centuries proved to be both a weakness and a strength. Thomas Merton observes:

When the monasteries of the Middle Ages lost their fevour the last observance that ceased to be properly carried out was the choral office. It may indeed have degenerated into a heartless routine, but the history of monasticism shows that long after the spirit of asceticism and of personal prayer has died in a monastery, the office may continue to be more or less devoutly and decently recited.

... [thus] ... reformers find themselves confronted with a more or less well organized structure of liturgy which, though the soul may have gone out of it, is still functioning in fairly good order. Hence it does not seem to require immediate attention. And so they look around for some other point at which to introduce the spearhead of reform.[11]

This must go some way to explain the conspicuous lack of thought and reflection given to the office in the life of the Church. Such a situation will no longer do in a society not static, but turbulent, mobile and questioning.

Obligation

Where the temptation to precise definition has not been resisted, the result has always been a diminishment. The office's calls upon us can never be absolute. In its classical form it is not for everyone. There is a tradition in Orthodox monasticism, originating on Mount Athos, which dispenses with the office on most days of the week, replacing it with communal recitation of the Jesus Prayer. The largest Orthodox monastery in Britain is of this type, and there the office is celebrated only on Sundays and festivals.[12] The eight- and thirty-day retreats in the Ignatian tradition (what could be more Catholic?) forbid the recitation of the office. It was very common in Roman Catholic communities until recently for lay religious, especially women, to have to make do with the rosary. So we have the paradox of Madame Acarie giving up the daily office to become a nun. Liturgical prayer needs such little pinches of salt: it has obvious pitfalls and can quickly turn into a framework for fear and guilt – a new and terrible subjection to law.

The concept of obligation which developed in the West has served many people well and continues to do so. This should on no account be undermined. And yet it is incomplete as it stands.

Jesus dismantled the Law, declaring the Sabbath to be for man, and all foods to be clean. Henceforth there are to be no externally imposed regulations breeding feelings of guilt when not fulfilled. Disciplines such as the daily office are only justified if chosen and entered into by free choice, exercised after a mature and responsible discernment of the vocations of individual and community. The daily office and its ilk are ways of covenanting our prayer to God in a transaction which involves the Church as a whole. Particular regulations about prayer cannot be tied to particular vocations such as priesthood – all we can seek is a covenant arising out of a context. The notion of obligation which assumes a fixed, precisely defined office is misleading. There is enough evidence from history to show that variety has always been around. The strict concept of obligation also brings an implication that those who failed in their obligation would be black sheep: in this way it ignores the particular needs and vocations of persons and communities. Rather do we need to seek an alliance between what the Church calls forth from people and what they can assent to with conviction. If a priest feels persistently guilty and dissatisfied about the daily office, and seems to be getting nowhere, that is probably a sign that the covenant needs revising, in consultation with spiritual director and bishop. None of us should be asked to do what is not within us to do. While prayer should tend towards struggle rather than ease, and testing rather than comfort, it still needs to be submitted to the acid test of asking whether in the long term it produces freedom, not slavery; growth, not confinement; joy, not depression; and peace, not frustration. There is no doubt that a sense of obligation should be there, and kept before the eyes of all, but it applies initially to the whole community rather than any one individual.

There is an obvious obligation on clergy to officiate where necessary at public worship. It is part of a priest's calling to do that regardless of personal needs, which are subsumed to the needs of the community. Any obligation is of that nature, the providing of a public service as part of one's job. When done alone, there may have to be modifications.

Wherever at all possible, the office needs to be rooted in some kind of community. The solitary priest praying alone is a relatively modern phenomenon, as we have discovered. The round of prayer is much easier kept up if supported by a group. Failing that, or in addition to it, it is a very good thing to have a relationship with a religious community, staying there occasionally to share in its worship. The cathedrals should ideally be such inspirational centres, but much needs to change if their potential riches are to nourish and encourage the clergy and people of their dioceses.

Office and Eucharist

We have found ourselves returning time and again to the unity of the Body of Christ and the understanding of Christian prayer as offered within the context of the Church. However important daily liturgical prayer is in sustaining this consciousness, it is not its source and fountainhead. For that we have to turn to the eucharist. The solidarity of the Church within itself and with its Lord is poured forth and sustained in the breaking of the bread and the sharing of the cup. The eucharist is the summit of all Christian prayer. It is here that Christ makes himself truly present and tangibly known. It is here that the Church is most fully the Church, here that the symbols of the Body and its unity reverberate most strongly. That has always been so well understood that there is no such thing as a people's or a monastic eucharist. It is the supreme liturgy of the whole Church, and the sacrament of unity.

We have seen that daily liturgical prayer is based on a strong sense of community: this sense of community is profoundly eucharistic. The unity of the Body in the prayer of the hours is that kind of unity which is exemplified in the liturgy of the Lord's table. It is natural to see, then, how Roman Catholic spirituality has seen the daily office as a kind of spinning-out of the Eucharist through the day. The Second Vatican Council states:

> The Liturgy of the Hours extends to the different hours of the day, the praise and prayer, the memorial of the mysteries of salvation and the foretaste of heavenly glory, which are offered us in the eucharistic mystery, the centre and culmination of the whole life of the Christian community.[13]

A French commentator has said that the eucharist 'inundates the day's prayer with its fires'.[14] A similar view to this is held in Orthodoxy. The eucharist indeed presents before our eyes the model of the Church's prayer, where Christ the High Priest offers and is offered in unity with his people. This sense of belonging is also profoundly baptismal, and it can be no accident that a daily ceremony at the font had an important history in many forms of vespers (see page 149f.). Baptism signals a beginning, which God sustains and carries forward not least through eucharist and office. Because of this rooting in the eucharist it is entirely natural that since time immemorial the altar has had an important place in the celebration of the office, through the act of facing towards it at certain parts of the service, and in prayers, processions and censings.

In all major traditions (Anglican included) the divine office has been inseparable from the eucharist on Sundays and greater festivals, and the bond between the two is seen particularly strongly at these times.

In the West attitudes on this matter have not been without their difficulties for the divine office, however. While the daily eucharist is certainly ancient practice, Robert Taft, in tracing its history, has shown that there can be no absolute laws about it.[15] Frequency is not necessarily commensurate with reverence. Before the Middle Ages the normal practice, even in Benedictine monasticism, was to celebrate the eucharist only on Sundays and feast-days. On weekdays communion was often made from the reserved sacrament. In Orthodoxy, which has preserved a similar attitude, daily celebration is unusual. Alexander Schmemann can even express unhappiness at the way in which in some traditions the eucharist has been made to descend into the daily round and become another daily office.[16] The French Benedictine Adalbert de Vogüé has come to the conclusion that:

> In itself the daily repetition of an act enhances it no more than does its renewal once a week. Frequency is not without ambiguity. To introduce a rite into the daily routine is

both to pay it homage and to make it commonplace – *quotidiana vilescunt* – to mark its importance and to weaken its impact. Inversely, spacing out the sacred celebration may seem either a sign of less interest – it is not worth spending time on every day – or a token of high esteem: the action is too sublime to be regarded, it should be reserved for solemn occasions.[17]

It therefore appears that open-minded consideration ought to be given to the problem of attaining the right balance between eucharist and office in each situation. Not many parishes, for instance, can sustain a daily mass and a public office, and have attendance at all of them. For some communities it will be felt that due honour is given to the eucharist by celebrating it daily, while for others greater honour and deference can be expressed by offering it only on certain days. For de Vogüé this is simply a choice of how to make the eucharist fruitful.[18] For St Augustine, too, it remains a difficult choice: in connection with making one's communion he says:

One, honouring it, dares not receive it daily, and the other, honouring it, dares not forgo a single day.[19]

Moreover, it is impossible to examine the nature of the daily office without alluding to this problem, because there is a sense in which we can judge whether or not we are giving due honour to the eucharist by the extent to which we are able to give due honour to the office. If the setting is imperfect, the jewel is marred; if the Eucharist is celebrated so often that there is no time for the daily office in which to reflect on it and 'spin it out', then we can become unable, as not a few Catholic Christians seem to be saying today, to see the real presence of Christ any more in what is the banquet of his Kingdom.[20]

It may be that we do not know what to do about the crisis of the divine office because we have not thought to stand back and look at what we are doing with the eucharist. In seeking to give due honour to the office, we are *ipso facto* giving honour to that mystery before which 'all mortal flesh should keep silence'. This is not to say *necessarily* that the daily eucharist cannot be a very good thing, and in some circumstances essential. Nor is it to seek to question the spirituality of Christians for whom it is central. It is simply to say that this sacrament, the living sustainer of the oneness of the Body, and the essential liturgical expression of the Church's self-understanding, cannot be considered in isolation from the honour which is due to the Church's ongoing life of prayer, whose backbone is the daily office. They have to be considered together, if they are to cohabit in a balanced order, and there may be some justification for speaking here of an *ecology* of Christian prayer. The spiritual traditions which the Church has inherited are an ecosystem which suffers if its delicate balance is disturbed.

It must seem by now that we have wandered far from the question which arose a few pages back – 'What is the daily office?' Yet such must be the answer, inscrutable perhaps as the utterances of a Shinto monk. It is determined by history and by geography, by who we are, and where we are. Its content is the outward ways in which inner attitudes are expressed. It is the building or room in which the prayer is offered, the people who are involved, and the music, gesture and spoken word they come together to make, in the traditions they have inherited. It is also a particular form of words – we should not forget that, but neither should we leave it stranded on a throne – words in poetry, prose and epigrammatic phrase, in cries and acclamations, greetings, blessings and silences. But above all the content is that *presentness* of the Church which is ever re-created at the Lord's table, the presence of Christ in his people as he prays in them and they pray in him to the Father of all.

In order to stimulate further thought and searching, it may be useful to come a little more down to earth than this, and so I offer below a picture of daily liturgical prayer which seems to me at this moment to emerge from the study of history, and from a personal experience of struggling, floundering and being caught up in the Church's daily liturgical prayer over quite a few years.

CHARACTERISTICS OF THE PRAYER OF THE CHURCH

1 Christian prayer is one. The prayer of the Church is the total prayer of all Christians. The separate prayers of all the members of the one Body make up a single whole, whatever form they might individually take. This prayer is Christ praying in his Church.

2 The varieties of prayer are many, but three categories are outstanding:
   (a) the sacraments, above all the eucharist;
   (b) daily liturgical prayer, which can be offered individually or with others;
   (c) the intimate prayer of individuals.

3 Daily liturgical prayer (category (b)) has three modes:
   (a) the daily office of the local church, which normally consists of two services, at the beginning and ending of the working day;
   (b) the monastic office, which divides the day into more frequent gatherings for prayer;
   (c) subsidiary liturgical prayer, celebrated by individuals and groups, which is inspired by the daily office and often consciously associated with it, and which can be twice or more per day according to circumstances.

4 Daily liturgical prayer is seen as a gift to the Father, covenanted and offered in its own right as a part of the prayer of the whole Body, irrespective of who is present or absent. So the public daily office is usually offered by a *quorum*.

5 As covenanted gift, it can be governed by no externally imposed legal

obligation, other than moral obligations arising from one's place in the one Body.

Personal motivation to pray is always founded in discernment of vocation and free response.

The *public* daily office is founded in the vocation of the whole community.

6 The daily prayer expresses by its content and manner of performance the bonds which unite the Church, in time (tradition) and space (the contemporary worldwide Church).

7 It varies widely in detail according to the vocation of the community which celebrates it. The only requirement of absolute necessity is that it should be *prayer*, offered at agreed *times*.

The fundamental structure of the main offices of the day is normally psalmody followed by intercessions.

8 Two outstanding differences of emphasis in the past have been found in the prayer of local communities and that of monasteries. The former has been selective in its use of the Psalter, and has employed all appropriate means to encourage the people to worship; the latter has been characterized by obedience and submission, and the quiet prayer of the psalms *in course*.

9 Daily liturgical prayer relates organically to other aspects of Christian living, especially: the eucharist; private prayer; Bible-study.

10 The daily prayer is indispensable to the life of the Church as a whole. While not all Christians are called to direct participation in it in its classical public form, all are called to make their contribution to the one prayer of the Church.

A note on the daily office in the Anglican Church

The Anglican Communion embraces a wide diversity, but it is perhaps possible in this particular field to assume that England is reasonably representative.

The present situation is mixed. On the positive side have to be included the still widespread understanding of the offices as public services to be performed in church where possible, and the important symbolic role played in this by the cathedral. To this we should add certain understandings about prayer: that it should have a liturgical backbone, should be rooted in the Scriptures, and should foster familiarity with them. In addition, despite the widespread collapse of Sunday mattins and evensong, many lay people are still familiar with these services, and have at least some opportunity to pray the psalms and the canticles and other elements of age-old tradition. These things are all bound together within a particular spirit which is difficult to define, but includes certain aesthetic standards concerning language and the manner in which services are performed. There is a formality and seemliness which at its worst can lead to unutterable dullness, but at its best is a precious and characteristic gift. The Anglican office also has in favour of it a very fine musical tradition.

On the negative side have to be weighed an array of problems more formidable than is often admitted, and which must be largely responsible for the disappearance of the Sunday offices in the majority of parishes, and the parlous state of the office on weekdays. Many churches have in fact been obliged to turn to the Roman 'Liturgy of the Hours' or other forms, for weekday use.

The problems include indiscriminate ploughing through the Psalter from Psalms 1 to 150, and massive amounts of Scripture-reading *in course*, reading four books of the Bible simultaneously, or, according to new alternatives, three books. The *preces* remain the sole form of intercession at the end of each office, inadequate as they are to cover all the objects that need the Church's daily prayer.[21] The sense of identity associated with this office tends to be overblown, setting it up as part of an independent rite comparable with the Roman or Byzantine, or even local uses such as Sarum. The text of the office in the form in which Anglicans have inherited it, however, can never be a runner in that league: (1) Its repertoire is too severely limited; it has no rich corpus of material such as responsories, hymns, canticles, non-biblical readings, and other variable and imaginative material such as characterizes the great independent rites, and little of the rich variety which follows the course of the seasons. (2) It has indeed no material distinctive to itself, bar a collect or two. (3) Both of these limitations arise from its simply being a pruning and rearrangement of the Roman office. All Cranmer did was reshuffle the cards, weeding handfuls of them out. There is nothing in its text or shape which other Christians can draw on, and nothing which has proved of any influence in the wider Church. Other Churches, not least that of Rome, have had to move quite far from the forms which prevailed among them until recently, and seen in that light the association of a particular form of the daily office with ecclesial identity is, in the Anglican Church, disproportionate. Drastic changes have been accepted in the eucharist, as demanded by our improved understanding of its history and origins. So it is not unreasonable to expect that similarly profound changes will have to affect the shape and verbal content of the office.

The way services are celebrated is also in need of thorough reappraisal. The set-piece Sunday evensong with organ and choir as it has been known needs to be revived, but in a very different form and style. Weekday services are also often performed in a way which is dry and uninspiring both to the clergy and to any people who might attend.

To all these problems we must add the Church's failure to attach sufficient importance to the office and to prayer, and to promote them with conviction. We say these things are vital, but do little to prove it. There is much to build on in the Anglican Church, but also much work to be done (and *metanoia* to be undergone) if any of this unique tradition is to survive the next few years. It is necessary to identify the areas where the tradition is strong, and those where it is weak. In the area of *content*, the most fruitful elements seem to be those which are no peculiarity of Anglicanism, but part of the wider Church's inheritance. In the areas of *understanding*, *practice* and *manner of celebration* the strengths are considerable and in some respects unique. Probably we should see these strengths as the best foundation for renewal, enriching them with treasures from the splendid and ancient storehouse of the Church catholic.

22

Prayer Today

Returns to roots can often lead to new departures: there is a distinct possibility today that the daily office needs to pass through one of those transformations which have occasionally swept over it, and there is no voice more prophetic on this subject than the very history of the office itself.

Those most historical of people, the religious orders, have been leading the way. Since the Second Vatican Council Roman Catholic and other communities, particularly the more monastic ones, have experimented to such an extent with the daily office that any community one visits is likely to be using a form which is peculiar to itself. There always has been diversity in the monastic tradition, each house having its particular uses, but recent experiment has been more bold. The guidelines published by the Benedictines in 1974 go so far as to state that

The Work of God and the celebrating community . . . should correspond so closely to each other that each community can be said to require its own proper liturgy.[22]

We have not made much reference to the religious orders in tracing the history of the office, but their experience and insights are essential to the Church as a whole, and should not be overlooked. Nor should they for their part forget that they are in a unique position to show a lead to the Church, and to explore paths which the secular Church is neither so free nor so equipped to do.

In experiment and exploration the divine office has lagged behind. It has undergone striking metamorphoses in the past in response to novel turns of events, and after the unprecedented transformations of the modern world it is very surprising that it has so far escaped any thorough reappraisal. In our developing understanding of the Christian faith it has come to a stop further back along the road, and there has been little, if any, growth in understanding of the daily office at the parish level, comparable with that of the eucharist or initiation or prayer in general, where a rediscovery of the past has provided seed for renewal. The problems here are of a particular difficulty, however, because the office affects the ordinary round of every day.

First, the daily office is concerned with time, and today we have considerable problems with time. We have no time, and our daily life has become so full of rival calls on our time, all of which demand energy and adrenalin, with powerful stimuli of sound, sight, colour, drama and tedium that any attempt to punctuate this turbulent flow with quiet pools of prayer is like trying to see our reflection in a river in spate. Apart from our enervated experience of the flow of time, daily routines and schedules nowadays are such that a twofold public office evolved in ancient times can match up to the timetables of relatively few people. So there is a problem of finding the best times for those who are willing to come together, and a more manifold approach to meet the more complicated situation.

Secondly, daily liturgical prayer, involving repetition of formulas, can be very difficult to take kindly to in a world of constant talk, monotonous repetition (e.g. TV adverts and news programmes), and empty words spoken with little reflection.

A discipline which is so intimately linked to the texture of daily life can only be amended and improved on the spot, in the particular circumstances of each local community. If that is to happen it will need to arise out of a sound understanding of what is at stake. It calls for a thorough programme of education, in theological colleges, parish groups, preaching, parish magazine articles, confirmation training, and teaching in schools and Sunday schools, concerned not merely with antiquarian study of old habits and practices, but with a rediscovery of *motives*, and the discovering of *vocation*. In particular, the demands which we allow prayer to make on us will correspond to the extent that we (a) allow God to be at the very centre, and (b) believe that direct access to God through prayer is important and possible.

Here we must take our eyes from the office for a moment, for we are in danger of putting the cart before the horse. Whether or not the office needs changing is ultimately a matter of opinion. What is not a matter of opinion is that first of all *we* must change. What most needs alteration is not the liturgy but ourselves. That may sound a paradoxical thing to say towards the end of a book devoted to practical understanding and practical change; and yet it seems unavoidable that it should be said, in order to indicate the spirit in which reform in prayer and worship has to be approached: the spirit not of a mechanic overhauling a machine, but of a Church coming in repentance before its God. For this reason alone, if for no other, it is necessary to dwell here at some length upon the point.

However much the modern Church says it believes in prayer, it so often behaves as if it has failed to surrender to God. The word 'surrender' is shorthand for Jesus' image of bride and bridegroom, and the total self-giving which is necessary in their coming together. Allowing God to be at the centre is something we all fail to do. We fail to wait utterly on God, to surrender all to him, and others then rightly see the Church as a busy, empty vessel. For we can often go to him in prayer without any idea of surrender, or any notion of disdaining our own will in order to be open to his; we go to be fed and watered according to our requirements. Meister Eckhart, less polite, said we treat God like a cow. We go to church to milk him, so we can come away with milk with which to make butter and cheese. Yes, God has expressly told us to do this, and he indeed feeds us when we ask, but it is always distasteful to exploit the generosity of others on demand whenever we want, without a commensurate love which includes a surrender of self. We reassure ourselves that God always forgives and his generosity comes without any strings attached. But perhaps we do not reflect what a relationship based purely on *receiving*, taking, does to us. It is immature, leaving us incapable of sharing with the Giver those deeper things which can only come where two mature people trust each other and are familiar with being alone together. The Church as a body is shy of being alone with its Lord in that direct access we call prayer, and diffident about the referral of important things back to him.

The Church has a poor sense of that alert waiting-on-God which vitalizes the Old and the New Testaments. It gives him insufficient room to inform and disturb its decision-making processes. We often seem to see the Church as a mechanism that just needs a bit of fiddling with. Prayer is a helpful extra which has to fit into spare holes in our timetables. Is this unfair? If it is, it should still be a matter of concern that there are not a few Christians who believe it to be fact. We, the Church, need to face some very awkward truths about our relationship with God when embarking on liturgical change.

Love is unruly, sweeping aside all obstacles in its path. Service of God through service of our neighbour may be a true outpouring of love; but such a relationship to God through our neighbour can only with difficulty be called *love* of God as St Paul speaks of it. Love seeks the beloved, and will be content with no side-ways. It can make no important decisions without referring them to the beloved, anxious for his approval.

But we have been challenged with two loves: love of God and love of our neighbour. Each needs the other, and only in the teasing dance between the two is there hope of a love liberated from sin and self-will. While many individuals have particular callings to excel at the one love or the other, the *Church* as a whole must reflect them both. They both make equal demands upon the Church's time and energy. Unless there is a superabundance in the Church of prayer, we will be failing our neighbours, giving them stones to build with when they need the bread of God in their viscera too.

Again, as well as direct surrender of each individual to God, there is the corollary that the Christian community can only surrender to him in so far as its members have surrendered to each other. Sometimes we seem to have too low a threshold of forbearance, and too much of the wrong kind of individualism in our congregations and our society. Unless we can work together self-effacingly in order that God may make of us a community where prayer is possible, it is useless trying to encourage individuals to pray in the modern world. In such a hostile environment prayer needs its own micro-climate. We have met many examples of this from history. Chapter 1 attempted to show the profound degree to which our modern culture renders us individually incapable of prayer. Other Christians in other ages have experienced similar difficulties. We only have to consider those of east Syria, of Transylvania, of the Greek Church under the Turks, the country minsters and parish teams of the Dark Ages, and the Roman Catholic recusants of post-Reformation England. All of these in different ways enabled prayer to be sustained by the creation of apposite environments, little worlds within the world. These were often physical, taking the form of monasteries and churches, but they were also human contexts formed by shared belief and shared ways of prayer. When rightly pursued, this has resulted not in a simple siege-mentality but in something more like the family home, where love is made possible and the members receive rooting and orientation which enables them to live in the world with confidence. We tend blithely to press on with prayer in an isolated way, and the resulting experience can be like trying to strike a match under water. Prayer needs air where it can breathe, it needs the Body of Christ: 'Without me you can do nothing' (John 15.5).

We need to face such questions as these before we can ever begin to talk about renewal in prayer and office. There is no more necessary step to be taken in any renewal than that of taking God more seriously. Without that, mere alteration of services is surely a waste of time. It is therefore with a great sense of unworthiness and unfaithfulness that we now turn to the practical steps which could accompany such a turning (*metanoia*) to the Father.

The following suggestions are merely ideas, and while some of them arise from personal experience, they are not put forward in any way as a programme or blueprint, but in the hope that, in conjunction with all that history gives us, and with the principles which seem to emerge from that history, they may help sow a few seeds from which future growth might gradually spring. They come under six headings: public worship in church; communal celebration outside the church; the prayer of individuals; the offices on Sundays; the role of the cathedral; and last, but not in any way least, comes official provision, because it seems to follow most naturally after the consideration of practical details.

1. Public worship in a parish church

The choice of the right translation of the Psalter is important, and by far the most successful one for the purposes of recitation is that of the American Episcopal Book of Common Prayer of 1979 (The Church Hymnal Corporation, New York). It is now used by many Anglican religious communities in Britain and elsewhere. We should not forget that there is more than one way of reading the psalms. For example, different people present could each stand up and read a psalm or part of a psalm, the book being passed from one to the other. A refrain might also be sung after every few verses. Each psalm should be followed by silence, and an extempore prayer could finally sum up the psalm in a few simple words.[23]

Reflection on the psalms and readings with the help of a commentary or theological book, or with an extempore meditation, can all be of help, but unless there are people with the time to prepare such things and do them well, they will not normally be possible every day in a busy parish.

It might be helpful to keep contingency forms of service available, suitable to bring out and use if a chance visitor comes, in a parish where the priest is trying to encourage people to start attending. Normally the office as provided would be said, but a more easily digestible form with carefully chosen psalms and readings, etc. could be kept by in case of need.

Music is so important in making the Word live that we should be prepared to go to considerable lengths to get it. With small groups, accompaniments on cassette can work well if there is at least one good singer, although people have to learn how to sing with a tape recorder. It is not much work to make a cassette with accompaniments for versicles and canticles for every day of the week – a job there for cathedral organists. If the office is worth doing well, it is worth spending money on. Small cassette recorders can be connected direct to reasonably powerful speakers, without the need for expensive amplifiers. If a pianist or organist with time to spare can be persuaded to accompany at least some of the daily services, even if not very well, they might receive a small honorarium. This should be thought worth it even if the normal attendance is only organist and priest.

A servers' rota could involve people of all ages – they would ring the bell, light candles, give out books, work the tape recorder, and lead certain parts of the service.

Regular teaching about daily liturgical prayer could lead to special fortnights when people sign up to come to individual services, with the aim of completely filling up the rota. In the summer holidays choir children could come in small groups to spend an occasional afternoon which would include practising some music, followed, after tea, by mini-choral evensong in church, even if unaccompanied. It may be possible to form a group or roll which anyone can join, whose job will be oversight and maintenance of the daily liturgical prayer, both public and private, with rotas for attendance or prayer in parallel, and regular meetings for common prayer.

The part of the church where services are held has to be considered carefully. It should be such that occasional visitors, finding themselves the only people there, will not feel too exposed or on the spot. It should be small enough to be intimate, but formal enough to make the kind of space in which we can be open to the Mystery of God. The officiant needs to beware of attracting too much attention to him or her self by making too many interjections, explanations and announcements. Much will depend on the character of the particular Christian community, obviously. In some parishes it will be appropriate for clergy to vest and use formal ceremonies, but in others it could be more natural to sit in an informal circle round a candle. Physical ritual may include the passing-round of an open Bible, each reading part of the passage or psalmody chosen. The interesting combination of informality with impressive liturgy which can be found at Taizé or at the church of St-Gervais in Paris provides another model; experiment with gesture, music and symbol in a formal rite intended to express the awesomeness of God's transcendence, and yet combined with informal sitting on the floor and relaxed relationships founded in loving community. This kind of experimental liturgy attracts criticism for a variety of reasons, but any attempt at recovering lost dimensions in worship will be bound to have its histrionic and self-conscious side, as Anglicans will know from some of the adventures of early Tractarianism. These stages have to be gone through. Attempts at evolving symbol and ritual appropriate to today will inevitably include mistakes and wrong directions.

Lighting is extremely important. Two spotlight bulbs can be connected to an ordinary domestic dimmer at very little cost, and would be quite adequate for a small worship area. Darkness gives a great sense of informality and repose, and the level of light can be adjusted as necessary for the various points of the service. Little light is needed for listening to psalms being read. Many parishes have teenagers who would be enthusiastic lighting consultants.

By tradition liturgical prayer has been represented in church with symbolic furniture, just as the eucharist is represented by the altar. Choirstalls are a secondary development, but the tradition of standing round a lectern may yet have some use left in it. In both East and West, this is the age-old way of celebrating the daily office. In some churches it may be possible to place a solid lectern in the middle of the area where the office is done. This could be a tall cupboard with a two- or four-sided reading-desk on top. The cupboard would be for keeping books, music, tape recorder, etc., and those who wish to join in would stand round the lectern, sharing two or three books. Others who prefer to be less active could remain in the background. There is something very good about sharing round a lectern which gives a strong sense of community and common task. A double or quadruple lectern with a revolving top makes it much easier to juggle with a collection of books. The breviary and its offspring have spoilt us, and in these days of pamphlets and loose-leaf folders there is a good deal of nostalgia for the days when services could be contained in one book. The easy-option, all-inclusive book requires, however, such a drastic reduction of resources and room for manoeuvre that liturgy can no longer be an offering of the very best: easier to perform, but limited and unimaginative. As Procter and Frere pointed out half a century ago, it is also a departure from the fundamental principles of Christian liturgy for all the participants to have their private, all-inclusive book.[24]

Turning now to more ancient ceremonies, it was not long ago that I was opposed to the revival of the lucernarium, feeling it to be unreal and antiquarian.

But then I had the experience of its daily use during a fortnight's mission in a parish. At first people were surprised, but by the end of a fortnight there was tremendous enthusiasm on all sides, and, with a daily attendance of 100 or more, plans were made to continue it after the mission had ended. We started by switching all the lights off. Two spotlight bulbs trained on a large crucifix were connected to an ordinary domestic dimmer switch and dimmed down as low as they would go. We started with relaxation exercises, sitting straight, breathing regularly, and relaxing the body stage by stage. Our attention was focussed on God's presence, and he was asked to sustain us in that awareness.

Then a quiet refrain was sung a few times. Someone entered with an enormous lighted candle, and a very short text on the theme of light was proclaimed, either from the Old Testament or from St John's Gospel. The candle was placed in its stand before the crucifix, and from it all lighted their individual candles. Then we had a psalm, read by one person. After each verse or group of verses all present sang a refrain. Then there was a long silence. Prayers and intercessions followed, sometimes with a sung refrain, then a long silence, time for individual prayers, the Lord's Prayer, another refrain, and so on, as long as seemed appropriate. We ended finally with a silence: those who wanted to pray by the light of the candle stayed as long as they liked; the others went through to the church hall for a cup of coffee. In their comments, people singled out the silence and raptness, the informality and the atmosphere of the darkness and the candles as something quite new for them, and very welcome. Their reaction was exactly the same as that of the people in the last parish where I served as a parish priest, when we introduced an all-night vigil before the Altar of Repose on Maundy Thursday. What we are all thirsting for, this seemed to say, is the sense of the presence of God, and to be enabled to attend to him in a state of inner quiet. The experience also showed how good it was to be liberated from fumbling with books, and demonstrated the power still inherent in the ancient practice of the use of refrains.

In parishes where the eucharist is regularly celebrated in the week, there is good reason for taking advantage of the provision for conflating this with the office of the hour. This does an injustice to the office, and is unsatisfactory from various points of view, not the least being that the office is not simply another liturgy of the Word, but something with its own distinct character and role. The great advantage of this procedure, however, is that it enables people to become familiar with the offices, and to come to know the psalms.

In areas where it is difficult to sustain a public daily office, something may be learnt from the old practice of passing it from church to church within a town (see page 181, n.2). Individual parishes in a deanery could serve a week by turns, during which they would ensure that the office was especially well done. This would mean that those churches where nothing was done would now have something at regular intervals; and this could have no detrimental effect on those where it was offered all the time anyway. It would be a challenge to parishioners, and a good expression of the solidarity of the Church in its continual offering of prayer.

Outside the church

The church, or, failing that, an oratory in the priest's house, has many things to recommend it as a venue for the community's daily prayer. Often, however, it is not practical. There can be problems with the building itself, or its location, heating in winter, or the sheer inappropriateness in some communities of having formal prayer in such a building. Sometimes it is possible to be flexible, using the church for a proportion of the services, or only in summer. The building is important, but not indispensable, and its many advantages may have to be sacrificed in favour of needs which are more urgent. This is nothing new. The east Syrian Church has a tradition of celebrating the daily office out of doors in the hot summer months, and the interplay between church and home which we find in the early Church has been mirrored in recent centuries by the freedom exercised by clergy to recite the daily office wherever is most convenient, even on the bus or in public places. The *Apostolic Constitutions* recommend that when the community cannot get to its church for any reason it should celebrate the daily services in people's homes (13).

In an ordinary parish there are various possible ways of doing this. One is for the daily office to be celebrated where people naturally assemble: before a parish council meeting, after choir practice, with the Mothers' Union or the youth club (with suitable adaptations, naturally). It should, even then, include something to sing as a matter of course. It may be possible to have a rota of households where services will be held, which, if it happens regularly enough, might eventually reach the point where the services go on willy-nilly whether the clergyman manages to turn up or not. For many elderly or housebound people the opportunity, say, of having a simple service at home once a fortnight, which was seen as a contribution to the whole parish's covenanted worship, could be very helpful and encouraging.

It is important that the parish 'team', which in an Anglican parish could consist of vicar, curate or part-time priest, reader, churchwardens and leaders of organizations, should have a shared discipline of prayer, which will include gathering either in small combinations or all together. In some places it is possible for the clergy in an area to come together regularly for the office. There may be something to be said for the revival in some form of the ancient office of parish clerk, a full- or part-time helper, one of whose primary tasks is to assist in the celebration of the daily services. This is not as eccentric as it may sound. If prayer is of central importance to the Church's life, it merits the commissioning of special people to support its maintenance.

Beyond such symbolic 'official' gatherings, the unit which cannot be ignored is the household or family. Even very devout people find it difficult to pray together at home. This is doubly difficult where there are older children in the family who need to be free if necessary to work through their scepticism and rebellion, or where only some of the family are practising Christians. The barrier at which all people seem to fall is the spoken word. In expecting prayer to consist of words spoken aloud in the presence of others we can be setting a standard which for most people is psychologically and emotionally impossible, at least as far as the English are concerned. If we look to other areas of life where the spoken word fails, we find ritual spontaneously being resorted to. Giving a present, sending a card, leaving flowers, winking, smiling, dancing, hanging on to keepsakes. The ancient people's office gave great importance to lighting of lamps, incense, gestures and symbolic objects, whether in church or home. It may be that similar symbols would prove useful today in a prayer of the hours which circumvents the need to speak.

External ritual can enable the participation of all ages – children, the deaf, and people with any kind of handicap – through being near enough to playing games not to be outlandish, while at the same time holding out the possibility of increasing confidence in expressing religious feeling. Such kind of prayer is obviously easily open to superficiality and eventual meaninglessness through unreflective repetition, and could probably only be justified if it were seen to be leading to the point where tongues would be freed, and prayer begin to be spoken. If a family were to attempt a wordless discipline of prayer, what would they do? Only families themselves can answer that one, and perhaps experiment may have to start in the families of clergy, where prayer together can be as difficult as anywhere. Here, however, is one suggestion for Lent. If special attention were drawn to daily liturgical prayer, so that it were part of the theme for that Lent, other exercises could be brought in as part of the scheme. Members of the congregation could each be issued with a candle (or, perhaps safer, a nightlight in a glass) at the Sunday service, which they are to put on the mantelpiece and light every day, preferably for the exact period that evensong is taking place in church (or at any time that they can manage it). It could have a board by it for members of the family to pin up pictures, prayers, newspaper cuttings, and anything else which expresses prayer, praise or intercession. Where possible, members of the family should read a special prayer, either together or individually, thinking of all the other people who are praying simultaneously. It could be worded accordingly, including the name of the parish.

An exercise like that might not amount to very much in the way of prayer, but it would be an experience of common observance in parallel with the rest of the Church at an agreed time (where possible), which is so marked for God. It would need to be very well prepared for, in a way which would enable the community to take it seriously as an exercise in consecrating time to God in a rhythmic and ecclesial framework. That Jerome advised people to do this thing in the fourth century can only be an encouragement (24).

The liturgical prayer of individuals

For reasons which have already been made clear, the daily office is often of necessity celebrated alone, mostly by clergy, but also by some laity.

To begin with the clergy: what is to be done when the priest has no one else to share in the offering of the Church's prayers? This is not to be seen as failure, but as one vocation among many. The daily office celebrated alone is still offered with the whole Church, even though no one else is physically present. It makes absolute sense to offer it as a quorum of one, offering the prayer the Church has covenanted, and it makes absolute sense, therefore, to offer it in exactly the same way as if the church were full. Wherever remotely possible, the offices should be offered in church, particularly when the priest is alone. The building is a necessary symbol of the community to itself, and a sign of it before the eyes of the world. It makes absolute sense to ring the bell, to vest, use candles, incense, music and appropriate gesture and symbol, liberating us from dependence on our purely intellectual powers of apprehending *words*. Cassette recorders enable us once in a while to listen to psalmody from a cathedral, or to special settings of the canticles, or an anthem. Here is a little poem by David Scott which recommends that the lone parson sing:

> I know the clergy around Llanfihangel
> are sometimes out of sorts with the full
> Morning and Evening Prayer, said each day.
> My suggestion is that they sing
> even alone in church, what they always say.
> It doesn't have to be Purcell
> or Pelham Humphryes; anything
> that touches the fancy will sound well
> and return a relish to praying.[25]

If the form of office used persistently fails to be kept to, it is evidently wrong and should be changed. In particular, the long Bible readings in course of the Anglican office can be totally inappropriate to the prayers of a hard-pressed parish priest, who may well find it better to omit readings altogether from the office and have instead a discipline of prayerful Bible-study at some other time every day. It is difficult to find time for all of these things, and often any attempt to be strict in saying the daily office can lack credibility in the face of the other important demands of the day. We can find ourselves picking away now and then at a discipline which is too much for us. Far better to do less and keep to it. The first priority is to maintain a daily rhythm. So long as that is kept, however little time may be spent on it, it is a going concern with a future in it. In building up a discipline of prayer we may have to start with something very skimpy indeed.

We here meet a problem which needs urgent resolution today: the lack of an integrated vision of the *life* of the parish priest. Clergy can tend to be assailed by competing demands on their time, and buy each demand off as best they can. It can feel like being surrounded by dogs barking for food. The first casualties tend to be the more sensitive and vulnerable ones: family life, study, prayer, time for relaxation. Whether married or single, what is really needed is a vision of the life of the priest, not as of dubious value unless justified by works, but as a state of being in itself which is part of God's economy. A parallel would be the monastic life, but the insights of a more unlikely band, those who are hermits, seem to be of particular help here, be it for clergy or for any other individual Christians ploughing a lonely furrow.[26] First of all, we see our life, our vocation as making sense in the eyes of God before we have done anything. After that we face the demands made upon us, and rationally apportion them the allotment of time they can have. In this way, essentials will still get done, although the vicar may have to cut down drastically in unexpected areas. But whatever the priest or minister is doing at the time, be it visiting, gardening, praying, shopping, preparing sermons, is understood as part of the life, and not as taking him or her away from other things their conscience is worried about. Within this economy prayer will have its rightful place, and it will have to be accepted that sometimes it will make people late for meetings or slow down pastoral work. Apart from the grace which will be opened up to us through greater faithfulness in prayer, and through allowing God to reign at the centre of things, it is this kind of balanced approach which leads to the least dissipation of energy, so that the end result can only be gain in achievement, not loss.

It is one thing to suggest nice tidy patterns and another thing to try to assemble them in a hurricane. The authorities who in former centuries turned the daily office into a legal obligation were not brought to do it without good reason. They knew that however good our intentions, the human will is weak and fails to keep to the standards it sets itself. We need objectively defined obligations, whether they be set by others or by ourselves. Sometimes we need subterfuges. Just as the young couple who felt their marriage was drifting apart saved the situation by signing up for a course in ballroom dancing, so Christians need to plot against themselves in order to keep to those standards their hearts and minds see to be right, but which their moods constantly betray.

It may be that ringing the church bell so that certain pre-warned spies can hear it and make a note when they do not, could be one way of helping clergy get daily to their knees. The parish group devoted to maintaining the daily office, which I have already suggested above, could meet with the parish priest once a month in the pub for half an hour, and each give an account of where they have succeeded or failed in their prayer. If unable to attend, a member would have to send a written note. Some element such as this, which helps our better nature to plot against our weaker, will for many people be necessary if any thing is to be done at all.

On some occasions, and particularly on days off, prayer ought to be allowed to drop into a lower gear. It is far better to do something less, than to do nothing at all, always bearing in mind that the main thing necessary is *prayer* at the appropriate times. On a day off there is no reason why the priest should not, say, go out into the garden and say a 'Glory be', offer the day silently to God for two minutes, and then say the Lord's Prayer and the Grace. Even a mere sign of the cross is better than nothing at all. The Church will be offering the office for you anyway. The 'lost' readings will have to be written off if you keep to the lectionary. A weekday lectionary which takes account of days off would be very useful here.

The part of daily liturgical prayer which has been most thoroughly lost is the remote participation of the laity. There is a certain amount of interest today in using forms of office such as compline for private prayer, and this needs to be encouraged and built somehow into the bandwagon of the local community's offering. Simple, rhymed forms of office which can be easily remembered, and yet which bear a recognizable link with the Church's services, would be of great help to many of us, and quietly singing one or two hymns to oneself could easily be given an ecclesial handle, and the praying or singing of any suitable prayers or songs could be understood as part of the same exercise. We need to distinguish two strands in the tradition: one is the prayer of *forms* which correspond to the Church's form of public prayer, thereby associating one's prayer with the Church; the other is prayer in parallel with the local church at the *time* they are praying. There is also the combination of the two, which has in the past particularly illuminated the prayer of the breviary for clergy.

There seems to be no reason why every baptized Christian should not have one or the other as a daily discipline, which would respond to a widespread need in the modern world to *belong*.

Sundays

We have seen the strength of Saturday and Sunday vespers in the past in all the major traditions, and with that the practice of beginning the worship on the Lord's day with mattins, sometimes preceded by a special vigil. This is still a central element of Orthodox practice, but also in the Anglican Church there is a unique tradition of sung mattins on Sundays which has helped to make English Christians, in a peculiar way, a people of the office. Mattins has gained a bad name here in having been seen as supplanting the eucharist, and has on that account experienced almost universal rejection. But the time has now come to give fresh consideration to something which has without question been central to the liturgical scheme of the Christian Sunday. The eucharist claims the place of honour, and merits the best of our time and energy, and in busy parishes clergy have enough verbiage to get through without having to start staging full-blown mattins as well. But in some places ways may be found for the offering of mattins by a small group which will provide a liturgical service of the Word too for those, who are not a few, who are not yet ready for the meat of the eucharist. The claims of evensong are perhaps even stronger. Instead of doing away with it when the congregation dwindles to half a dozen, we should be glad of what is a very presentable quorum, and use it as a basis on which to build new understandings and new approaches, which can be taught and urged with confidence and commitment. The resulting form of worship may be very different in style from anything we have known before.

In many parishes evensong is sacrificed in favour of an evening eucharist. While recognizing the need to provide the eucharist for all in a complex and mobile society, we have made the mistake of assuming the simplest answer is to sacrifice the delicate balance of the Church's liturgy. It is as if the radio broadcast nothing but news, in order that all may hear it, or a mother of a large family never left the kitchen because there is always someone coming in wanting something to eat. The ecological balance of 2000 years is lost. It is very regrettable, therefore, that Sunday evening eucharists, for all their merits, should have replaced traditions of sung vespers which have in places been very strong: it has caused, for instance, the widespread disappearance of Sunday *nieszpory* among Polish Roman Catholics, and even solemn vespers in cathedrals the world over. There must be a way of making a better compromise so that the balance is not completely lost.

5 . The cathedral

Any vision of a daily office of the future would be incomplete without some reference to that central pillar of the Church's prayer, the cathedral. Perhaps one may be permitted to make three pleas: (1) that cathedrals preserve their traditions in order to maintain living contact with the roots: the old offices of the Anglican Church and the Latin and Gregorian chant of the Roman offices should be kept in vigour, even if reformed and adapted in accordance with present insights; (2) that the worship be open too to experiment, in the quest for renewal, in the rediscovery of ancient models, texts and usages, and their interpretation for the modern Church (I am sure the canons of Milan would be delighted to give guidance to an English cathedral on how to offer an occasional celebration of the glorious Ambrosian vespers (31) with its unique chant); cathedrals have resources which parishes can never hope to have, and are in a position to give inspiration and example to their dioceses in the search for a liturgical prayer for our time; (3) that there be sufficient connection between cathedral and parish so that it is evident they belong together, and so that parishes may look to the cathedrals as the hub of the diocese's prayers, and feel that they and it are on the same wavelength.

Parishioners should be encouraged to go to the cathedral for a weekday evensong occasionally, the parish priest perhaps offering a lift once a month. The replacement of sung mattins in English cathedrals by a said service is a sad loss. Even though the canons who say it together may not have the voices of angels, there is no reason why some things should not be sung with the accompaniment of a chamber organ. At Westminster Roman Catholic Cathedral weekday services are sung with the use of chamber organ and a small men's choir, at times when the choristers are away. This sets a very encouraging example for other churches where resources can sometimes be modest.

Official provision

Perhaps the Church needs to provide a kind of 'kit', letting local communities get on with using it as they see best (as various churches such as the Church of England have already begun to do in their recent revisions). In practice, even if not in theory, that is how the Byzantine office often seems to function, and I have heard it expressed as a matter of pride that in true Orthodoxy things go rarely according to the exact letter. A Romanian abbot once told me a little jingle which they have in his church with regard to this:

> Everything may be according to the book,
> And yet the soul be empty.[27]

The 'kit' should perhaps include the following:

(a) A basic order or framework for the service, with indications as to what is most important.

(b) A variety of systems for praying the psalms and other similar texts, both selective and *in course*, with some possibility of thematic treatment. (Return to the ancient fixed psalms is problematic: few people would be keen to repeat such psalms as 63 and 141 every day.)

(c) A variety of lectionaries providing one, two or three readings per day, and spread over one, two, three or even more years, with some guidance on reading from other sources, ancient and modern, to aid reflection. Such lectionaries would be flexible enough to be usable by clergy or groups who pray the office less than seven days a week (taking account of days off, weekends, etc.). In particular, one suggestion: a simple office of readings which gives Bible reference, one suggestion on other reading (or a brief quotation), a hymn and a collect.

(d) A rich collection of hymns, responsories, and other forms, and a good selection of litanies and other types of prayer; a proportion of these should be reasonably but not always too obviously thematic, with indications of appropriate psalms, readings, etc. (from (b) and (c)) which could accompany them.

(e) Generous provision for observing the Church's year and holy days.

(f) Music suitable for unaccompanied singing or for limited resources. Also cassettes, especially with settings of parts of the office, in the form of accompaniment and of music to listen to.

(g) Guidance on modes of celebration and ceremonies, and provision for additional observances such as the lucernarium and resurrection vigil.

(h) Provision of forms of prayer for daily use by families and individuals. They should be simple, memorable, and at least in part set to music, and should reflect in some way the content of the office, or at least include an explicit expression of unity with it and with all in the parish and the wider Church at prayer. Guidance could also be given on gestures and ceremonies for use in private or domestic prayer.

It would be an excellent return to tradition if renewal in daily liturgical prayer were pursued in co-operation with the cathedrals, drawing on their expertise and their potentiality for fostering that sense of solidarity and 'praying-with' which has emerged so often in this book. It would be sad if this role of cathedrals could not find new life. It is this, rather than simply gathering clergy and bishop together now and again, which would mark a realistic return to the norm which was set by the city-office in the early centuries.

The process can not but involve a patient slowness, and in the parishes themselves one way forward may be for the diocese to help set up pilot schemes, wherever possible ecumenical, providing not simply new services but also formation, guidance and support.

All of these suggestions can no doubt be easily added to and improved upon, but even as they stand they would demand an undertaking of enormous proportions which could only be tackled ecumenically, and over a long time.

23

Prayer is Belonging

'I may speak with the tongues of men and angels . . . but if I have not love, I am worth nothing.'[28] Expertise is ashes if it be not in the service of love: not simply some romantic, high-flown love, which we are thrown into on the rebound from things dry and lifeless, but love that is found in the living reality of the world *as it is*; the love we find in our neighbour, incomplete if shadowed from that greater light, the realness of God. We have no business to be seeking anything other than the *real*, and the things we have investigated in this book only have value if they help us to find a way into the real. Of all the qualities with which the real is invested, the greatest, and the most real, is love.

We play around with encountering God. We give lip-service to things we fail to do. We play at putting things in God's hands, making sure that in *reality* the reins stay firmly in ours. If we were truly open to him our hearts would sink.

> By His power He stilled the sea;
> by His understanding He smote Rahab.
> By His wind the heavens were made fair;
> His hand pierced the fleeing serpent.
> Lo, these are but the outskirts of his ways;
> and how small a whisper do we hear of Him!
> But the thunder of His power who can understand?[29]

The awe, of which the modern world knows so little, the voltage in relationships human and divine, which have been lost in our informality, where shall we find them?

The Fathers of the Second Vatican Council serenely point to an outrageous clue:

The Liturgy of the Hours . . . is 'the voice of the bride addressing her bridegroom'.[30]

At first sight a fanciful and romantic conceit, this image looks back over a long tradition of using the language of human love to describe prayer, traceable through centuries of reflection for instance on the Song of Songs, and back to the very words of the Lord himself. The image of bride and groom is a striking indicator of the level at which we are called to relate to God. Today we find it difficult to take this God seriously, and our prayer and worship are often consequently trivial, banal and all too human, with little conception of marriage-like surrender to the God who is plunged deep in the centre of all that is real. 'Behold, the bridegroom comes – go out to meet him.'[31] The prayer of the Church stems from the command to pray, a command inseparable from the call to love. No ideal on the earth is worthy to stand at the centre of our life other than this: an image reflected in human love, but whose source is him who is the Mystery within and beyond all things, hardly felt nor seen if not known in the pilgrimage of prayer; not any prayer either, but that which is rooted in the accumulated wisdom and mistakes of centuries, lived and suffered in darkness until he brings us into 'another circle of existence'[32] and through us, the Church, of all people the least in the heavenly realm, light is shed for humanity on the path towards what is promised.

Not all are called to be great pray-ers, but the Church as a body is indeed, and all its individuals are its organic members; so that the prayer of the Body, like a ladder of Jacob joining heaven and earth, belongs to all of us; through it we belong together and together we belong with God.

An earnest of its fullness is given and received when we share the bread and the cup at the wedding-banquet of the Lord, celebrating the memory of his saving deeds. The spinning-out of that earnest is the prayer of the Church. This escapes all simple definition – ordered but free, binding but liberating, a contradiction, an enigma, an unlikely place where those can meet who have long been strangers, time can live which long seemed dead, and coals which fade to a dim glow in their isolation shed forth their glory in a place where fire is shared. This prayer has always gone on and always will, half hidden, half recognized, the offering by the few which is the offering of all. It can live with the throng, it can do without them. It does not depend on our bright ideas. The prayer of the Church is in the hand of him who is our Father: it is his, not ours, and it asks of us not simply effort or change, but surrender, the giving of each to the other in a covenant grounded in the very sources of life abundant.

PART V

Sources

Sources

The section which follows seeks to do two things:

1. To give a bird's-eye view of how daily liturgical prayer has evolved, and a handy means of reference when the reader is unclear about points of detail. This is necessary in a subject so wide and complex that the general reader can often be left unable to see the wood for the trees.

Any tabular summary such as this can only pass lightly, of course, over the many complications involved in the interpretation of ancient texts. This needs to be borne very much in mind in using this part of the book. In especially difficult instances, however, the reader is referred in the footnotes to further reading.

2. To encourage the reader to go to the sources, most of which are not too difficult of access. The passages from the Fathers in particular can give a taste of how their contemporaries thought and prayed which can only be gained through a reading of the sources themselves. The reader is particularly encouraged to read sections 6 to 15 and 23, 24, 27 and 28. (For a good introduction to reading the Fathers, see the book by Ramsey, bibliography no. 59.)

The presentation attempts to be reasonably consistent, but is not entirely so; the degree of detail included depends to some extent on the nature of each entry, and the likely needs of the reader in each particular case. Wherever possible the order of services follows the traditional sequence, beginning the liturgical day with vespers. Where more than two or three services are involved, however, this has not been followed in the interests of simplicity.

Abbreviations

Mn	Midnight, or any office in the hours of darkness
Cc	Cockcrow
M	Morning office, mattins (in Roman use: lauds)
P	The first hour (prime)
T	The third hour (terce)
S	The sixth hour (sext)
N	The ninth hour (none)
E	Evening office (vespers, evensong)
C	Completion of the day (compline)
SF	Sundays and feast-days

List of sources

1   First-century Judaism

Shema' two times per day (morning and evening):
'Hear, O Israel: the Lord our God is one Lord; and you shall love the Lord your God with all your heart, and with all your soul, and with all your might.' This was recited by every adult male, morning and evening.

Prayer three times per day (morning, afternoon and evening):
Origin usually attributed to Ma'amadoth (see below). Some, however, connect it with Daniel 6.10 and 9.21, and Psalm 55.17. Content: *berakah*-type of prayer (esp. the *Tefillah*). Could be either individual or in synagogue (see Matt. 6.5).

Temple:
Two sacrifices: morning and evening (later, morning and afternoon). Three on Sabbaths, new moons and festivals: morning, afternoon and evening.

Ma'amadoth:
Priests and Levites were organized in rotas to spend a fortnight in Jerusalem and be present at the sacrifice, accompanied by a lay delegation. Other laymen who stayed at home gathered at the time of the morning sacrifices to pray in parallel with them.

Synagogue:
Services on Sabbath. Also some synagogues on Mondays and Thursdays (market days). Daily services in some synagogues? Content: Psalms? *berakah*-type prayer; blessing; reading from Law (and Prophets on Sabbath) sometimes with exposition.

2   Relevant references in the OT

Day and night
Psalm 1.2; 42.8; 77.2; 92.2

Morning
Psalm 5.3; 59.16; 88.13; 143.8

Evening
Psalm 141.2

Night
Psalm 16.7; 63.6; 77.6; 88.1; 119.55, 62, 148; 134.1

Early hours
Psalm 130.6

Three times a day
Psalm 55.17; Daniel 6.10

Seven times a day
Psalm 119.164

Coinciding with evening sacrifice
Daniel 9.21; Judith 9.1ff.

3   Relevant references in the NT

Prayer without ceasing

Luke 21.36, etc.	Watch at all times.
Luke 18.1ff.	Pray always, without losing heart (parable of the persistent widow).
1 Thess. 5.17	Pray without ceasing.
Col. 1.9	We have not ceased to pray for you.
Acts 10.2	Cornelius prayed constantly to God.

Persevering in prayer

Luke 18.1–8	The persistent widow.
Acts 1.14	All persevered in prayer.
2.42	Persevered in the apostles' teaching and fellowship, to the breaking of bread and the prayers.

Rom. 12.12	Persevere in prayer.
Col. 4.2	Persevere in prayer.
Eph. 6.18	Keep alert with all perseverance.
Acts 20.31	Stay alert . . . I did not cease day or night to admonish . . .

Content

Matt. 6.9–13	The Lord's Prayer.
1 Cor. 14.26	A hymn, an instruction, a revelation, a tongue . . .
Col. 3.16/Eph. 5.19	Psalms and hymns and spiritual songs.
Acts 4.25ff.	(A prayer which includes a Psalm).
1 Tim 2.1	Supplications, prayers, intercessions and thanks . . . for all men, for kings . . . and all in high positions.

In private houses

Acts 2.1	All in one place.
4.31	The place in which they were gathered together was shaken.
12.12	The house of Mary . . . where many were gathered . . . praying.

In the Temple

Luke 24.53	They were continually in the Temple blessing God.
Acts 2.46	Day by day attending the Temple and breaking bread in their houses.
3.1	Peter and John were going up to the Temple at . . . the ninth hour.
5.12	They were all together in Solomon's portico.

Night/Night and day

Matt. 25.1–13	(Wise and foolish virgins).
Mark 4.35ff.	(Stilling of the storm).
13.35	Watch . . . in the evening, or at midnight, or at cockcrow, or in the morning.
14.32ff., etc.	(Gethsemane).
14.38	Watch and pray.
Luke 2.37	(The prophetess Anna – fasting and prayer, night and day).
Luke 6.12	All night he continued in prayer to God.
9.32	(Transfiguration: they were heavy with sleep).
12.35ff.	Be awake . . . if he comes in the second or third watch.
18.7	Will not God vindicate his elect, who cry to him day and night?
Acts 12.12	(Prayer during night at house of Mary).
16.25	About midnight Paul and Silas were praying and singing hymns.
20.7ff.	(Night-time Eucharist).
26.7	Our twelve tribes . . . worship night and day.
2 Cor. 6.5	Labours, watching, hunger . . .
1 Thess. 3.10	Praying earnestly night and day.
5.6	Let us not sleep, as others do, but let us keep awake and be sober.

2 Pet. 3.10	The day of the Lord will come like a thief.
1 Tim. 5.5	She who is a real widow ... continues in supplications and prayers night and day.
Rev. 3.3	If you will not awake, I will come like a thief.
16.15	I am coming like a thief! Blessed is he who is awake.

Early hours (cockcrow?)

Mark 1.35	In the morning, a great while before day, he rose and went to a lonely place, and there he prayed.
6.48	About the fourth watch of the night he came to them, walking on the sea.

Dawn

Mark 16.2, etc.	(Resurrection).
Luke 1.78	(Benedictus): The dayspring from on high shall dawn upon us (see also 2 Pet. 1.19).
John 21.4	Just as day was breaking, Jesus stood on the beach.

Third hour

Mark 15.25	(Crucifixion).
Acts 2.15	(Pentecost).

Sixth hour

Mark 15.33, etc.	(Crucifixion: darkness until the ninth hour).
Acts 10.9	(Peter praying on the rooftop).
22.6 and 26.13	(Conversion of St Paul).

Ninth hour

Mark 15.30	Eloi, Eloi ...
Acts 3.1	Peter and John were going up to the Temple to pray.
10.30	(Cornelius the centurion prays at the ninth hour).

Sunset

Matt. 14.23	(Jesus praying alone).
Mark 14.17	(Last supper).
Luke 9.12ff.	(Feeding of 5000).
24.29	(Road to Emmaus).
John 20.19	(Resurrection appearance).

Lamps

Matt. 25.1–13	(Wise and foolish virgins).
Luke 11.33ff.	(The lamp).
12.35	Let your loins be girt and your lamps burning.
John 8.12	I am the light of the world.

THE EARLY CENTURIES

4 Clement of Rome (from a letter written *c.* 96):
We should do in order everything that the Lord commanded us to do at set times. He has ordered oblations and services to be accomplished, and not by chance and in disorderly fashion but at the set times and hours.

5 Didache (? first century ? second century)
The Lord's Prayer should be said three times every day.

6 Clement of Alexandria (*c.* 150–*c.* 215)
M/T, S, E/N, Mn, on rising, on going to bed, mealtimes.[a]
Psalms and readings at mealtimes and evening.
Ephesians 5.14 is cited as part of a Christian hymn.[b]

'We are bidden to worship ... not on special days as some do, but continuously all our life through, and in all possible ways ... Wherefore it is neither in a definite place nor special shrine, nor yet on certain feasts and days set apart, that the gnostic honours God ... but he will do this all his life in every place, whether he be alone by himself or have with him some who share his belief ... Accordingly all our life is a festival: being persuaded that God is everywhere present on all sides, we praise him as we till the ground, we sing hymns as we sail the sea, we feel his inspiration in all that we do.'[c]

'If there are any who assign fixed hours to prayer, such as the third, sixth and ninth hour, yet the gnostic at all events prays all his life through.'[d]

7 Origen (Alexandria, *c.* 185–*c.* 254)
M/T, S, E/N, Mn.[a]

'Thus alone can we accept prayer without ceasing as a practicable saying, if we speak of the whole life of the saint as one great unbroken prayer: of which that which is commonly called prayer is a part. This ought to be engaged in not less than three times every day, as is clear from the case of Daniel ...'[a]

'... if our business does not allow us to withdraw and offer the prayer that is due, it is permitted to pray without even seeming to do so ... in order that he may perform the act of prayer in quiet without distraction, each one can select in his own house, if possible, a place set apart, of a sacred character ... There is a place of prayer which has charm as well as usefulness, the spot where believers come together in one place, and, it may be, angelic powers also stand by the gatherings of believers, and the power of the Lord and Saviour himself, and holy spirits as well, those who have fallen asleep before us, as I think, and clearly also those who are still in this life, although 'how' it is not easy to answer ... we must not despise the prayers that are made there, since they have a singular value for him who joins genuinely in common worship ... the superiority of the place where the saints meet when they assemble devoutly together in church.'[b]

'We ... affirm, and have learned by experience, that they who worship the God of all things in conformity with the Christianity which comes by Jesus, and who live according to his gospel, using night and day, continuously and becomingly, the prescribed prayers, are not carried away either by magic or demons.'[c]

8 Tertullian (Carthage, *c.* 160–*c.* 225)

No fixed prescription, but recommended are: M, T, S, N, E, Mn, and mealtimes.*

'We have the right, after rehearsing the prescribed and regular prayer as a foundation, to make from other sources a superstructure of petitions and additional desires.'*b*

'Concerning times of prayer, no rules at all have been laid down, except of course to pray at every time and place ... But concerning time, we shall not find superfluous the observance from extraneous sources of certain hours also – I mean those common ones which mark the periods of the day, the third, sixth and ninth hours ... Although these hours simply exist without any command for their observance, it is still good to establish a presumption that might reinforce the admonition to pray, and tear us away from our affairs for this duty as if by law, so that we might worship not less than three times per day ... in addition of course to our statutory prayers which without any behest are due at the coming in of daylight and night.'*c*

'The more conscientious in prayer are accustomed to append to their prayers Alleluia and such manner of psalms, so that those who are present may respond with the endings of them ... So let us never proceed unarmed: by day let us remember the station, by night the vigil. Beneath the armour of prayer let us guard our Emperor's standard.'*d*

Should include prayer for emperors, their ministers, all in authority, the welfare of the world, the prevalence of peace, and the delay of the final consummation.*e*

Husband and wife should sing psalms to each other.*f*

9 Cyprian (Carthage, *d.* 258)

M, T, S, N, E, Mn.*a*

Prayer and Psalms also at mealtimes.*b*

'Before all things the teacher of peace and master of unity would not have prayer to be made singly and individually; so when someone prays he does not pray for himself alone. For we say not "My Father which art in Heaven," nor "Give me this day my daily bread"; nor does each one ask that only his debt be forgiven him ... Our prayer is public and common; and when we pray we pray not for one, but for the whole people, because we the whole people are one ... This law of prayer the three children observed when they were shut up in the fiery furnace, speaking together in prayer, and being of one heart in the agreement of the spirit ... they spoke as if from one mouth.'*c*

10 Hippolytus (Rome, early third century)

Most information on hours of prayer is in the section whose authenticity is disputed.

M, T, S, N, E (agape?), C, Mn, Cc.

If not at home at these hours, the Christian should pray to God in his heart. Most of these prayer-times seem to be domestic, except that M can be replaced by a teaching-session.

The agape begins with the lucernarium.

11 Eusebius (Caesarea, Palestine, *c.* 260–*c.* 340)

First person to mention explicitly the public celebration of the daily office.

'Throughout the world in the churches of God in the morning, at sunrise and in the evening, hymns, praises and truly divine pleasures are constituted to God. The hymns which everywhere in the world are offered in his Church at the morning and evening hours are a pleasure to God. Therefore it is said ... "the lifting up of my hands is an evening sacrifice..." '[a] (Written between 327 and 340)

'The practice of singing psalms in the name of the Lord is observed everywhere; for this commandment to sing psalmody is in force in all the churches existing among the peoples, not only the Greeks, but also among the barbarians ... In the whole world, in towns and villages as well as in the fields, in a word, in all the Church, the peoples of Christ gathered in all the nations sing with a loud voice hymns and psalms to the only God announced by the prophets, in such a manner that the voice of the psalm-singers is heard by those outside.'[b]

'The Emperor Constantine himself, as a sharer in the holy mysteries of our religion, would seclude himself daily at stated hours in the innermost chambers of his palace, and there, in solitary converse with God, would kneel in humble supplication, and entreat the blessings of which he stood in need.'[c]

A canon of psalms attributed to Eusebius prescribes twenty-four psalms, one to be said at each hour of the day and night. Elsewhere it gives for the morning Psalms 63, 141 and 142, and for the evening the 'lucernarium Psalms' (*psalmoi lychnikoi*) 130, 141 and 13 (or 113).[d]

12   John Chrysostom (Antioch and Constantinople, c. 347–407)

Chrysostom writes about both Antioch and Constantinople, monastic and people's offices. It is difficult to separate out these different strands, but the general picture is consistent:[a]

Mn	M	T, S, N (monastic)	E
Ps. 134	Hymns, incl. Ps. 63	Psalms and	Psalms
Isa. 26.9ff.	Gloria in excelsis	hymns[d]	Ps. 141
Variable psalmody	Dismissal of		Dismissal of
(Apparently) Pss.	catechumens		catechumens
148–150[b]	Prayers of the		Prayers of the
	faithful[c]		faithful[c]

The prayers of the faithful include supplication for the bishop, those present, all people, the whole world, the Church, kings and those in authority (not necessarily in that order).[f]

He frequently encourages people to attend all the offices daily, or, failing that, to pray at home. They should get up (children included) for the night prayers.[g]

People should attend all the offices regularly because: 'Just as, in preparing a meal, when we make a drink, so if warm water goes cold, we warm it by bringing it over to the fire ... You say, "How is it possible for a secular man detained in the tribunal to pray at the three hours of the day and run to church?" It is possible, and it is very easy. For even if it is not easy to run to church, it is possible to pray standing there while still detained in the courtroom.' He seems to have had difficulty persuading people that it was possible to pray without using their voice.[h]

'Where there is a psalm, a prayer, a choir of prophets, a faithful band of singers, one would not be wrong in saying that there is the Church.'[i]

13 Apostolic Constitutions (? Syria, ? fourth century)

This may have been compiled from various sources and presents the following picture:[a]

M	T, S, N	E	Cc on Sundays
Ps. 63	(private)	Ps. 141, 'of the	Includes gospel of
Prayer for catechumens, etc.		lucernarium'	resurrection and
Dismissal of catechumens, etc.		Prayer, etc.	three psalms
Prayers		Dismissal, etc.	
Solemn morning prayer		Prayers	
Deacon: 'Bow for the imposition		Solemn evening prayer	
of hands'		'Bow...'	
Blessing		Blessing	
Dismissal		Dismissal	

Gloria in excelsis given for morning prayer, and a prayer including Te Decet Laus and Nunc Dimittis for evenings.[b]

'If because of unbelievers it is impossible to go to the church, meet as you can in a house – let no pious person enter the church of the impious ... If you are unable to meet either in the church or a house, let each individual sing, read and pray by himself, or together with two or three ... When evening comes, gather the Church, O bishop, and when you have said the lucernarium Psalm, let the deacon recite the prayers for the catechumens, energumens, competents and penitents ...'[c]

14 Basil (Cappadocia, c. 330–79)

Basilian monastic communities were closely involved with the local community, and the offices he refers to were therefore of a mixed type. His references to the offices are only fragmentary:[a]

Mn	M	T	S	N	E	C
Prayers	Ps. 51		Ps. 91		Lucernarium	Incl.
Antiphonal psalmody	Hymns and		Also Ps. 55?		Phos hilaron, etc.	Ps. 91
Responsorial psalmody,	canticles				Homily at	
etc., each psalm ending					weekends	
with a prayer					? Litany	

Speaks of the hymn 'Hail, gladdening light' (Phos hilaron), which the people sing when the lamps are lit, as an ancient hymn.[b]

15 Gregory of Nyssa (Cappadocia, c. 330–c. 95)

(Describing the death of St Macrina):

... But the voice of the choir was summoning us to the evening service and, sending me to church, the great one retired once more to God in prayer. And thus she spent the night ...

... As she said these words she sealed her eyes and mouth and heart with the cross. And gradually her tongue dried up with the fever, she could articulate her words no longer, and her voice died away, and only by the trembling of her lips and the motion of her hands did we recognize that she was praying.

Meanwhile evening had come and a lamp was brought in. All at once she opened the orb of her eyes and looked towards the light, clearly wanting to repeat the thanksgiving sung at the lighting of the lamps. But her voice failed and she fulfilled her intention in the heart and by moving her hands, while her lips stirred in sympathy with her inward desire. But when she had finished the thanksgiving, and her hand brought to her face to make the sign had signified the end of the prayer, she drew a great deep breath and closed her life and her prayer together.

THE OFFICE IN THE EAST

16   Egeria (visit to Jerusalem, *c.* 380)
Cc, M, S, N, E (no S and N on Sundays)

M
Morning hymns;
Arrival of bishop and clergy;
'The prayer for all' (inside screen);
Commemoration of names *ad lib.*;
Blessing of catechumens;
Prayer;
Blessing of faithful;
All come to bishop's hand.

S and N
Psalms and antiphons while bishop is
   sent for;
Bishop enters;
Recites prayer (inside screen);
Blessing of faithful;
All come to bishop's hand.

E
Lucernare Psalms and antiphons;
Bishop sent for;
He enters, and he and presbyters sit;
Hymns and antiphons;
Bishop stands in front of screen;
Deacon commemorates individuals
   (choir's response: *Kyrie eleison*);
Bishop recites prayer;
Deacon bids catechumens stand and bow
   heads;
Bishop blesses them;
Deacon bids faithful stand and bow heads;
Bishop blesses them;
Individuals come to his hand.

Station at the cross:
Bishop is then led to the cross with hymns;
People follow.
Prayer,
Blessing of catechumens,
Prayer,
Blessing of faithful.
All go behind cross;
Above blessings and prayers repeated.
All come to bishop's hand.

Sunday vigil
All gather outside ('as if it were Easter');
Hymns and antiphons, each ending with
   a prayer;
Cock crows – Bishop enters cave;
Doors open;
All enter;
Three responsorial psalms with prayers;
Commemoration of all;
Offering of incense;
Gospel of resurrection;
Procession to the cross;
One Psalm with a prayer;
Blessing and dismissal;
All come to bishop's hand.

'Monazontes' return to church;
Psalms and antiphons until daybreak.

Lent – Friday-night vigil
Responsorial psalms;
Antiphons;
Readings.

(Alternating throughout the night until
   morning)

17   East-Syrian

VESPERS

PRELIMINARY PSALMODY	Glory to God in the highest (three times). And on earth peace and a good hope to men at all times and for ever. Amen. Kiss of peace. Farced Lord's Prayer. Prayer. First Marmita (usually three Psalms in course). Second Marmita (usually three Psalms in course).	
PEOPLE'S VESPERS	Laku Mara (Hymn to Christ). First Shuraya (about six Psalm-verses with Alleluias). First Anthem (strophes reflecting on Shuraya). Psalms 141, 142, 119.105–12, and 117. Second Shuraya. Second Anthem. Triple Litany. Trisagion. Prayer. Prayer of Inclination.	*Veil opened.* *Procession with light and* *incense* *Cross and Gospels placed on* bema, *where entire service is* *celebrated* *Veil closed*
STATION	Evening anthem (Sundays and feast-days: 'Basalike' procession). Psalm-verses. Farced Lord's Prayer. Martyrs' anthem. (Not Sundays and feast-days). Each priest present says a prayer. Three prayers: of Mary, the Apostles, the patron saints. Blessing with the cross. Kiss of peace. Nicene Creed.	*Procession to Martyr's tomb*

MATTINS

FESTAL VIGIL (Sundays only)	Glory, etc. (as vespers). Farced Lord's Prayer. Prayers. Psalmody. Anthem. Variable psalm (refrain: 'Glory to you, O God'). Hymn of praise. Litany.	*At* bema *All sit. Procession from* bema *to altar* *All stand*
PEOPLE'S MATTINS	Two collects. Psalms: 100, 91, 104.1–15, 113. Psalm 93. Pss. 148–150 and 117.	*(SF: at Ps. 113, lamps lit,* *procession to* bema)

Hymn with incense. (Laku Mara) Psalm 51. Hymn of penitence	} ferias	Anthem with incense Hymn of light Benedicite Gloria in excelsis	} SF

Trisagion.
Prayer of Inclination.

STATION   Martyrs' anthem.
Each priest says a prayer.
Three prayers (as vespers).
Blessing with cross.
Kiss of peace.
Nicene Creed.

EXAMPLES:

(a) Lord's Prayer

All: 'Our Father who are in heaven, hallowed be your name, your kingdom come, Holy, Holy, Holy are you, our Father who are in heaven, heaven and earth are full of the greatness of your glory.

The angels and men cry to you holy, holy, holy, are you,

Our Father who are in heaven hallowed be your name, your kingdom come, your will be done on earth, as it is in heaven.

Give us this day the bread that we need, forgive us our debts and sins as we have forgiven our debtors, lead us not into temptation but deliver us from the evil one, for yours is the kingdom and the power and the glory, for ever and ever – Amen.'

President: 'Glory be to the Father and to the Son and to the Holy Ghost,'

Answer: 'From everlasting unto everlasting amen and amen' – 'Our Father ...' (as above up to holy, holy, holy are you).

(b) Laku Mara

'We give thanks to you, Lord of all and we glorify you Jesus Christ, for you are he who raises up our bodies and you are the Saviour of our souls.'

This hymn 'Laku Mara' is repeated 3 or 5 times but the first time without a psalm verse. Here are the psalm verses of Laku Mara:

ON SUNDAYS AND MEMORIALS	ON THE FEASTS OF OUR LORD
1 'I rejoiced when they told me we are going to the house of the Lord' (Ps. 122.1)	1 'I was glad while they were saying'. 2 'That we are going to the house of the Lord'.
2 'Gloria Patri...' and 'A Saeculo...'	3 'Gloria Patri...' 4 'A Saeculo...'

The hymn 'Laku Mara' is concluded by a prayer:

'You O Lord are truly he who raises up our bodies, the good saviour of our souls and the constant preserver of our life and (O Lord) we are bound to thank, adore and glorify you at all times, Lord of all, for ever – Amen.'

(c) Trisagion, Prayer and Prayer of Inclination
Now the deacon, who recited the litany, invites the people to sing the trisagion: 'raise your voices all you people and glorify the living God'. All sing loudly:

'Holy God, holy Almighty one, holy immortal one have mercy on us'
'Gloria Patri...'   Holy God...
'A Saeculo'   Holy God...
'Let us Pray, peace be with us'; then follows the oration after trisagion.

ON SUNDAYS AND FEASTS	ON MEMORIALS
'O holy one who are by nature holy and glorious in your Being and high and exalted above all by your divinity, a nature holy and blessed for ever, we confess, adore and praise you at all times Lord of all Father, Son and H. Ghost – Amen.'	'O holy, glorious, powerful and immortal one, who dwell in the saints and whose will finds its pleasure in them we beseech you, turn my Lord and have mercy on us as it is customary to you at all times, Lord of all Father, Son and H. Ghost for ever – Amen.'

The prayer of Inclination:
At the end of the above quoted prayer the deacon says loudly:

'Bless my lord – Bow your heads for the laying of hands and receive the blessing.'

The president then blesses the deacon:

'May Christ glorify (give fruit to or make shine) your service in the kingdom of heaven'. And then turning to the people, continues: 'And as our souls are perfected by one perfect faith in your glorious Trinity, may we all in one unity of love be worthy to raise to you glory, honour, praise and adoration at all times, Lord of all, Father, Son and H. Ghost for ever – Amen.'

(d) Blessing with the cross
PRIEST: 'Glory to you, Jesus our conquering king, the brightness of the eternal Father, begotten without beginning before all times and things which came into being, we have no hope and expectation unless it be in you the creator. By the prayer of the just and elect who have been approved by you from the beginning, pardon our sins and forgive our offences, deliver us from our afflictions, answer our requests and bring us to the glorious light, and deliver us by thy living sign from all harm, hidden and open, Christ the hope of our nature now and at all times and for ever – Amen.'
PEOPLE: 'May Christ hear your prayer. May Christ make your priesthood glorious in the kingdom of heaven.'

(e) Synagogue service (ninth century)
The Sabbath morning service in the oldest extant Jewish prayer book (ninth century) opens with the following Psalms: 91, 100, 104 (part), 113 (part), 93, 145–150, 29, 92, 34, 90, 135 and 136. Cf. Mattins above.

18   The Old Byzantine people's office

VESPERS

PRELIMINARY	1 'Blessed be the Kingdom ...'
PSALMODY	2 Litany
In narthex	3 Eight Antiphons: (1) Psalm 86
	(2)–(7) Variable psalmody
	(8) Psalm 141 *Doors open. All enter nave*

EVENING	4 Prokeimenon (responsory)
HYMNS	5 Litany
At ambo in	6 Three 'Little Antiphons' (Pss. 115–117)
middle of nave	7 (On festivals: the Lessons)

THE PRAYERS	8 (Litany of Catechumens on certain days, especially in Lent)
At sanctuary	9 Litany of the Faithful
	10 Final prayers
	11 Prayer of Inclination

STATION	12 (In some places: procession to stations at relic-house and baptistery)

MATTINS

PRELIMINARY	1 'Blessed ...'
PSALMODY	2 Litany
In narthex	3 Eight Antiphons: (1) Psalms 3, 63 and 134
	(2)–(7) Variable psalmody
	(8) Benedicite *Doors open. All enter nave*

MORNING	4 Litany
HYMNS	5 Psalm 51
At ambo in	6 Psalms 148–150
middle of nave	7 Benedictus (and Nunc Dimittis on Saturdays)
	8 Gloria in excelsis
	9 Trisagion
	10 (Sundays: Prokeimenon and resurrection gospel)

THE PRAYERS	11 (Litany of Catechumens, on certain days, especially in Lent)
At sanctuary	12 Litany of the Faithful
	13 Final prayers
	14 Prayer of Inclination

Note: Surviving documents, while agreeing in most details, witness to such a wide variety of usage that it is not possible to map out a completely standard scheme. The one given here, however, is typical

19   Byzantine

VESPERS

Origin:		
PRELIMINARY PSALMODY	1 'Blessed be our God at all times, now and for ever and unto ages of ages. Amen.' 'Come, let us worship . . .' (3 times)	*(SF: Censing)*
	2 Psalm 104	*3 venerations by all. During Ps. 104 priest reads 7 secret prayers, standing before doors with head uncovered*
	3 Great Litany	
	4 Kathisma of Psalter (not on Sundays)	
	5 Little Litany	
PEOPLE'S VESPERS	6 Psalms 141, 142, 130 and 117 with strophes	*Censing. Priest robes, doors opened, lamps lit (SF: Entrance procession). 2 candles are stood before the royal doors*
	7 (SF: Processional hymn to the B.V.M.)	
	8 Phos hilaron	
	9 Prokeimenon (Responsory)	
	10 (On certain days, and in Lent: the Lessons)	
	11 Litany	*(SF: Litany augmented with no. 18)*
	12 Prayer of Inclination	
FURTHER PRAYERS	13 Aposticha (Psalm-verses and strophes)	
	14 Nunc Dimittis	
	15 Trisagion	
	16 Lord's Prayer	
	17 Apolytikion (Troparion [hymn] of the day)	
	18 Litany (ferias only)	*(SF: Blessing of bread, wine and oil)*
	19 Versicles	
	20 Blessing and Dismissal	

MATTINS

ROYAL OFFICE (Omitted when vespers and mattins are joined together)	1 'Blessed . . .' 'O Come . . .' (3 times)	
	2 Psalms 20 and 21	
	3 Trisagion and Lord's Prayer	
	4 Prayers for the rulers and church authorities	*Censing*
	5 Litany for the authorities	
MONASTIC VIGIL	6 Glory to God in the highest . . . towards men. (3 times) O Lord, open my lips . . . (2 times)	
	7 Hexapsalmos: Psalms 3, 38, 63. Psalms 88, 103, 143.	*Hexapsalmos read by reader in nave. During 2nd trio of Psalms: 12 secret prayers are read by priest; nos. 4 to 12 are read before royal doors with head uncovered.*
	8 Great Litany	
	9 Isaiah 26.9, 11, 15 (SF: verses from Ps. 118)	
	10 Trinitarian hymn (SF: Apolytikion, as no. 30)	
	11 1st Kathisma of Psalter and hymn 2nd Kathisma of Psalter and hymn (3rd in winter)	

PEOPLE'S FESTAL VIGIL (Omitted on ferias)	12 Polieley (verses from Pss. 135 and 136) or sometimes Ps. 119	*Usually only a few verses.* *Censing. Priest robes, doors opened, lamps lit.*
	13 Evlogitaria (Resurrection responsory)	
	14 Little Litany	
	15 Hymn	
	16 Anabathmoi (short hymn based on Pss. 120–134)	
	17 Prokeimenon (responsory)	
	18 Gospel of resurrection	*(SF: Gospels enthroned in centre of church veneration of Gospels and distribution of bread)*
	19 Resurrection hymn	
PEOPLE'S MORNING OFFICE	20 Psalm 51	
	21 (SF: Solemn prayer)	
	22 Canon of the day:	*Censing.*
	Odes 1 to 3, Little Litany, hymn.	*Ode no. 9 is Magnificat and Benedictus (the latter is usually omitted)*
	Odes 4 to 6, Little Litany, hymn.	
	Odes 7 to 9, Little litany, and:	
	23 Exapostilarion and Pss. 148–150	
	24 Gloria in excelsis	
	(SF: Resurrection hymn	
	Gloria in excelsis	
	Trisagion	
	Apolytikion (as no. 10)	
	Litany no. 31)	
	25 Litany	
	26 Prayer of Inclination	
FURTHER PRAYERS (Ferias only)	27 Aposticha (Psalm-verses and strophes)	
	28 Trisagion	
	29 Lord's Prayer	
	30 Apolytikion (Troparion [hymn] of the day)	
	31 Litany	
CONCLUSION	32 Blessing and Dismissal	

Note: The word 'hymn' has been used here to denote any poetic material, and should not be simply understood in the Western sense of the term.

THE PEOPLE'S OFFICE IN THE WEST

20   Clement of Rome (see 4)

21   Hippolytus (see 10)

22   Egeria (Gaul or Spain, *c.* 380. See 16)
. . . called by us *Lucernarium.*

23 Ambrose (Milan, *c.* 339–97)

M	*S*	*E*
Hymns, canticles, psalms	'On very many days'	'Hour of incense'
Beatitudes	'Hymns'	'Evening sacrifice'[c]
Benedicite[a]	Eucharist[b]	

Metrical hymns were used.[d] He makes many references to the hours of prayer either at home or in church.

The psalm is our 'armour by night, and teacher by day . . . The dawn of day resounds with the psalm, and with the psalm re-echoes the sunset.'[e].

'Let our mind be ever with Christ; let it never depart from his temple, from his word. Let it be ever engaged in reading the Scriptures, in meditations, in prayers, that the Word of God may always operate in us, and that, daily proceeding into the church, or addressing ourselves to domestic prayers, we may begin with him and end with him.'[f]

'Certainly our solemn prayers ought to be said with giving of thanks, when we rise from sleep, when we go forth, when we prepare to receive food, after receiving it, and at the hour of the incense, when at last we are going to rest. And again in your bedchamber itself, I would have you join psalms in frequent interchange with the Lord's Prayer, either when you wake up, or before sleep bedews your body.'[g]

There were special all-night vigils before festal days, which included psalms, readings, and, sometimes, a sermon.[h]

24 Jerome (Italy and Palestine, *c.* 342–420)

M, T, S, N, E, Mn[a]

'Prayers, as everyone knows, ought to be said at the third, sixth, and ninth hours, at dawn, and at evenings. No meal should be begun without prayer, and before leaving the table thanks should be returned to the Creator. We should rise two or three times in the night and turn over (*revolvenda*) the parts of Scripture which we know by heart.'[b]

Laeta 'ought to rise at night to recite prayers and psalms; to sing hymns in the morning; at the third, sixth, and ninth hours to take her place in the line to do battle for Christ; and lastly to kindle her lamp and to offer the evening sacrifice. So let the day be passed, and so let the night find her at her labours. Let reading follow prayer, and prayer again follow reading.'[c]

Speaks of the 'rule of psalmody and prayer which you must always observe at the third, sixth, and ninth hours, at evening and in the morning.'[d]

An effort should be made to attend the all-night vigils on the eve of feasts.[e]

25 Niceta (Remesiana, present-day Yugoslavia, *c.* 370–414)

Describes Saturday and Sunday vigils consisting of prayers, 'hymns' and 'readings'. He gives a list of nine canticles which were in use in his diocese, apparently the following:

Exod. 15.1	Isa. 26.9	Lam. 5.1
Deut. 32.1	Habakkuk 3	Dan. 3.57 (Benedicite)
1 Sam. 2.1	Jonah 2.3	Luke 1.46 (Magnificat)

26 Cassian (*c.* 360–435)
In Gaul and Italy:

M	T, S, N,	E
Ps. 51 (Gaul)		'The eleventh hour,
Ps. 63		by which the hour
Pss. 148–150		of the lucernarium
Ps. 51 (Italy)		is denoted.'

27 Arnobius Junior (North Africa, fifth century)
On Psalm 148: 'In all the world, by the daily sound of this psalm we call everything in heaven and earth to praise and bless God.'

28 Augustine (Hippo, North Africa, 354–430)
His mother omitted 'on no day the oblation at your altar, coming to your church twice a day, morning and evening, without any intermission, not for idle stories and useless chit-chat, but to hear you in your discourses, and that you might hear her in her prayers.'[a]

... 'he thought to himself and said, "I will rise daily, I will go to church, I will say one hymn in the morning and another in the evening, and third or fourth in my house; daily I offer the sacrifice of praise, and immolate to my God." You do indeed do well if you do this. But take heed lest you become careless ... take care lest you chant well, but live ill.'[b]

(On the Lord giving and the Lord taking away in good times and bad:) [in winter] the ant falls back on what she has gathered in summer; and within her secret store, where no man sees, she is replenished from her summer toils. When during the summer she was gathering these stores for herself, everyone could see her: when she feeds on them in winter, no one sees. What is this? See the ant of God – he rises day by day, hastens to the church of God, and hears a reading and sings a hymn, and ruminates on what he has heard. By himself he thinks on it, and stores within the grains gathered from the threshing-floor. They who providently hear those very things which even now are being spoken of, do like this, and are seen by all to go to church and come back from church, to hear a sermon, to hear a reading, to choose a book, to open and read it, all these things are seen when they are done.'[c]

29 The fifth to the seventh centuries
(a) *Council of Toledo 1 (400)*
Every priest, deacon and cleric must attend the offices daily. A virgin dedicated to God, or a widow, may not, in the absence of a bishop or priest, sing the antiphons at home with her servant or cantor. The lucernarium may only be celebrated in church; if it is celebrated at home, a bishop, priest or deacon must be present.

(b) *Council of Vannes (465)*
Clergy who live within the city walls and are discovered absent from mattins without good excuse are to be excommunicated for seven days. The order of the daily office and its psalmody are to be uniform throughout the province.

(c) Council of Agde (506)
(Under Caesarius, Bishop of Arles). The morning and evening hymns are to be sung every day and in a uniform manner.

Mattins	Vespers
Antiphons (With collect after each, recited in order by bishops or priests)	Antiphons (as at mattins)
The Morning Hymns	The Evening Hymns
Capitella (see page 170)	Capitella
Collect	Collect
(? Prayer of Inclination)	Prayer of Inclination (by the bishop)

Compare this with Mozarabic mattins (30), where the 'morning hymns' are the Benedicite and Psalms 148–150. Compare also with local monastic usage at mattins and lucernarium (44). There was also a daily vigil service immediately preceding mattins, but this was poorly attended. Special efforts were made to encourage attendance at it in Advent and Lent.

(d) Council of Tarragona (516)
'Priests and deacons of country churches are to keep weeks with the lesser clerics, i.e. in one week the priest, in the other the deacon, with the condition that on Saturdays all clerics must appear at vespers, so that the solemnity of the Lord's Day may be celebrated with all present. Mattins and vespers are to be celebrated every day, as when clergy fail to do this, basilicas have been discovered where not even the lamplighting is administered.' (nec luminaria ministrari)

(e) Council of Gerona (517)
The whole province must follow the usage of the Metropolis; The Lord's Prayer is to be added to the end of mattins and vespers, and the priest is to recite it aloud.

(f) Council of Vaison 2 (529)
In favour of Roman usage. All priests in parishes must, as is already the custom in Italy, receive the young unmarried lectors into their house, to instruct them in the psalms, lessons, and the law of the Lord, that they may have able successors. If such a lector decides to marry, he must be permitted. If the priest is hindered from preaching, a deacon should read a homily by a Father of the Church. As in Rome, all the east and Italy, so also here Kyrie eleison must be frequently sung, with great feeling and compunction, at mattins, mass and vespers. As in Rome, all the East, Africa and Italy, on account of the [Arians] . . . As it was in the beginning is to be added to the Gloria.

(g) Fulgentius, Bishop of Ruspe (N. Africa, c. 530)
Everyone is to attend the daily vigils, as well as mattins and vespers.

(h) Mid-sixth-century Rome
Bishops at their consecration have to promise to 'celebrate the vigils every day in church, from the first cockcrow until the morning, with every order of my clergy'.

(i) Council of Braga (563)
Pro-Roman. At mattins and vespers the same psalmody is to be used throughout the region, without adding monastic usages. Hymns are forbidden. The same lessons are to be read everywhere at festal vigils.

(j) *Council of Toledo 4 (633)*

Sought to undo the work of Romanizing Council of Braga. Liturgical uniformity for the whole of Spain and Narbonne. Some Spanish clerics omit the Lord's Prayer on weekdays. Any who persist in this are to be deposed. Hymns are permitted. The Song of the Three Children is to be sung daily. Instead of *Glory be to the Father* ..., which some use, *Glory and honour to the Father* ... shall be used. If a chant is joyful, the Gloria is added; if it is sad, the beginning is to be repeated.

(k) *Council of Toledo 8 (653)*

Clergy are to learn the Psalter, canticles, hymns and the order of baptism by heart.

(l) *Council of Merida (666)*

At festal vespers, immediately after the oblation of the light and the singing of the *vespertinum*, the *sonus* shall be sung (30). All Clergy must have a group of clerics, according to the parish's means, with whom to offer the praise of Almighty God.

(m) *Council of Toledo 11 (675)*

All clerics must read Scripture diligently. Worship must everywhere be held as in the Metropolis. Only monastic houses may have some special uses with the bishop's permission. The monastic forms of mattins and vespers are suppressed, and all monasteries must use the cathedral form for those two offices.

30   Mozarabic

VESPERS

'In the name of our Lord Jesus Christ, light with peace – Thanks be to God.'

†Lucernarium
  Collect
†Sono
†Antifona
†Collect
†Lauda
†Hymn
†Supplication
†Collect
  Lord's Prayer
  Prayer of Inclination

MATTINS

Introduction as at vespers
Hymn
Collect
Psalm 3 with ant. (Sundays also Pss. 51 and 57)
Collect

†Antifona ⎤
†Collect   ⎥
†Antifona ⎥ 'MISSA' – several missae
†Collect   ⎥ on great feasts
†Antifona ⎥
†Collect   ⎦

†Responsory
†Collect
†Canticle with ant.
  Benedicite
†Sono
  Pss. 148–150
†[OT Lesson]
†Hymn
†Supplication
†Final collect
  Lord's Prayer
  Prayer of Inclination

† = Variable

EXAMPLES:[a] (for third Sunday after Pentecost)

LUCERNARIUM
With you, Lord, is the fount of life: and in your light R︮ We see light. V︮ The sons of
men have hoped in the protection of your wings: and were satisfied with the riches of
your house, and you gave them to drink of the torrent of your pleasure. R︮ We see ...

COLLECT
O Lord with whom is the fount of life, and in whose light we see light: raise up in us
the splendour of your knowledge, that when we are thirsty you may give us living
water, and restore the darkness of our minds with your heavenly light. Amen.

SONO
The darkness is not dark to you, R︮ and the night is as clear as the day, Alleluia.
V︮ Your eyes saw my imperfections, all of them were written in your book: they were
fashioned day by day. Alleluia. R︮ And the night ...

ANTIFONA
Your throne, O God, is inestimable, and your glory incomprehensible: before whom
all the army of angels stands in trembling. R︮ Whose appearance dried up the abyss,
and whose anger causes the mountains to melt. V︮ Lord God of strength, who is
like you? You are mighty, O Lord, and yours are the ways of truth. R︮ Whose
appearance ...

LAUDA
You are just, O Lord: Alleluia. R︮ Righteous are your judgements, Alleluia. V︮ Your
Word endures O Lord for ever in the heavens. Alleluia, alleluia. R︮ Righteous are ...
V︮ Glory be ... R︮ Righteous are ...

SUPPLICATION
Let us pray to the redeemer of the world: our Lord Jesus Christ; with all supplication
let us pray: that he may increase the faith of his Holy Catholic Church, and grant it
peace and protection.
R︮ Grant this, O God almighty and eternal. 3 Kyries.

The Mozarabic office has close affinities with the Ambrosian use, and also with the
liturgies of the East, where the Goths who occupied Spain in the fifth and sixth
centuries had received their Christianity. This office seems to have evolved between
the fifth and seventh centuries, and thereafter remained unaltered in essentials. It
brings together in a combined muddle a monastic office of twelve daily services, and a
people's office comprising solely mattins and vespers. It was used by the whole Spanish
church until the end of the eleventh century, at which time the secular rulers imposed
the Roman usage on the whole country. The old rite continued in use here and there,
however, until interest revived in the fifteenth century. The Bishop of Segovia founded
a community for its celebration in 1436, and at the end of the century Archbishop
Ximenez of Toledo with the Pope's encouragement endowed a chapel in the cathedral
for its celebration in perpetuity. In 1502 he published the first printed Mozarabic
breviary.[b]

The people's offices of mattins and vespers bear little obvious resemblance to their
Roman equivalents, and make use of liturgical terminology which will be strange to
many. The small use that is made of psalmody is particularly noticeable, especially at

vespers, where the Psalter is not used at all. Also in Orthodoxy, particularly in the Slav use, psalmody is frequently reduced to a few verses, often interspersed with refrains, and so becoming in effect short responsories. Here in the Mozarabic office they probably derive from antiphonal and responsorial psalms. During the lucernarium a candle used to be held aloft. The *supplication* is all that is left of the litany. Its petitions vary with the calendar.

The first part of mattins is probably ancient: a monastic-type vigil, but assumed into this office at an early stage. As in many other traditions, the psalmody is followed by canticles, and the heart of the people's mattins probably starts with the Benedicite. The lesson is unusual, and does not appear in all the sources. I have followed Pinell in putting it in square brackets.[c] There seems to have been a diversity of local usages.[d] Until the end of the eleventh century the Mozarabic people's office, with characteristic usages such as the lucernarium, preserved much of its ancient vigour in the everyday life of Spain. Its beautiful texts abound in rich imagery, very much in the spirit of praise and joyful thanksgiving, but at the same time with a powerful sense of awe at the holiness of God.

31 Ambrosian

VESPERS

PEOPLE'S   †Lucernarium
VESPERS   †(Sundays: Antiphon in the Choir)
      †Hymn
      †Responsory

Sundays and ferias	*Saints' Days*
†5 Psalms*	Proper Psalm
	Pss. 134 and 117*
	Proper Psalm*

Magnificat*
(12 Kyries, sometimes)

———

STATION   †Responsory*
      †Psallendae (processional chants) with stations at the two baptisteries*
      Blessing

MATTINS

VIGIL   Hymn
      †Responsory (= invitatory)
      Benedictus es (Daniel 3.28ff.)

Weekdays	*Saturdays*	*SF*
†Pss. 1 to 109	Exodus 15.1–19*	Isaiah 26.9–20*
in 10 groups,	Psalm 119 (half	1 Sam. 2.1–10*
5 each week*	each Saturday)*	Habakkuk 3.2–19 (summer:
		Jonah 2.2–9)*

†Reading
†Responsory
†Reading
†Responsory
†Reading
Benedictus
†(SF: Antiphon at the Cross and Exodus 15.1–19*)

PEOPLE'S MORNING OFFICE	*Weekdays*	*Saturdays*	*SF*
	Psalm 51*	Psalm 118*	Benedicite*

Psalms 148–150 and 117*
†'Direct' Psalm
Gloria in excelsis*
†Hymn
12 Kyries

STATION †Responsory*
Station at baptisteries (with psallendae only on Sundays)
†Psalm verses*

Blessing

† = Variable material.
* = Accompanied either before or after by a collect or other act of prayer.

EXAMPLES of Lucernarium:*

Ordinary Sundays
℣ You, O Lord, light my lamp.
℟ O my God, illuminate my darkness.
℣ For in you shall I be delivered from temptation.
℟ O my God ...
℣ You, O Lord ...
℟ O my God ...

Ordinary ferias
℣ The Lord is my light
℟ And my salvation; whom then shall I fear?
℣ The Lord is protector of my life;
℟ And my ...
℣ The Lord is my light
℟ And my ...

Fridays in Lent
℣ Let my prayer be set forth in your sight as the incense, and the lifting up of my hands
℟ An evening sacrifice.
℣ Lord, I call to you, hear me and listen to the voice of my prayer.
℟ An evening sacrifice.
℣ Set a watch before my mouth, O Lord.
℟ An evening sacrifice.
℣ Let my prayer ...
℟ An evening sacrifice.

The Ambrosian rite of the diocese of Milan is a marvellous and too little-known example of living local liturgy. The office underwent considerable changes at the time of Charlemagne in the ninth century, and we cannot be completely clear on what it was like before that date (23). There seem originally to have been no lesser hours, but simply a morning office and an evening lucernarium, with a weekend people's vigil and occasional nocturnal vigils. How this form of office arose nobody knows for certain, but its many eastern characteristics point to direct contact between Milan and the East. There are close similarities too with the Mozarabic office (30) and with the Celtic people's office as it appears in the Antiphoner of Bangor.[b] The Ambrosian rite itself had wide influence in the middle ages, and there were other, closely related rites, such as that of Augsburg, which had close affinities with the Ambrosian, and continued in use until 1584.[c]

Vespers

Nowadays the lucernarium is only accompanied by a light-ritual on Sundays and feasts, and employs a portable oil-lamp rather than a candle. On certain feasts the Archbishop presides, vested in a chasuble. A large number of the lucernarium texts not unnaturally reflect the theme of light. The one prescribed for Fridays in Lent, on the other hand, is based on Psalm 141, and may perhaps indicate that this psalm was originally used in full at this point. The five variable psalms are latecomers. The Magnificat, too, still omitted at certain times, is a borrowing from the Roman office. The twelve Kyries are the remnant of a concluding litany, and the procession to the baptisteries here and at the end of mattins has relatives in many rites of East and West, and no doubt an ancestor in the comparable procession in Egeria's Jerusalem.[d] (16)

Mattins

The opening section of mattins, with its psalmody and readings, is originally a people's festal vigil, extended later to all the days of the week, and rather clumsily adapted to accord with Roman usage in the process. On Sundays it retains the form of a resurrection vigil, whose gospel of the resurrection has been replaced by the gospel of the day in the Roman fashion.[e] This ends with an antiphon at the cross, occasionally preceded by an antiphon before the cross, which exactly parallels the procession to Golgotha in Egeria's Jerusalem, with stations before and behind the cross.[f] This procession evolved into an elaborate ceremony involving processional crosses with candles fixed to their extremities.[g] On Saturdays, the use of the Exodus canticle with Psalm 119 is Jewish – both are still read together today in the synagogue Sabbath service.[h] On Sundays this canticle follows the antiphon at the cross, accompanied by a kind of lucernarium. A large candle, called *columna* (probably representing the pillar of fire in the wilderness), is lit, together with twelve candles in choir, from the flame on top of the processional cross.[i] Mattins is dominated throughout by the theme of light, in a similar way to vespers, something we meet with time and again in offices of both East and West. The *Gloria in excelsis* is slightly different from that used in the mass, and has a long versification added to it which, with some similarities of wording, is also there in Byzantine mattins and in the Antiphoner of Bangor.[j] The offices are sprinkled throughout with groups of triple *Kyrie eleisons* (see also 29f). There is frequent use too of the acclamation: 'Blessed are you, O God, Amen', and the psalms and other main pieces are frequently preceded or followed by variable collects, centring them in acts of prayer.

The Ambrosian office today

The Ambrosian liturgy is in use throughout the diocese of Milan; in 1983–4 a five-volume vernacular breviary came into use, very much richer in content than the Roman 'Liturgy of the Hours'.[k] The offices are sung daily in Milan cathedral by the canons, and solemnly with the proper ceremonies on Sundays, when the Ambrosian chant is performed by the cathedral's large resident choir. Much waits to be restored, however: the processions to the baptisteries are never performed, for example, although the texts are always recited. In parishes, public celebration is very rare. The office is simply a private breviary for clergy or small groups. A book containing the ferial office is proving successful with small groups of laity who say the office together.[1]

The Ambrosian office is an astonishing survival, yet the new breviary, despite its many excellences, has continued the process of assimilating the offices ever more closely to the Roman form. This unique living deposit of the ancient memory of the Church has yet to receive a just restoration in the light of modern scholarship, and also deserves to be much better known in the Church at large.

32   The Roman Office and its derivatives

(a) By the fifth century the great Roman basilicas had acquired communities living a quasi-monastic life. Various forms of office were in use, among which was to be found the ancestor of the medieval Roman office. Its form in the sixth century seems to have been:

Nocturns	Mattins	P, T, S, N	Vespers	Compline
Versicle,	Psalm 51,	Psalm 119	5 Psalms (from	Pss. 4, 91 and
Ps. 95,	Ps. of day,	(3 sections)	110–147),	134
12 Psalms, from	Pss. 63 and 67	Lesson,	Versicle,	Versicle,
1–109,	(1 Gloria),	Responsory,	Magnificat,	Kyrie,
Versicle,	OT Canticle,	Versicle,	Litany,	Lord's Pr.
3 lessons with 3	Pss. 148–150,	Kyrie,	Lord's Pr.?	
resp. Pss.	(1 Gloria),	Lord's Pr.		
Litany?	Versicle,			
	Benedictus,			
	Litany,			
	Lord's Pr.?			

(b) *Synod of Whitby (664)*
Britain becomes the first country in Europe to pass over completely to the Roman rite.

(c) *Synod of Cloveshoe (747)*
British clergy are to celebrate daily the seven canonical hours.

(d) *Charlemagne (from 790 onwards)*
Campaign to impose the Roman rite in Germany, France and Italy. Amalarius of Metz played a crucial role in introducing the Roman rite and its chant.

(e) *Spain (1085)*
Abolition of the Mozarabic rite in Spain, and introduction of the Roman.

(f) *Papal Chapel (eleventh to thirteenth centuries)*
The curia had made private arrangements for saying the daily office in a simple, businesslike manner, rather than attend the elaborate ceremonies of the basilicas. This papal daily office evolved in its own way, independent of the Roman churches.

1223 – The Franciscans adopt this form of daily office.
1241 – Their revision of it is taken by them all over Europe in the breviary which they used and propagated.

(g) *Quiñones breviary (1535)*

A swingeing reform of the breviary was carried out by the Franciscan Cardinal Quiñones:

Antiphons and responsories were abolished:
Psalter to be read straight through in one week;
3 Psalms to every office, including Vigil;
3 readings at Vigil (OT, NT, non-biblical);
Hymn placed at beginning of every hour;
Variations for feasts and saints' days reduced to an absolute minimum.

Though enjoying enormous success, it was suppressed in 1568.

(h) *The Anglican office (1549, 1552 and 1662)*

A drastic reform, partly inspired by Quiñones. Monastic-type recitation of the Psalter once a month, and long lessons, *lectio continua*. Partially successful in reviving the people's office tradition.

MATTINS		EVENSONG
	Sentence	
	Exhortation	
	Confession	
	Absolution	
	Lord's Prayer	
	———	
	Versicles	
	Gloria	
	Versicle	
Venite →		
	Psalms of the day	
	OT Lesson	
Te Deum or Benedicite →		← Magnificat or Psalm 98
	NT Lesson	
Benedictus or Psalm 100 →		← Nunc Dimittis or Psalm 67
	Apostles' Creed	
	Kyries	
	Short Lord's Prayer	
	Preces	
	Collect of day	
	2 collects	
	———	
	Anthem	
	Further prayers	
	The Grace	

(i) *Council of Trent (1568)*

All forms of office less than 200 years old abolished.

(j) *The seventeenth to nineteenth centuries in France and Germany*
Many local reforms, some in the vernacular, and a limited revival of the offices as public worship. Return to the Roman office in latter part of nineteenth century.

(k) *Pius X (1911)*
Complete restructuring of the Psalter and standardization of the vigil (ferial: 9 psalms and 3 lessons; Festal: 9 psalms and 9 lessons). There was some strong criticism of the dispersal of the Laudate Psalms (148–150) against ancient tradition, and of introducing variable psalmody to compline.

33   The Roman Office in its classic form

VIGIL ('Mattins')

> Pater, Ave, Creed
> O Lord, open my lips ...
> O God, make speed ...
> Gloria Patri
> Alleluia
> Psalm 95 and ant.
> Hymn

Sundays and Feasts			Weekdays
1st nocturn:	*2nd nocturn:*	*3rd nocturn:*	*Nocturn:*
12 Psalms and ants. (Feasts: 3)	3 Psalms and ants.	3 Psalms and ants.	12 Psalms and ants.
Versicle	Versicle	Versicle	Versicle
Lord's Prayer	Lord's Prayer	Lord's Prayer	Lord's Prayer
Collect	Collect	Collect	Collect
Blessing	Blessing	Blessing	Blessing
3 lessons (Bible) and responsory after each	3 lessons (Patristic or hagiographical) and responsory after each	3 lessons (Homily on a text from the day's gospel) and responsory after each	3 lessons (Bible) and responsory after each (Lauds follows)
		Te Deum	
		(Lauds follows)	

Note: The 3 readings in a nocturn usually consist of a single passage divided into 3 sections, with responsories coming in between. For example, the lessons in the first Nocturn on the Fifth Sunday after Epiphany are: 1 Tim 1.1–4; 5–11; 12–16.

MORNING OFFICE (Lauds)	PRIME
O God, make speed ...	Pater, Ave, Creed
Gloria Patri	O God, make speed ...
Alleluia	Gloria Patri
4 Psalms	Alleluia
OT Canticle	Hymn
Pss. 148–150 under one Gloria	3 Psalms
Capitulum	Athanasian Creed (Sundays)
Hymn	Capitulum
Versicle	Responsory
Benedictus and ant.	Kyrie
Kyries*	Lord's Prayer
Lord's Prayer*	Creed
Preces*	Preces
Ps. 130*	Officiant's confession
Versicles*	Community's confession
	Versicles
Collect of the day	Collect
Commemorations	Grace

PRIME (continued, 'CHAPTER OFFICE'):

- Martyrology-reading
- Versicle
- Collect
- O God, make speed ... (3 times)
- Gloria Patri
- Kyrie
- Lord's Prayer
- Versicles
- Gloria Patri
- Collect
- Blessing

MORNING OFFICE (continued):

- Commem. of the Cross*
- Marian antiphon
- Versicles
- Blessing

*=Weekdays in Lent, Ember days and vigils which are fasts.

TERCE, SEXT, NONE	VESPERS	COMPLINE
Pater, Ave	Pater, Ave	Blessing
O God, make speed ...	O God, make speed ...	Capitulum
Gloria Patri	Gloria Patri	Versicle
Alleluia	Alleluia	Lord's Prayer
Hymn	5 Psalms	Officiant's confession
6 sections of Ps. 119	Capitulum	Community's confession
Capitulum	Hymn	Versicle
Responsory	Versicle (Ps. 141.2a)	
Kyries*	Magnificat and ant.	O God, make speed ...
Lord's Prayer*	Versicle	Gloria Patri
Preces*	Kyries*	Alleluia
Collect	Lord's Prayer*	4 Psalms
Blessing	Preces*	Hymn
	Ps. 51*	Capitulum
	Preces*	Responsory
	Collect of the day	Versicle
	Commemorations	Nunc Dimittis and ant.
	Commem. of the Cross*	Kyries
	Marian antiphon	Lord's Prayer
	Versicles	Preces
	Blessing	Collect
		Blessing
		Marian antiphon

* = Weekdays in Lent, Ember days and vigils which are fasts.

LESSER OFFICES

Little office of the B.V.M.
This provides a complete range of hours, including the vigil, with a simple scheme of Psalms and readings. It was to be said on all ferial days, each office being attached to the beginning or end of the corresponding ordinary office.

Office of the dead
This consists of vigil and lauds (called 'Dirige' or 'Dirge') and vespers only. it was to be said on the first ferial day of the month, and in Advent and Lent on the first ferial day of every week.

The gradual Psalms
Psalms 120 to 134 are said in 3 groups of five, each group ending with versicles and a collect; to be said on every Wednesday in Lent.

The seven penitential Psalms
Psalms 6, 32, 38, 51, 102, 130 and 143, followed by the Litany; to be said, kneeling, every Friday in Lent. The Litany alone is said on St Mark's Day and on the three Rogation days.

PSALMODY in the Roman Daily Office

From the Middle Ages to 1911

	VIGIL	LAUDS	PRIME	TERCE	SEXT	NONE	VESPERS	COMPLINE
Sunday	1–3, 6–21	93, 100, 63, 67 Benedicite 148–150	54, 118, 119.1–32	119.33–80	119.81–128	119.129–end	110–116.9	4, 31.1–6, 91, 134
Monday	27–38	51, 5, 63, 67 Isaiah 12.1–6 148–150	54, 24 119.1–32	ditto	ditto	ditto	116.10–end, 117, 120, 121	ditto
Tuesday	39–42, 44–50, 52	51, 43, 63, 67 Isa. 38.10–20 148–150	54, 25 119.1–32	ditto	ditto	ditto	122–126	ditto
Wednesday	53–62, 64, 66, 68	51, 65, 63, 67 1 Sam. 2.1–10 148–150	54, 26 119.1–32	ditto	ditto	ditto	127–131	ditto
Thursday	69–80	51, 90, 63, 67 Exod. 15.1a–19 148–150	54, 23 119.1–32	ditto	ditto	ditto	132, 133, 135–137	ditto
Friday	81–89, 94, 96, 97	51, 143, 63, 67 Habak. 3.2–19 148–150	54, 22 119.1–32	ditto	ditto	ditto	138–142	ditto
Saturday	98–109	51, 92, 63, 67 Deut. 32.1–43 148–150	54, 119.1–32	ditto	ditto	ditto	144–147	ditto

The Benedicite always replaces the weekday OT canticle on feasts and in Eastertide.

After 1911

	VIGIL	LAUDS	PRIME	TERCE	SEXT	NONE	VESPERS	COMPLINE
Sunday	1–3, 8–11	93, 100 (51, 118), 63 Benedicite (Benedictus es) 148	118/54* (93, 100) 119.1–32	119.33–80	119.81–128	119.129–end	110–116.9	4, 91, 134
Monday	14, 15, 17–21, 30	47 (51), 5, 29 1 Chron. 29.10–13 (Isa. 12.1–6) 117	24, 19.1–15 (47)	27, 28	31	32, 33	116.10–end 120–122	6, 7
Tuesday	35, 37–39	96 (51), 43, 67 Tobit 13.1–7 (Isa. 38.10–20) 135	25 (96)	40	41, 42	44	123–127	12, 13, 16
Wednesday	45, 46, 48–51	97 (51), 65, 101 Jud. 16.13–17 (1 Sam. 2.1–10) 146	26, 52, 53 (97)	54, 55	56–58	59, 60	128–132	34, 61
Thursday	62, 66 68, 69	98 (51), 90, 36 Jer. 31.10–14 (Exod. 15.1–23) 147.1–11	23, 72 (98)	73	74	75, 76	133, 136–138	70–71
Friday	78, 79, 81, 83	99 (51), 143, 85 Isa. 45.15–25 (Hab. 3.2–19) 147.12–20	22 (99)	80, 82	84, 87	89	139–142	77, 86
Saturday	105–107	149 (51), 92, 64 Ecclus. 36.1–16 (Deut. 32.1–69) 150	94, 108 (149)	102	104	109	144, 145	88, 103

Items in brackets ( ) replace what immediately precedes them at certain penitential times.
* Ps. 54 replaces Ps. 118 at Prime on certain major feasts and important days.

MODERN REFORMS

34 Roman (1971)

Invitatory	*M*	*E*
(To be used before the first	O God, make speed ...	O God, make speed ...
office of the day, replacing	Gloria Patri	Gloria Patri
O God, make speed ...	Alleluia	Alleluia
Gloria and Alleluia)	Hymn	Hymn
	Psalm	2 Psalms
	OT Canticle	NT Canticle
	Psalm	Short reading
O Lord, open my ...	Short reading	Responsory
Ps. 95 or alternative	Responsory	Magnificat
	Benedictus	Intercessions
	Intercessions	Lord's Prayer
	Lord's Prayer	Collect
	Collect	

'Day Office'	*Compline*	*Office of Readings*
O God, make speed ...	O God, make speed ...	O God, make speed ...
Gloria Patri	Gloria patri	Gloria Patri
Alleluia	Alleluia	Alleluia
Hymn	Act of penitence	Hymn
3 Psalms	Hymn	3 Psalms
Reading	Psalm(s)	Versicle
Versicle	Reading	Biblical reading
Collect	Responsory	Non-biblical reading
	Nunc Dimittis	Responsory
	Collect	Te Deum
		Collect

(This office is to be said at any convenient time of day.)

35   Anglican

The various member-churches of the Anglican Communion have all carried out their own reforms. The English Alternative Service Book (1980) has abbreviated the lectionary and psalm-cycle, and in addition to a new office which differs little from that of 1662, it also provides alternative shorter forms, as follows:

M	E
O Lord, open our lips...	Confession
Let us worship the Lord...	Absolution
Gloria Patri	O Lord, open our lips...
Venite/Jubilate/Easter Anthems	Let us worship the Lord...
Psalms of the day	Gloria Patri
OT Reading	Psalms of the day
NT Reading	NT Reading
Variable canticle	Variable canticle
Creed	Lord's prayer
Lord's Prayer	Collect of the day
Collect of the day	Evening collect
Morning collect	

MONASTICISM

The East

36   Cassian (*c.* 385)

His report seems to be an amalgam, but claims to describe the offices at Scete in Lower Egypt.

E	M
12 Psalms	12 Psalms
(The last one	(The last one
with Alleluia	with Alleluia
refrain)	refrain)

2 readings after each office is over
    (weekdays: OT and NT; weekends:
    both NT)

Method of psalmody
Each psalm is read by one brother while
    the rest sit.
After each psalm:

   {
    All stand for silence
    Prostration (except Sundays and
      Eastertide)
    All stand for silence
    Improvised collect.

Gloria Patri after last psalm

37 Pachomius (Upper Egypt, c. 290–346)

Two daily offices. They included use of Psalm 95, general use of the Psalter (and perhaps other Scripture passages) read out by a reader, with silences and prostrations. Little else is known.

38 Palestine and Syria (report by Cassian c. 380)

Mn and M	Second M ('New service')	T, S, N	E
Ends with Pss. 148–150	Psalms 51, 63 and 90	3 Psalms each	? Lucernarium ? Psalm 141

Fridays: Mn
3 antiphons
3 responsorial psalms } by turns?
3 readings

39 De Virginitate (? Cappadocia. ? Late fourth century)

Mn	M	T, S, N	E ('Duodecima')
Ps. 119.62	Ps. 63	Hymns and	'If you come'... a
Ps. 51	Benedicite	praises	'greater and longer
As many psalms as possible standing, each followed by genuflection and prayer. Alleluia after every 3 Psalms	Gloria in excelsis 'and the rest'		synaxis', alone if necessary

40 Basil (see 14)

41 Byzantine (see 19)

The West

42 Columbanus (Ireland, late sixth century)

Duodecima	Mn	Cockcrow	T, S, N
12 Psalms	12 Psalms	24–36 Psalms, according to season (Sats. and Suns.: 36–75)	3 Psalms Intercessions (with psalm-verses instead of Kyries)

Psalms recited Egyptian fashion in groups of 3, each 3rd psalm with an antiphon, and genuflection for prayer after each psalm.

43 Ordo Monasterii (?N. Africa. ?Follower of Augustine. ?Mid–fifth century)

Nov.–Feb.	Mar.–Apr./Sept.–Oct.	May–Aug.
12 Antiphons	10 Antiphons	8 Antiphons
6 Psalms	5 Psalms	4 Psalms
3 readings	3 readings	2 readings

M	T, S, N	Lucernarium	C
Psalms 63, 5 and 90	Responsorial Ps. 2 Antiphons Reading A prayer	Responsorial Ps. 4 Antiphons Responsorial Ps. Reading A prayer	'The Customary Psalms'

44 Aurelian (Bishop of Arles 546–53) Revision of the Rule of Caesarius his predecessor.

Caesarius claimed to base his office on that of Lérins. The following is a summary of the typical ferial office. Differences between this and the original rule of Caesarius, and between different types of community, and variations according to the season, make it difficult to give a succinct summary.[a]

Nocturns	*2nd Nocturns* (winter)	*Mattins*	*Prime*[b]
Psalm 51	Psalm 57	Canticle	6 Psalms
18 Psalms	18 Psalms	Psalms 43 and 63	Antiphon
3 little antiphons	3 little antiphons	Psalms 145–150	Hymn
2 readings	2 readings	Hymn	2 readings
Hymn	Hymn	Capitellum	Capitellum
Capitellum	Capitellum	12 Kyries	

T, S, N.	*Lucernarium*	*Duodecima*	*Compline*
12 Psalms	Invitatory Psalm	Ps. 104.19bff.	Psalm 91
Antiphon	3 antiphons	18 Psalms	'Customary
Hymn	Hymn	3 little antiphons	capitella'
Reading	Capitellum	2 readings	
Capitellum		Hymn	
		Capitellum	

In winter:
  3 missae after 2nd nocturns
All Fridays:
  6 missae after Duodecima
  3 missae between nocturns and *M*
All Sundays:
  6 missae after nocturns

> *Missa* (floating unit)
> 3 readings, each followed by a prayer
> 1 antiphon-psalm
> 1 responsorial psalm
> 1 antiphon-psalm

Readings: Except in nocturns and missae, all are brief memory-readings.[c]

Resurrection Gospel: In the first missa after nocturns on Sundays, the resurrection gospel is read from each evangelist in turn, in a four-week cycle.

Sunday mattins is expanded to include, among other things, the Te Deum, Magnificat and Gloria in excelsis.

Kyrie eleison is to be recited thrice before each office, thrice after its psalmody, and thrice at its end.

45 The Rule of the Master (Provence or Italy, c. 500–525)[a]

Mn	M	P, T, S, N	Lucernarium	C
Versicle	7 Psalms	4 Psalms	7 Psalms	4 Psalms
Ps. 95	Versicle	Apostle reading	Versicle	Apostle reading
15 Psalms	Apostle	Gospel reading	Apostle	Gospel reading
(summer: 11)	'Gospels'	Versicle	'Gospels'	Prayer
Apostle reading	Prayer	Prayer	Prayer	Versicle
Gospel reading				
Versicle				
Prayer				

While typical of its era in being obscure in many points of detail, the Rule of the Master presents particular difficulties of interpretation. The main one concerns the content of mattins and lucernarium. Does 'Gospels' mean a gospel canticle, as in Benedict, or a gospel reading? The matter remains unresolved.[b]

All the readings in the above offices were recited from memory.

There was a weekly all-night vigil on Saturday nights at which the Bible was read systematically from the book.

The 7 'psalms' at mattins included Ps. 51 and Pss. 148–150, and the rest were canticles. It is not sure whether the Master considered 148–150 to be one psalm or three. At lucernarium the psalms were *in course*.

46 Benedict (Italy, c. 480–c. 550. Rule written c. 540)

Given here is the office as Benedict describes it in his Rule. It was considerably elaborated and adapted in subsequent centuries, particularly by Benedict of Aniane (c. 750–821), whose revision was approved for the Carolingian Empire in 817.

Mn
O Lord, open ... (3 times)
Psalm 3
Psalm 95 with antiphon
Hymn

Weekdays

1st nocturn
6 Psalms and antiphons
Versicle
Blessing
3 readings, with responsory
after each
Gloria

2nd nocturn
6 Psalms and Alleluias
Apostle (memory-reading)
Versicle
Kyries

Sundays and feasts

1st nocturn
6 Psalms and antiphons
Versicle
Blessing
4 readings, with
responsory after each
Gloria

2nd nocturn
6 Psalms and antiphons
Versicle
4 readings, with
responsory after each
Gloria

3rd nocturn
3 OT canticles and
Alleluia
Versicle
Blessing
4 lessons, with responsory
after each

Te Deum
Gospel of the day
Te Decet Laus
Blessing

M	P, T, S, N	E
Ps. 67 (directaneus)	O God, make	4 consecutive psalms
Ps. 51	speed...	Apostle reading
2 Psalms	Gloria	Responsory
Canticle	Hymn	Hymn
Psalms 148–150	3 Psalms	Versicle
Apostle reading	Reading	Magnificat
Responsory	Versicle	Litany
Hymn	Kyrie	Lord's Prayer (aloud by Superior)
Versicle	Lord's Prayer	
Benedictus	(silent)	C
Litany		Gloria
Lord's Prayer (aloud by		Psalms 4, 91 and 134
Superior)		Hymn
		Blessing

From Easter to 1 November the weekday Mn readings are replaced by one memory-passage from the OT.

Notes

Numbers in brackets refer to the Bibliography.
Numbers in bold type refer to Part V: Sources.

I. Prayer and human nature

1 Psalm 123.2
2 Charles Davis, 'Ghetto or Desert ...', in *SL* 7.2–3 (1970) pp. 14ff.
3 See Thomas Kuhn: *The Structure of Scientific Revolutions* (2nd edn), Chicago 1970
4 See G. Gutierrez, *A Theology of Liberation* (1974), pp. 91f., 113f., 116f. and 269f.
5 Peter Berger, *A Rumour of Angels* (1970), pp. 20f.
6 Anthony Bloom, *Living Prayer* (1966), p. 23
7 Thomas Merton, *Climate of Monastic Prayer* (1969), p. 35
8 *Church, World, Mission*, New York 1979, p. 84
9 Eliade (29) 32f.
10 G. Dix, *The Shape of the Liturgy* (2nd edn, 1945), 744ff.
11 *Mere Christianity* (1952), p. 65
12 Ibid., p. 111
13 M. Eliade, *The Forbidden Forest* (1978), p. 508
14 Quoted in Fischer (55) p. 166, from *Gesammelte Werke von F. Kafka* (ed. Max Brod), New York/Frankfurt 1958, vol: *Briefe von 1902–1904*, p. 28
15 Bouyer (4) p. 120
16 *Moralia in Job* 20.1 (*PL* 76.135); *Hom. in Ezek.* 7.8 (*PL* 76.843)
17 Welte (47) pp. 1f.
18 Quoted in J. Bowker, *Problems of suffering in religions of the world* (1970), p. 91
19 Thekla (135) p. 6
20 J. Dominian in *The Tablet*, 11 Feb. 1984, p. 127
21 Mowinckel (41) 116
22 H. Mühlen, *Geistesgaben heute* (Topos Taschebüchen 1982), pp. 123–7
23 Heiler (34) pp. 11f.
24 W. Pelz, *Distant strains of triumph* (1964), p. 155
25 Crichton (7) p. 9
26 L. Bouyer, *The Meaning of the Monastic Life*, New York 1955, p. 142
27 C. Barr, *Im Christlichen Orient* (1934), p. 202
28 See (15)
29 J. Leclercq, *The Love of Learning and the Desire for God* (1978), p. 90. (See also pp. 16ff. and 89ff.)
30 E. Von Severus, 'Dem heiligen Benedikt heute begegnen' (in *Erbe und Auftrag*, Beuron, 56 (1980), pp. 289–95), p. 293f.

31 W. H. Vanstone, *Love's Endeavour, Love's Expense* (1977), chs. 5 and 6
32 Mowinckel (41) p. 59
33 B. Schellenberger, *Nomad of the Spirit* (1980), p. 95
34 T. Merton, *Climate of Monastic Prayer* (1969), pp. 84f.
35 M. Carrouges, *La Liturgie à l'heure de Ioneso* (Unam Sanctam 66, 'La Liturgie après Vatican II', Y. Congar *et al.* 1967), p. 180
36 C. S. Lewis, *Letters to Malcolm* (1969), p. 12
37 Guardini (32) pp. 20f.
38 See David Keirsey and Marilyn Bates, *Please understand me : Character and Temperament Types*, Prometheus Nemesis Books, Del Mar, CA 92014 (USA), 1978
39 Ibid., p. 34
40 Ibid., p. 36
41 Cyprian, *De Dom. Orat.* 8
42 T. Ware, *The Orthodox Church* (1963), p. 310
43 P. Dumitriu, *To the Unknown God* (1982), pp. 152f.
44 Rev. 5.13f.
45 Augustine, *Enarrationes in Psalmos*, 85 (86).1
46 R. Vernay OSB, 'On the desert place of the inner sanctuary', a paper, 1974
47 Damian (28) pp. 60–75
48 M. Furlong, *Travelling in* (1971), p. 103
49 J. Macquarrie, *Paths in Spirituality* (1972), p. 105
50 Guardini (32) p. 60
51 Thomassin (24) chapter 25 (based on words in Augustine's commentary on Psalm 88 (89))
52 John 17.21
53 See 1 Cor. 12.12–27
54 H. A. Hodges and A. M. Allchin, *A Rapture of Praise: Hymns of John and Charles Wesley* (1966), no. 136, pp. 152–3

II. The history of daily prayer

 1 Delling (53) p. 181
 2 See Bradshaw (5), chapters 1 and 2
 3 See Fischer (55)
 4 Clement, *Stromateis* 7.7
 5 See Walker (61)
 6 I am grateful to the Revd Dr Alan Amos for this information
 7 See Luykx (71) pp. 67–81
 8 Vogüé (76) pp. 128f.
 9 Quoted in Uspensky (113) pp. 64f. See also Egender (119) vol. 1, p. 65
10 See Grosdidier (120) pp. 191–4
11 See Dekkers (66)
12 Egeria 24.1, as given in Bradshaw (5) p. 77
13 Egeria 24.2, as above, pp. 78ff.
14 See Bradshaw (5) p. 82
15 Uspensky (113) pp. 96ff.
16 See ibid., p. 34
17 See page 150
18 For further details on its origins see Taft (23) p. 37
19 See pages 149ff.
20 Atiya (82) p. 240

21 On the *bema* see Bibliography. Relative structures have been found at Boppard on the Rhine, and in Trier Cathedral

22 Illustrations from J. Lassus, *The Early Christian and Byzantine World* (1967), pp. 40, 42

23 See page 172

24 See page 150

25 See page 149

26 See page 184

27 E. Werner, *The Sacred Bridge* (1959), p. 150. See also W. O. E. Oesterley and G. H. Box, *A Short Survey of the Literature of Rabbinical and Mediaeval Judaism*, (1920), p. 149f.

28 See note accompanying (26) for parallels

29 Mateos (93) p. 27

30 Such collects are a characteristic of the daily office in the East, but also feature in the non-Roman rites of the West. See page 173

31 P. Sigal, 'Early Christianity and Rabbinic Liturgical Affinities', in *New Testament Studies* 30 (Jan. 1984), pp. 63–90

32 Maclean (90) pp. 212ff.

33 Uspensky (113) p. 73

34 Illustration from *DACL: Byzance*

35 Uspensky (113) p. 32

36 See Winkler (104) pp. 61f.; Bradshaw (5) p. 74; Taft (23) pp. 42–4, and in this book, page 184

37 It has been discovered that the modern Byzantine vespers of the Presanctified in Lent contains two services of vespers, each with a lucernarium, one of which is clearly in origin a people's office (see Janeras (122)). Was there a ceremony with light in the old Byzantine vespers which had been dropped by the time of our earliest documents?

38 See Egender (119) vol. 1, p. 53

39 Arranz (115) p. 85; (see also Arranz (116) 63–end; Egender (119) vol. 1, pp. 46ff.; Uspensky (113) p. 91)

40 Arranz (114) p. 118

41 See Winkler (104) p. 76, and Bradshaw (5) pp. 91f.

42 See Egender (119) vol. 1, p. 71

43 Mateos (129) pp. 22ff.

44 Arranz (115) pp. 409f.

45 The use of Psalm 51 in this position is very common. Cf. 14, 18, 19, 26, 30, 31, 32a, 33, 38, 39, 44, 45, 46

46 See page 157

47 Cf. 17, 18, 26, 27, 30, 31, 32, 33, 38, 44, 45, 46

48 See page 158

49 Illustration by John Perret, from *Roumanian Pilgrimage*, by M. R. Loughborough (1939) p. 78

50 Prudentius, *Liber Cathemerinon* v, 'Hymnus ad Incensum Lucernae'. (Works, trans. H. J. Thomson (1969), vol. 1, p. 47)

51 In Psalm 64 (65).12 (*PL* 9.420)

52 Sermon 77.7 (as given in translation by Bernard Peebles, Catholic University of America *The Sermons of Caesarius*)

53 E.g. Sermon 75.2 and 3; 137.1

54 Sermon 136.1–4; see also Hilary, In Ps. 64.12

55 E.g. Sermon 72; 77.6

56 Sermon 300.1

57 *DACL* vi.560

58 See 23, 26, 27, 29c, j, 30, 31. Taft's opinion in (23) ch. 8 that Ps. 141 was used in the Western

vespers cites very uncertain evidence. The opening verses receive some use, but use of the psalm as a whole seems to have been rejected as unsuitable from very earliest times. (See Winkler (104) pp. 91ff., and Magistretti (157) p. 156)

59 Addleshaw (137) p. 9
60 See A. Friedmann, *Paris, ses rues, ses paroisses, du moyen-âge à la Révolution* (1959), pp. xxivf.
61 Tour (166) p. 129
62 *PL* 125.775 cap. IX
63 *PL* 97.323f.; see also Leo IV (*PL* 115.677), Theodulf (*PL* 105.193), Riculf (*PL* 131.19), Gregory IX, *Decr.* IX, bk. 3, tit. 1, cap. iii, etc
64 See, for example, Hincmar of Rheims, *PL* 125.779 cap. XI
65 The 'Canons of Edgar' 45 (in B. Thorpe, *Ancient Laws and Institutes of England* (1843), p. 399)
66 Quoted in Ditchfield (151) p. 17
67 Ibid., ch. 2, 3 and 4; see also relevant parts of Gasquet (175), and C. Atchley, 'The parish clerk, and his right to read the liturgical epistle', *Alcuin Club Tracts* 4 (1903)
68 Ditchfield (151) p. 36
69 Ibid., p. 23
70 Temperley (184) p. 8
71 See Gasquet (175) pp. 150f.
72 Temperley (184) p. 8
73 Burgess (170) p. 52
74 Ibid., p. 54
75 Catalogue of All Saints' deeds, Bristol Record Office, NA 46 (229)
76 Archdale A. King, *Liturgies of the Past* (1959), pp. 203–5
77 *Monumenta Germaniae Historica* (*Scriptores*) pp. 106f.
78 Quoted in *DACL* 1312 n. 9
79 Ibid., n. 7
80 Quoted in Thomassin (25) p. 251, col. 2. I have been unable to trace the original
81 *Monumenta Germaniae Historica (Leges) Capitula Regum Francorum I*, 91, p. 106
82 Peter Damian, *De Horis Canonicis*: introduction (*PL* 145.223)
83 Salmon (20) p. 13
84 Ibid., pp. 16–20 and 140 n. 68
85 Ibid., p. 19
86 See Humbeeck (178), Anson (168), and Clement F. Rogers, *Sitting for the Psalms*, Church Historical Society and SPCK (1931), pp. 18–23
87 H. Bradshaw and C. Wordsworth, *Statutes of Lincoln Cathedral* (1897), vol. 1, p. 392. See also on Hereford Cathedral ibid., vol. 2, pp. 72 and 80
88 Canon 45
89 See page 264, n. 24
90 From E. L. Cutts, *Scenes and Characters of the Middle Ages* (1926), p. 74f.
91 Salmon (20) p. 19
92 See Dijk (172) pp. 37–42
93 Ibid., p. 40
94 *DACL*, 'Livres d'Heures', col. 1836
95 Dijk (172) p. 40
96 Nicholaus de Plove: *Tractatus Sacerdotalis* ... (1476) 1508 edition, under 'De modo dicendi horas canonicas'
97 Quoted in Wordsworth (186) p. 78
98 Rock (179) vol. iv, p. 141
99 Cited in Rock (179) p. 165
100 See Salmon (20) p. 133 n. 20

101 *The Teaching of the Abyssinian Church*, trans. A. F. Matthew (1936), p. 61
102 Maclean (90) p. 233
103 *Ep.* 207
104 See A. Lagarde, *The Latin Church in the Middle Ages* (1915), p. 80
105 See L. Pritchard, *The Life and Writings of Father Baker* (Catholic Records Society, vol. 33), p. 261
106 E.g., Caesarius *Serm.* 75.3, 133.1, 136.1
107 E. Bishop (142) pp. 330f.
108 See L. Oliger (ed.), *Regula Reclusorum Angliae et Quaestiones tres de Vita solitaria saec. XII–XIV*; *Antonianum* 9 (1934), pp. 37–84, 243–68, 79
109 Jungmann (193) French edn., p. 182, n. 26
110 Stadlhuber (196) 319f. and n. 227
111 Jungmann (193) French edn., p. 81 (*PL* 101.509)
112 *PL* 101. 465ff., 509ff., 569ff., etc
113 See, for example, *PL* 101.1383, and A. Wilmart (ed.), *Precum Libelli Quattuor Aevi Karolini*, *EL* 1940
114 *A relation or rather a true account of the Island of England ... about the year 1500* (probably Venetian, *c.* 1497), Cambridge Camden Society, 1847
115 Hoskins (192) p. xvi
116 Ibid., pp. xvi and xviii
117 England is unique in that the production of vernacular primers completely dried up in the fifteenth century, not emerging again until the early sixteenth. This was probably due to the English Church's problems with dissent and the translation of Scripture. See Blom (201) pp. 3f.
118 *De Inst. Laic.* 1.12 (*PL* 106.145–7)
119 Schnitzler (195) p. 79; Jungmann (193) French edn., p. 175, n. 50; *PL* 106.113
120 Stadlhuber (196) p. 306
121 See Schnitzler (195) and Stadlhuber (196)
122 *Conditor alme siderum*, English Hymnal No 1, verse 3, trans. J M. Neale
123 Jungmann (154) p. 105
124 Heinz (191) p. 55; Stadlhuber (196) p. 319, n. 221
125 Schnitzler (195) p. 82
126 Bouyer (4) p. 105
127 RB 20
128 *Moralia in Job* 5.54f.
129 Bouyer (4) p. 62
130 *Festal Menaion* (126) p. 65
131 C. Butler, *Benedictine Monachism* (1919), p. 305
132 Vogüé (76) p. 149
133 T. Merton, *The Climate of Monastic Prayer* (1969), pp. 65 and 85
134 See W. Legg (206) pp. 30–5
135 See, for example, B. T. Mudge, 'Monastic Spirituality in Anglicanism', *Review for Religious*, vol. 37, no. 4 (July 1978), 505ff.; and R. Hale, *Canterbury and Rome – Sister Churches* (1982), ch. 3
136 G. E. Aylmer and R. Cant, *A History of York Minster* (Oxford 1977), pp. 260–3
137 Staley (209) pp. 240f. Two similar bequests in Leicestershire are mentioned in the preface to William Beveridge's *The great necessity and advantage of public prayer and frequent communion* (1709)
138 J. Paterson, *Pietas Londinensis*, 1714. A single sheet folio in the British Museum (cited in Legg (206) p. 107 n.) gives information for 1692, but it is not clear how complete it is. The corresponding numbers it gives for this table are: 9, 26, 4, 1, ?, ?, ?

139 Best (200)
140 *London Parishes*, published by Weed and Jeffery, 1824. The two which had both services daily were St Andrew's, Holborn and St Sepulchre's. The three services daily were celebrated at St James's, Piccadilly and St Martin-in-the-Fields. The five which had one daily service were:
    St Antholin, Watling St (evensong)
    St Dunstan's, Stepney (mattins)
    St Giles-in-the-Fields (mattins)
    St George's, Hanover Square (mattins)
    St James's, Clerkenwell (mattins)
The church with one service per week was St Katharine Cree, with mattins on Wednesdays at 11.30 am. These figures are in addition to cathedrals and collegiate establishments
141 C. Mackeson, *Guide to the Churches of London*, 1866
142 *A letter of advice to members of the Church of England to come to divine service morning and evening every day*, 1708 edn., p. xxxvii (first published 1688)
143 The *Guardian*, no. 65, 26 May 1713
144 S. Pepys, *Diary*, 14 July 1664
145 Legg (206) p. 91
146 The *Spectator*, no. 14, 16 March 1710 (1711)
147 Canon 15 (see Jones (15) pp. 406f.)
148 J. N. Cardwell: *Two Centuries of Soho* (1898), p. 156
149 Best (200) p. 46. Also Legg (206) p. 100
150 F. R. Raines and F. Renaud, *The Fellows of the Collegiate Church of Manchester*, Chetham Soc. (1891), part ii, p. 213
151 J. Wallis, *The Natural History and Antiquities of Northumberland* (1769), vol. II, pp. 224–34
152 See G. W. O. Addleshaw and F. Etchells, *The Architectural Setting of Anglican Worship* (1948), pp. 91 and 185. See also p. 43
153 Izaak Walton, *Lives* (Nelson 1903), p. 270
154 J. H. Pruett, *The Parish Clergy under the Late Stuarts – the Leics. Experience* (Illinois 1978), pp. 115f.
155 F. C. Mather, 'Georgian churchmanship reconsidered', in *JEH* (April 1985), p. 277
156 W. Benham (ed.), *Letters of Wm Cowper* (1884), pp. 9 and 16
157 *Sermons by the Late Reverend George Berkeley Ll.D.*, 1799. Introduction by Eliza Berkeley, pp. xxiff.
158 Ibid.
159 Quoted in J. H. Overton: *English Church Life in the 19th Century*, p. 142
160 A. J. B. Beresford Hope, *Worship in the Church of England* (1874), p. 20
161 Bateman's life of Wilson, p. 264
162 E. B. Pusey, *Tract 18*, new edn (1840), p. 8
163 *A Companion to the Altar*, 1718 edn., p. 32
164 Legg (207) p. 22; E. V. Lucas, *Life of Charles Lamb*, 2nd edn (1905), p. 25; E. G. Sandford, *Memoirs of Abp. Temple* (1906), vol. I, p. 18
165 See note 162
166 An elderly bachelor, *Not Many Years Ago* (1898), 2nd edn., p. 11
167 Parker Society 1852
168 *Devotions in the Ancient Way of Offices*, with a preface by George Hickes, edn. of 1846
169 For further information, see Hoskins (192), and Blom (201) pp. 264ff.
170 See Blom (201)
171 Crichton (203) p. 171
172 Ibid., p. 161
173 Blom (201) pp. 147f. and 161f.

174 Crichton (204) p. 11
175 J.-B. Le Brun-des-Marettes, *Voyages liturgiques de France, ou recherches faites en divers villes du Royaume par le Sieur de Moléon* . . . (Paris 1718), p. 183 (misprinted as 203)
176 Ibid., pp. 386–418
177 Ibid., p. 410
178 Ibid., p. 408
179 L. Sheppard, *Barbe Acarie* (1953), p. 102f.
180 François de Sales, *Introduction to the Devout Life*, II, ch. 15
181 From the parish of St-Romain
182 Collette (214) pp. 283f.
183 N. Abercrombie, *The Life and Work of Edmund Bishop* (1959), p. 37
184 I am grateful to Mgr J. D. Crichton for this information
185 E.g. *Nouveau Paroissien, Latin et François* . . . : Local ('Gallican') use of the diocese of Rouen, published by the Archbishop of Rouen in 1843. Or *Office Paroissial . . . contenant les messes et les vêpres pour tous les jours de l'année* . . . : Roman rite, diocese of Bourdeaux, 1872
186 Collette (214) p. 293. The 'eight tomes' were the eight *tones* of the chant
187 Brémond (212) vol. x, ch. 5, p. 214
188 *Exercices du pénitent* (Paris 1758), p. 355; Brémond (212) p. 209
189 From Brémond (212) p. 217
190 Popp (217) p. 115
191 Ibid., p. 137
192 Bäumer (1) vol. 2, pp. 360f.
193 Popp (217) p. 208
194 Ibid., 137
195 Ibid., 133
196 Ibid., 175f.
197 Ibid., 178
198 Ibid., 334ff.
199 See Schnitzler (195) pp. 75–8; also Kopeć (225) pp. 208f.
200 Roth (220) pp. 122ff.
201 Ibid., 170
202 Ibid., 204
203 Ibid., 267
204 Ibid., 81
205 Ibid., 214
206 Ibid., 205
207 Ibid., 213
208 Ibid., 257
209 Ibid., 258
210 M. Chorzępa: *Gorzkie Żale, ich geneza i rozwój historyczny*. Nasza Przeszłość (Cracow) 12 (1960), pp. 221–257
211 Gülden (224) p. 61
212 Ibid., 161f.
213 Pronounced 'goj-inki'
214 See, for example, under *godzinki* in the standard Polish encyclopaedias, e.g. (223)
215 Maria Konopnicka, *Nowele i Obrazki* (Warsaw 1951), vol. II, p. 202
216 Gloger (223) p. 197
217 Gülden (224) p. 180
218 See Bäumer (1) vol. II, pp. 73–85
219 See Ruch Biblijny (222) p. 177
220 Referred to in Thomassin (25) p. 283, col. 2

221 Schnitzler (195) p. 75
222 Kopeć (225) 208–11
223 Schenk (226) p. 78
224 Kopeć (225) p. 203
225 Schenk (226) p. 165
226 Gülden (224) pp. 166f.
227 Ibid., 165
228 *DACL* (6)
229 See, for example, Crichton (7) pp. 50–55; Jones (15) pp. 381–6

III. The Content of Daily Prayer

1 See page 156, n. 9, and also 36, 37, 39, 42, 45. The Psalms in the Byzantine office are each followed by similar exercises
2 L. Fischer (ed.), *Bernhardi ... ordo officiorum Ecclesiae Lateranensis*, Munich 1916 (*Historische Forschungen und Quellen* 2 and 3) p. 4, etc (more examples in index)
3 See 16, 17, 18, 31. For parallels in the Byzantine office see Uspensky (113), who connects it with the *Lity* (pp. 35, 51–4 and 79ff.) and Egender (119 vol. 1) who sees a vestige of it in the *Aposticha* (pp. 139f. and 370f.). There are vestiges of it too in the Mozarabic office: see Pinell (162) p. 426. For a possible Celtic example in the antiphoner of Bangor, see Curran (149) p. 186. On the stations in the Ambrosian office, see Magistretti (157) pp. 150 and 165–71, and *Sources*, note 31(f) = subsection.
4 See 13, 16, 17, 18, 19, 29c, 30
5 See 14, 17, 18, 19, 26, 30, 31, 32a, 33, 38, 39, 44, 45 and 46
6 A. Louth, *Discerning the Mystery*, 1983
7 *GILH* 15
8 For example, in the Book of Alternative Services of the Anglican Church of Canada (1985), Anglican Book Centre, Toronto, pp. 705–909; the *Psautier de la Bible de Jérusalem* (Paris 1961), (collects by J. Gélineau and D. Rimaud); *St Augustin prie les psaumes*, A. G. Hamman (Paris 1980); B. Magee, *The Psalm Collects* (Dublin 1978). For the ancient collections, see P. Verbraken, *Oraisons sur les 150 psaumes*, Paris 1967; and A. Wilmart and L. Brou, *The Psalter-collects from 5th- and 6th-century sources*, Henry Bradshaw Society 83 (1949)
9 Sermon 76.1, as quoted in Taft (23) p. 153
10 This question is taken up again on p. 187
11 The full list of Mozarabic canticles is given in Mearns (236) pp. 71–4
12 Ibid., 59f.
13 Taft asserts in (23) p. 313 that the Magnificat was first introduced into vespers by Benedict, but gives no evidence
14 Eusebius, *Eccl. Hist.* 5.28.5
15 A. Wilmart (ed.), *Precum Libelli Quattuor Aevi Karolini*, EL 1940, p. 91. The Gloria is given as part of a private morning office which follows a 'Gallican' form, including also Psalms 148–150, the Benedicite and the Te Deum
16 Hoskins (192) p. ix
17 See Agobard's reform of the Lyons antiphoner (9th cent.) in *PL* 104.329ff.; and *Breviarium S. Lugdunensis Ecclesiae*, 1737
18 See W. H. Frere, *The Winchester Troper* (introduction) 1894; Baumstark (2) ch. 6; Bäumer (1) vol. I pp. 418–24; C. S. Phillips, *Hymnody Past and Present*, 1937
19 J. M. Neale, *Hymns of the Eastern Church* (3rd edn., 1918), Introduction, pp. [27] and [33]
20 For example, in *Festal Menaion* (126) p. 75
21 See Vogüe (76) 140ff.
22 Basil, *Ep.* 207

23 Gelineau (233) pp. 151ff. (esp. 154)
24 *DACL* I, col. 2309
25 See Gelineau (233) pp. 151ff.
26 Ibid., 158f.
27 The term is used by Gelineau and others
28 Caesarius, *Reg. Virg.* 15; Aurelian, *Reg. Virg.* 23 and *Reg. Mon.* 29. See Vogüé (76) p. 166, n. 44
29 Cassian, *Inst.* 2.6
30 Compare 12, 13, 14, 16, 17, 18, 19, 23, 26, 29c, 30, 31, 38, 39, 42 (no readings) with 32, 33, 43, 44, ?45, 46 (memory-readings) and [30 mattins], 35 and ?45 (?systematic reading).
    Taft in (23) pp. 34ff. cites evidence of regular readings in the Egyptian cathedral offices. There is no indication, however, of how the Bible would have been treated in such readings, and the texts cited are too fragmentary and isolated (they are separated by centuries) to indicate anything more than a possibility
31 Taft (23) pp. 347–61
32 *PL* 95.1584 (translation as given in Bradshaw (5) p. 137)
33 Heiming (70) p. 140
34 Taft (23) p. 165 and ch. 10
35 RB 10. On transference of readings to the refectory see *PL* 95.1584 note j
36 Zerfass (63) p. 182
37 See Bradshaw (5) pp. 66–71, 90–92, 121f., 152f., and *passim*; also Taft (23) ch. 9. Zerfass has also shown that where readings occur in Eastern offices, they are there to give a sense of occasion to the offices of feast-days (Zerfass (63) 107 and 114)
38 Ep. 12.24 (*PL* 77.1234)
39 E.g. Isidore, *De Eccl. Off.* 1.10.3 (*PL* 83.745)
40 Crichton (7) p. 96
41 Egeria 24.6
42 Translations of the original Latin do not always bring out this difference in Benedict's terminology
43 Bäumer (1) vol. II, p. 440
44 Jungmann (153) pp. 191ff.
45 Pudichery (98) pp. 34f.

IV. Interpretating the Facts

1 Schmemann (133) p. 67. The quotation is from Tertullian, *Apol.* (1.) 39
2 See Taft (23) p. 145, n. 23, and p. 224, n. 13
3 *GILH* 33
4 Field (11) section 23, p. 39
5 See Bradshaw (5) 12ff.
6 See pp. 68, n. 26 and 74, n. 36. See also Winkler (104) pp. 61f. and 68, and Bradshaw (5) p. 74
7 See Kniazeff (123)
8 W. Durandus, *Rationale of the Divine Office* (ed. J. M. Neale 1843) Book I, 'Proeme' 14, p. 11
9 Pages 30 and 33
10 Shortly before going to press I was pleased to discover an essay by Carl Dehne ('Roman Catholic popular devotions', in *Christians at Prayer*, ed. John Gallen, Notre Dame, USA and London 1977, ch. 5, pp. 83–99) who arrives at broadly similar conclusions to those given here, with differences which are also interesting. For Dehne, Christian people's prayer is: (1) expression rather than edification: the worshipper is subject rather than object; (2) persons-centred rather than theme-centred, grounded in a lively sense of the communion of saints; (3) Christocentric; (4) given to clarity of expression; (5) circular or spiral rather than

straight-line: things do not follow logically or inevitably; the themes are not collected, segregated, concentrated or ordered; (6) relatively highly ceremonialized; (7) unvarying in form, with a good deal of repetition

11 Merton, *Climate of Monastic Prayer* (1969), p. 87
12 Monastery of St John the Baptist, Tolleshunt Knights, Essex
13 *GILH* 12
14 D. de Reynal, *Théologie de la Liturgie des Heures* (Paris 1978), p. 28
15 See Taft, 'Frequency of the Eucharist throughout History', in D. Power, *Can we always celebrate the Eucharist?* (Concilium 1982). Also in: R. Taft, *Beyond East and West*, Washington 1984
16 Schmemann (133) pp. 151ff.
17 Vogüé (76) p. 161
18 Ibid.
19 Ibid., n. 171 (Augustine *Ep.* 54.3)
20 See, for example, *Worship* 58.2 (March 1984), pp. 164ff. and 61.1 (Jan. 1987) pp. 2–15
21 The new American BCP provides one alternative litany, and the Canadian book (see p. 262 n. 8) over a dozen
22 Field (11) p. 40
23 See p. 262, n. 8 for collections of Psalm-collects
24 P. Procter and W. H. Frere, *A New History of the Book of Common Prayer* (1941), p. 6
25 'Bishop Taylor's remedies against tediousness of spirit', by David Scott, in *A Quiet Gathering* (Bloodaxe Books 1984), p. 75. The reference in the title is to Jeremy Taylor (1613–67), *Holy Living*, VII, 6.2
26 See pages 40ff.
27 Toate merg după Tipic, Dar în suflet nu-i nimic
28 1 Cor. 13.1f.
29 Job 26.12ff.
30 *GILH* 15 and *Constitution on the Sacred Liturgy* (Sacrosanctum Concilium) n. 84
31 Matt. 25.6
32 See D. H. Lawrence, *The Rainbow* (Penguin 1949), ch. 3, pp. 95f.

V. Sources

Unless otherwise indicated, translations are the author's, many of them based on those given in Bradshaw (5).

4 1 Clem. 40.1–4 (trans. Taft (23) 14)
5 Didache 8.3
6 a. *Strom.* 7.7; *Pedagogue* 2.9–10
 b. *Protrept.* 9.84
 c. *Strom.* 7.7 (trans. Library of Christian Classics, ed. J. E. Oulton and H. Chadwick (1954), p. 114)
 d. *Strom.* 7.40
7 a. *De Orat.* 12 (trans. as 6c p. 262)
 b. *De Orat.* 31.2, 4, 5 and 7 (trans. ibid., pp. 324ff.)
 c. *Contra Celsum* 6.41 (trans. Ante-Nicene Christian Library, ed. A. Roberts and J. Donaldson (Edinburgh 1872), p. 380)
8 a. *De Orat.* 25, *Ad Uxor* 2.4.2, *De Jejun* 10
 b. *De Orat.* 10 (trans. E. Evans (1953), p. 15)
 c. *De Orat.* 24 and 25 (trans. ibid., 35)
 d. Ibid., 27 and 29 (trans. ibid., 37 and 39)
 e. *Apologeticus* 39
 f. *Ad Uxor* 2.8

9 a. *De Dom. Orat.* 34–6
   b. *Ep.* 1.16
   c. *De Dom. Orat.* 8 (trans. A. Roberts and J. Donaldson (eds.) (Edinburgh 1868), p. 403)
10 *Ap. Trad.* 15, 18, 19, 25, 26, 35, 39, 41
11 a. In Ps. 64(65).9b
   b. In Ps. 65(66).2
   c. *Vita Constantini* 4.22
   d. *Can. Diur.* (*PG* 23.1395)
12 a. See Taft (23) 42ff., 48, 80–84
   b. Homily on 1 Tim. 4
   c. Hom. 68(69) on Matt. 3; In Ps. 140(141).1
   d. Hom. 14 on 1 Tim. 4; 5.9
   e. Ps. 140(141).1
   f. Hom. 6 on 1 Tim. 1; *On the Obscurity of Prophecies* 2.5
   g. Sozomen, *Eccl. Hist.* 8.7f.; Palladius, *De vita Chrysos.* 5. Hom. on Acts 26.3f.
   h. *De Anna* 4.5f.
   i. Expos. in Ps 41(42).2
13 a. 2.59 and 8.34–9
   b. 7.47f.
   c. 8.34
14 a. Longer Rule 37.2–5
   b. *On the Holy Spirit* 29(73)
15 *Life of St Macrina* 22 and 25 (trans. W. C. Clarke (1916), pp. 52 and 57)
16 Egeria 24.2–7, 8–12, 27.8
17 a. Pudichery (98) p. 19
   b. Ibid., p. 26
   c. Ibid., pp. 39f.
   d. Ibid., p. 59
   e. E. Werner, *The Sacred Bridge* (1959), p. 150
21 *Ap. trad.* 25 and 35 (see Taft (23) pp. 21–7) (trans. G. Cuming, Grove Liturgical Study 8 (1976), sections 25, 35, 41 and 42)
22 Egeria 24.4
23 a. Expos. in Ps. 118(119)19.32
   b. Ibid., 8.48; on the possible use of Psalm 119 at this service see Bradshaw (5) p. 113 (but Borella in (146) p. 250 says that Ps. 119 was introduced into the little hours much later, under Roman influence)
   c. *De Virg.* 3.4.18–20; In Ps. 1 *enarr.* 9; In Ps. 118(119).8; see Winkler (104) pp. 92–5, and Taft (23) pp. 142f.
   d. *Ep.* 21.34
   e. *Enarr.* in Ps. 1.9
   f. *De Abraham* 2.5.22
   g. *De Virg.* 3.4.18
   h. *Ep.* 20.11–13; Paulinus, *Vita Ambrosii* 13; Augustine, *Confessions* 9.7
24 a. In Ps. 118 (119); see also b, c, d
   b. *Ep.* 22.37
   c. *Ep.* 107.9
   d. *Ep.* 130.15
   e. *Contra Vigilantium* 1.9ff.; *Ep.* 107
25 *De Psalm. Bono* 11 (text in *JTS* 24 (1923), p. 239)
26 *Inst.* 3.3–11. The question of mattins is complicated: see Taft (23) 96ff., 195ff. (and also 76ff.). Taft takes the mention of Ps. 51 after the Laudate Psalms in Italy as a mistake (p. 128),

but there are parallels in the Mozarabic office, which can put this Psalm here (see Jungmann (153) pp. 142f.) and in east Syrian mattins (17)

27 *Comment.* in Ps. 148

28 a. *Confessions* 5.9
   b. *Enarr.* in Ps. 49(50).23
   c. Ibid., 66(67).3

29 Summaries of the acts of these councils can be found in C. J. Hefele, *A History of the Councils of the Church* (Edinburgh 1895), vol. IV. Wherever possible I refer here to *PL*, which is probably the most accessible source, even if not necessarily the standard text (collection attributed to St Isidore)
   Passages not in inverted commas are summaries
   a. Canon 5 (*PL* 84.329) and Canon 9 (ibid., 330)
   b. Canons 14 and 15 (Hefele (see note above) p. 17)
   c. *Mattins and vespers:*
      Canon 30 (*PL* 84.267)
      Vigils
      Sermons 72.1–3, 76.1–3, 86.5, 118.1, 188.6, 195.4, 196.2,4, 211.5, 212.6
      Prayer of Inclination
      Sermons 76.2, 77.5 and 7
   d. Canon 7 (*PL* 84.312)
   e. Canon 1 (*PL* 84.313); Canon 10(11) (*PL* 84.316)
   f. Canons 1–5 (*PL* 84.261f.)
   g. (*PL* 65.147)
   h. (*PL* 105.71)
   i. Canons 1, 2 and 12 (*PL* 84.565–7)
   j. Canons 2, 10, 13, 14, 15, 16 (*PL* 84.365–372)
   k. Canon 8 (*PL* 84.421)
   l. Canons 2 and 18 (*PL* 84.616 and 623)
   m. Canons 2 and 3 (*PL* 84.458)

30 a. (*PL* 86.702f.)
   b. *Breviarium Gothicum* (see *PL* 86). The principal sources in the Bibliography are the entries 143, 148, 150, 153, 160, 161, 162, 163, 167
   c. Pinell (162) p. 19; see also Jungmann (153) pp. 144ff.
   d. See Bruyne (148)

31 a. Borella (146) pp. 252f.
   b. See Curran (149) p. 186 and *passim.* I am grateful in the following account to Dr Cesare Alzati for clarification on certain points. The principal sources in the Bibliography are the entries 143, 144, 146, 149, 150, 157, 167
   c. Bäumer (1) vol. I, p. 347
   d. See pages 63, n. 19 and 149f.
   e. Mateos (58) p. 304
   f. For an analysis of this part of the office see M. Navoni, *Antifona ad Crucem. Contributo all storia e alla liturgia della Chiesa milanese nei secoli V–VII*, Ricerche storiche sulla Chiesa Ambrosiana XII (Archivio Ambrosiano LI) (1983), pp. 49–226
   g. Such usage is very ancient: see Socrates, *Eccl. Hist.* 6.8
   h. Borella (146) p. 229
   i. Ibid., 242f.
   j. Ibid., 245
   k. *Liturgia Ambrosiana delle Ore* (5 vols.), Centro Ambrosiano di Documentazione e Studi Religiosi, Piazza Fontana 2, 20122 Milano
   l. *Diurna Laus* (1982), publisher as above.

32 a. Vogüé (75) pp. 483–98; Bradshaw (5) pp. 136ff.
    g. J. Wickham Legg (ed.), *Breviarium Romanum a Francisco Cardinali Quignonio*, Cambridge 1888
36 Cassian, *Inst.* 2.1–12, and 3.1f.
37 A. Veilleux (trans.), *Pachomian Koinonia*, vol. 2, pp. 199f. For a summary of the present state of knowledge see Taft (23) 62ff.
38 Cassian, *Inst.* 3.1–6,8. It is difficult to know whether Pss. 148–150 formed part of a morning office, or simply came at the end of the vigil. See Taft (23) pp. 76–80 and ch. 10
39 Pseudo-Athanasius, *De Virg.* 12, 16, 20
42 Columbanus, *Regula Monachorum* 7; *Reg. Coenobialis* 9
43 Text in D. de Bruyne (ed.), *The First Rule of St Benedict*, Revue Bénédictine 42 (1930), pp. 318–25
44 a. Caesarius, *Reg. Virg.* 68–70, 48–65
        Aurelian, *Reg. Mon.* 28, 29, 31, 56, 57, 59
    b. Prime is only prescribed for weekends and feasts in Caesarius, but every day in Aurelian
    c. See Heiming (70) pp. 119f.
45 a. *Regula Magistri* 33–49
    b. I have tried to avoid disquisitions on matters of detail, but it would be impossible to give a breakdown of the Master's office in tabular form without some attempt to justify the interpretation I have chosen, so I will try to do this briefly.

    Taft (*E and W*, p. 127) accepts the arguments of E. de Bhaldraithe (*The Morning Office in the Rule of the Master*, Regula Benedicti Studia 5 (1976), pp. 201–23) which conclude that 'Gospels' refers to a gospel reading. The article provides very useful insights, and presents a persuasive argument, but falls short, in my view, of being decisive. Much of the supporting evidence is too ambiguous: the precise meaning of the word 'antiphon', the question of inheritance of practices from the synagogue, the scattered examples of gospel readings in Eastern and other rites, and their relationship to the resurrection vigil, the station at the baptisteries (see pp. 149f.) which was brought forward into the vesperal psalmody at Rome in Easter week, and the nature of what was sung there; these remain too unclear to provide strong evidence. The Master can be very inexact and circuitous in expressing himself, and this must compromise the use of internal evidence. So the details of the psalmody at mattins have to remain a puzzle. Taft's solution, which follows de Vogüé in separating Psalm 148 from its companions Taft (23), (128f.), seems improbable. The assumption that Psalms 148–150 were performed separately, first made by de Vogüé, relies on the Master's injunction against joining psalms: yet he may take for granted that these are not such psalms, being, by tradition, 'hymns', in a class apart. For the interpretation of a difficult text we perhaps rely too much on its own author's clarity of mind! The interpretation of the word *lectiones* could come under similar strictures. There remain other unresolved matters too, such as what, if anything, was replaced by the *Benedictiones* on feast-days. As more than one view, therefore, seems to be tenable, I have attempted simply to reflect the text as it stands
46 RB 8–19

Select Bibliography

General

1   Bäumer, S., trans. R. Biron, *Histoire du Bréviaire* (Paris 1905), 2 vols.
2   Baumstark, A., *Comparative Liturgy*, 1958.
3   Bouyer, L., *Life and Liturgy*, 1956.
4   — et al., *History of Christian Spirituality*, 1963–8.
5   Bradshaw, Paul, *Daily Prayer in the Early Church*, 1981.
6   Cabrol, F., and Leclercq, H. (eds.), *Dictionnaire d'Archéologie Chrétienne et de Liturgie*, Paris 1907–53 (*DACL*).
7   Crichton, J. D., *Christian Celebration: The Prayer of the Church*, 1976.
8   — In Jones (no 15), pp. 369–89.
9   — 'A Historical Sketch of the Roman Liturgy', in L. Shepphard, *True Worship*, 1963.
10 Cutts, D. and Miller, H., *Whose office? Daily prayer for the people of God*, Grove Books, Nottingham (Liturgical Study 32), 1982.
11 Field, A. (ed.), *Directory for the Celebration of the Work of God* (drawn up by the Benedictine Confederation), 1981.
12 *GILH* (*General Instruction on the Liturgy of the Hours*) with a commentary by A. M. Roguet; trans. P. Coughlan and P. Purdue, 1974.
13 Grainger, R., *The Language of the Rite*, 1974.
14 Grisbrooke, W. Jardine, 'A contemporary liturgical problem: the divine office and public worship', *SL* 8.3 (1971–2), pp. 129–68; 9 (1973), 3–18 and 81–106.
15 Jones, Cheslyn et al. (ed.), *The Study of Liturgy*, 1978.
16 Jungmann, J. A. (ed.), *Brevier Studien* (Trier) 1956.
17 Martimort, A. G. (ed.), *The Church at Prayer*, vol. IV: *The Liturgy and Time*, 1985.
18 Mateos, J., 'The morning and evening office', *Worship* 42 (1968), 31–47.
19 Mullett, J., *One People, One Church, One Song*, 1968.
20 Salmon, P., *The Breviary through the Centuries*, Collegeville 1962.
21 — 'La prière des heures', in A. G. Martimort, *L'Église en prière*, 1965.
22 Storey, W. G., 'The Liturgy of the Hours: Cathedral versus monastery', *Worship* 50 (1976), pp. 50–70.
23 Taft, R., *The Liturgy of the Hours in East and West*, Collegeville, 1985.
24 Thomassin, R., *L'Office Divin dans ses rapports avec l'oraison mentale* (17th cent.), Ligugé 1894.
25 — *Ancienne et nouvelle discipline de l'Église* (1679), 7 vols. (Paris 1864), vol. II.

Prayer and Human Nature

26 Allchin, A. M. (ed.), *Solitude and Communion – Papers on the Hermit Life*, Fairacres, Oxford 1977.

27 Allmen, J.-J., *The Theological Understanding of Common Prayer, LMD* 116 (1973), pp. 74–88.
28 Damian, Peter, on 'The Lord be with You', in *Writings* (trans. P. McNulty) 1959.
29 Eliade, M., *The Sacred and the Profane*, 1959.
30 — *Myths, Dreams and Mysteries*, 1977.
31 Gelineau, J., 'Les Formes concrètes de la Prière commune', *LMD* 116 (1973), pp. 59–73.
32 Guardini, R., *Liturgische Bildung*, 1923.
33 — 'Vom Liturgischen Mysterium', in *Die Schildgenossen* (1925), pp. 385–414.
34 Heiler, F., *Prayer*, 1932.
35 Hildebrand, D. von, *Liturgy and Personality*, Baltimore 1960.
36 Huizinga, J., *Homo Ludens*, 1956.
37 Leclercq, J., *Prière des Heures et Civilization contemporaine LMD* 105 (1971), pp. 34–45.
38 Leeuw, G. van der, *Phänomenologie der Religion*, Tübingen 1970.
39 Maur, H.-J. auf der, *The Difficulties of Common Prayer Today, SL* 10.3/4 (1974), p. 167ff.
40 Meyer, H. B., 'Time and the Liturgy', in *Liturgical Time* (ed. W. Vos and G. Wainwright), Rotterdam 1982.
41 Mowinckel, S., *Religion und Kultus*, Göttingen 1953.
42 Schnitzler, T., 'Das Stundengebet als Memoria', in *Heiliges Dienst* 33 (1979), pp. 14–17.
43 — 'Das Stundengebet als Segen', ibid., pp. 59–61.
44 Tippmann, R., 'Zeit und Ewigkeit in der Liturgie', in *Theologie und Glaube* (1950) no. 5, pp. 448–54.
45 Wainwright, G., 'Sacramental Time', in *Lit. Time* (see Meyer), 135–45.
46 — *Doxology* 1980.
47 Welte, B., 'Zeit und Gebet', in *Erbe und Auftrag* 56 (1980).

The Early Church

48 Bäumer (no. 1) vol. I, pp. 45–205.
49 Bradshaw (no. 5) ch. 1–4.
50 Crichton (no. 7) pp. 29–41.
51 Cullmann, O., *Early Christian Worship*, 1978.
52 Cuming, G. J., 'The New Testament foundation for common prayer', *SL* 10 3/4 (1974), pp. 88–105.
53 Delling, D. G., *Worship in the New Testament* 1962.
54 Dugmore, C. W., *The Influence of the Synagogue on the Divine Office*, Alcuin Club 1964.
55 Fischer, B., 'The common prayer of congregation and family in the ancient Church', *SL* 10 (1975), pp. 106–24.
56 Mateos, J., 'Office de minuit et office du matin chez S. Athanase', *OCP* 28 (1962), 173–80.
57 — 'The Origins of the Divine Office', *Worship* 41.8 (1967), 477–85.
58 — 'La Vigile Cathédrale chez Égerie', *OCP* 27 (1961), 281–312.
59 Ramsey, B., *Beginning to read the Fathers* (1986), ch. IX: 'Prayer'.
60 Taft (no. 23) ch. 1–3, 8–10.
61 Walker, J. H., 'Terce, Sext and None an Apostolic Custom?' in *Studia Patristica* 5 (1962), pp. 206–12.
62 Wilkinson, J., *Egeria's Travels*, 1971.
63 Zerfass, R., *Die Schriftlesung im Kathedraloffizium Jerusalems*, Münster 1968.

Monasticism

64 Bhaldraithe, E. de, 'Problems of the monastic conventual mass', *Downside Review* 90 (1972), 169–82.
65 Bradshaw (no. 5) ch. 5 and 7.

66 Dekkers, E., 'Les anciens moines cultivaient-ils la liturgie ?', *LMD* 51 (1957), pp. 31–54.
67 Fischer, B., 'Prière commune institutionnelle et Prière personelle libre dans la Règle de Saint Benoît', *LMD* 143 (1980), 153–73.
68 Grisbrooke, W. Jardine, 'The formative period – cathedral and monastic offices' in Jones (no. 15), pp. 358–68.
69 Hanssens, J. M., 'Nature et Genèse de l'office des matines, *Analecta Gregoriana* LVII, Rome 1952.
70 Heiming, O., 'Zum Monastischen Offizium von Kassianus bis Kolumbanus', *ALW* VII.1 (1961), pp. 89–156.
71 Luykx, B., 'L'influence des moines sur l'office paroissal', *LMD* 51 (1957), pp. 55–81.
72 Mateos, J., 'L'Office monastique à la fin du 4me siècle', *OC* 47 (1963), pp. 53–88.
73 Taft, R., 'Praise in the Desert: The Coptic Monastic Office Yesterday and Today', *Worship* 56.6 (November 1982), pp. 513–36.
74 — (no. 23) ch. 4–7, 10–11.
75 Vogüé, A. de, 'La Règle de St Benoît' (*Sources chrétiennes*) (1971), vol. 5, ch. III.
76 — *The Rule of St Benedict, A doctrinal and spiritual commentary* (Kalamazoo, Michigan 1983), ch. VIII.

The East (general)

77 Casper, J., 'Les Heures canoniales dans les rites orientaux', *LMD* 21 (1950), 83–98.
78 Leeb, H., *Die Gesänge im Gemeindegottesdienst von Jerusalem*, vom 55. bis 8. Jahrhundert, Vienna 1970.
79 Martimort (no. 17) pp. 233–42.
80 Raes, A., 'Note sur les anciennes matines byzantines et arméniennes' *OCP* 19 (1953), pp. 205–10.
81 Taft (no. 23) ch. 12–17.

East Syrian

82 Atiya, A. S., *A history of eastern Christianity* (1968), ch. 12–16, 21 and 22.
83 Badger, G. P., *Nestorians and their rituals*, 2 vols., 1852.
84 Cutts, E. L., *The Assyrian Christians*, 1877.
85 Dacl (no. 6) *Syrie.*
86 Dalmais, I. H., 'Le thème de la lumière dans l'office du matin des églises syriennes-orientales', *LO* 40 (1967), pp. 257–76.
87 Dauvillier, J., 'L'archéologie des anciennes églises de rite chaldéen', *Parole de l'orient* 6/7, 1975/6 (1978), pp. 357–86.
88 Hambye, E. R., 'Survival and revival: East-Syrian Christianity yesterday and today', *Ostkirchlichen Studien* 19 (1970), pp. 312–38.
89 Maclean, A. J., *East Syrian daily offices*, 1894.
90 Maclean, A. J. and Browne, H., *The Catholicos of the East*, 1892.
91 Martimort (no. 17) p. 235f.
92 Mateos, J., 'L'office paroissal du matin et du soir dans le rite chaldéen', *LMD* 64 (1960), pp. 66–89.
93 — 'L'office divin chez les chaldéens', *LO* 35 (1963), pp. 253–82.
94 — 'Les matines chaldéens, maronites et syriennes', *OCP* 26 (1960).
95 — 'Les différentes éspèces de vigiles dans le rite chaldéen', *OCP* 27 (1961), pp. 46–63.
96 — 'Lelya-Sapra: essai d'interprétation des matines chaldéennes', *OCA* 156 (1959).
97 Pathikulangara, P. V., 'The divine office in the Malabar liturgy', *EL* 88 (1974), pp. 131–41.

98 Pudichery, S., 'Ramsa: an analysis and interpretation of the Chaldean vespers', *Dharmaram College Studies* 9 (1972).
99 Surma d'Bait Mar Shimun, *Assyrian Church Customs*, 1920.
100 Taft (no. 23) ch. 13.
101 — 'Some notes on the *bema* in the east- and west-Syrian traditions', *OCP* 34 (1968), pp. 326–59.
102 Vellian, J., 'The Church as Bride in the east Syrian Liturgy', *SL* 11 (1976), pp. 59–64.
103 — *East Syrian evening services*, Kottayam 1971.
104 Winkler, G., 'Über die Kathedralvesper in den verschiedenen Riten des Ostens und Westens, *ALW* 16 (1974), pp. 53–102.
105 — 'Das Offizium am Ende des 4. Jahrhunderts und das heutige chaldäische Offizium, ihre strukturellen Zusammenhänge', *Ostkchln Studien* 19 (1970), pp. 289–311.

The old Byzantine 'chanted office'

106 Arranz, M., 'L'Office de l'Asmatikos Hesperinos', *OCP* XLIV (1978), pp. 107–30 and 391–419.
107 — 'L'Office de l'Asmatikos Orthros', *OCP* 47 (1981), pp. 122–57.
108 Darrouzès, J., 'Sainte-Sophie de Théssalonique d'après un rituel', *Revue d'Etudes Byzantines*, 34 (1976), pp. 45–78.
109 Grisbrooke, W. J., ibid., (see *general*) 8.3 pp. 145ff.
110 Hannick, C., 'Etude sur l'Akolouthia Asmatiké'; *Jahrbuch der österreichischen Byzantinistik* 19 (1970), pp. 243–60.
111 Mateos, J., *Le Typicon de la Grande Église*, 1962.
112 Strunk, O., *The Byzantine Office at Hagia Sophia*, Dumbarton Oaks Papers 9–10 (1956), 175ff.
113 Uspensky, N., *Evening Worship in the Orthodox Church* (New York 1985), ch. 5–7 and *passim*.

Byzantine

114 Arranz, M., 'Les Prières sacerdotales des Vêpres byzantines', *OCP* 37 (1971), pp. 85–124.
115 — Les prières presbytérales des matines byzantines, *OCP* 37 (1971), pp. 406–36.
116 — 'Les grandes étapes de la liturgie byzantine', *Bibliotheca 'Eph. Lit.' Subsidia* (1976), pp. 43–72.
117 — 'La liturgie des heures selon l'ancien euchologie byzantin', *Studia Anselmiana* 68, Rome 1979.
118 Baumstark, A., 'Denkmäler der Entstehungsgeschichte des Byzantinisches Ritus', *OC* (1927), pp. 1–32.
119 Egender, N., Introductions to *La Prière des Églises de rite Byzantin*, vol. 1 (*La Prière des heures*) and vol. 3 (*Dimanche*), Chevetogne 1975.
120 Grosdidier de Matons, J., 'Kontakion et canon: Piété populaire et liturgie officielle à Byzance', *Augustinianum* 20 (1980), pp. 191–203.
121 Hapgood, I. F., Service-book of the Holy Orthodox-Catholic Apostolic Church, 5th edn., New Jersey, 1975 (festal only).
122 Janeras, V., 'La partie vespérale de la liturgie des Présanctifiés', *OCP* 30 (1964), pp. 193–222.
123 Kniazeff, A., 'Ad libitum du Supérieur', *Bibliotheca EL Subsidia* 7 (1976), pp. 169–81.
124 Kniazeff, A., 'La lecture de l'Ancien et du nouveau Testament dans le rite byzantin', *LO* 35 (1963), pp. 201–51.
125 Martimort (no. 17) pp. 238f.
126 Mary, Mother, and Ware, K., *The Festal Menaion*, 1969.

127 — *The Lenten Triodion*, 1978.
128 Mateos, J., 'La synaxe monastique des vêpres byzantines', *OCP* (1970), pp. 248ff.
129 — 'Quelques problèmes de l'Orthros byzantin' *Proche-orient Chrétien* 11 (1961), pp. 17–35 and 201–20.
130 — 'La célébration de la parole dans la liturgie byzantine', *OCA* 191 (1971), pp. 127–47.
131 Mercénier, E., 'Le Bréviaire dans l'église orientale', *Les Questions liturgiques et paroissiales* (1950), pp. 204–8.
132 Radovic, A., 'Réformes liturgiques dans l'Eglise de Grèce', *Bibliotheca EL Subsidia* 7 (1976), pp. 261–74.
133 Schmemann, A., *Introduction to Liturgical Theology* 1966.
134 Taft (no. 23) ch. 17.
135 Thekla, Sister, *The service of Vespers; Prayers of the Day* (Library of Orthodox Thinking, nos. 3 and 4), 1976 and 1977.
136 Uspensky (no. 113) Parts I and III.

The 'Dark Ages' in the West

137 Addleshaw, G. W. O., *The early parochial system and the daily office*, Alcuin Club 1957.
138 — *The beginnings of the parochial system*, St Anthony's Hall Publications (York), no. 3, 1953.
139 — *The development of the parochial system from Charlemagne to Urban II*, ibid., no. 6, 1954.
140 Bäumer (no. 1) vol. I, pp. 188–433.
141 Beck, H. G. J., 'The pastoral care of souls in south-east France during the 6th century', *Analecta Gregoriana* 51, Rome 1950.
142 Bishop, E., *Liturgica Historica* 1917.
143 Bishop, W. C., *The Mozarabic and Ambrosian Rites*, Alcuin Club 1924.
144 — 'The Ambrosian Breviary', *Church Quarterly Review* 23 (1886), pp. 83–112.
145 — 'A service book of the seventh century', *Church Quarterly Review* 37 (1894), pp. 337–63.
146 Borella, P., *Il Rito Ambrosiano*, Milan 1964.
147 Bradshaw (no. 5) ch. 6.
148 Bruyne, D. de, 'Un système de lectures de la liturgie mozarabe', *Revue Bénédictine* 34 (1922), pp. 147–55.
149 Curran, M., *The Antiphonary of Bangor*, Irish Academic Press 1984.
150 DACL (no. 6), 'Paroisses rurales', 'Bréviaire', 'Office divin', 'Mozarabe', 'Ambrosien', 'Gallicane', etc.
151 Ditchfield, P. H., *The Paris Clerk*, 1913.
152 Fernandez Alonso, J., *La cura pastoral en la Espana romanovisigoda* (Rome 1955), pp. 337–44.
153 Jungmann, J., *Pastoral Liturgy*, 1962.
154 — *The Early Liturgy to the Time of Gregory the Great*, 1959.
155 — Ch. 36–8 in 'The Church in the age of feudalism' (*History of the Church* (1980), vol. III), H. Jedin and J. Dolan (eds.).
156 Lafont, G., 'The Eucharist in monastic life', *Cistercian Studies* XIX (1984), no. 4, pp. 296–318.
157 Magistretti, M., *La liturgia della chiesa milanese nel sec. IV*, vol. I, Milan 1899.
158 Martimort (no. 17) pp. 242–52.
159 Monachino, V., *S. Ambrogio e la cura pastorale a Milano nel sec. IV* (Milan 1973), pp. 139–51.
160 Pinell, J., 'Unité et Diversité dans la liturgie hispanique', *Bibliotheca 'Eph. Liturg.' Subsidia* 7 (1976), pp. 245–60.
161 — 'Vestigis del Lucernari a Occident', *Liturgica* I, pp. 91ff.
162 — 'El oficio hispano-visigotico', *Hispania Sacra* 10 (1957), pp. 385–427.
163 Prado, G., *Manual de liturgia hispano-visigotica o mozarabe*, Madrid 1927.

164 Taft (no. 23) ch. 8–11.
165 Thomassin, L., (no. 25)
166 Tour, I. de la, *Les paroisses rurales du IVe au XIe siècle*, Paris 1900.
167 Winkler (no. 104) pp. 53–102.

Medieval

168 Anson, P. F., 'The evolution of the monastic choir', *Downside Review*, Spring 1949, pp. 183–93.
169 Bäumer (no. 1) vol. II, pp. 1–138.
170 Burgess, C., 'For the increase of divine service': chantries in the parish in late medieval Bristol, *JEH* 36.1 (Jan. 1985), pp. 46–65.
171 Crichton (no. 7) pp. 46–51, and in no. 15, pp. 369–82.
172 Dijk, S. J. P. van, and Walker, J. H., *The origins of the modern Roman liturgy*, 1958.
173 Eisenhofer, L and Lechner, J., *The Liturgy of the Roman Rite*, 1961.
174 Fransen, G. 'L'obligation du bréviaire en occident', *Les Questions liturgiques et paroissiales* (1950), pp. 200–204.
175 Gasquet, F. A., *Parish Life in medieval England* 1906.
176 Gy, P.-M., 'L'unification liturgique de l'occident et la liturgie de la Curie romaine', *Bibliotheca 'Eph. Lit.' Subsidia* 7 (1976), pp. 155–67.
177 Hughes, A., *Medieval manuscripts for Mass and Office: a guide to their organization and terminology*, Toronto 1982.
178 Humbeeck, D. van, 'Origine et Évolution des Stalles', in *Les Questions liturgiques et paroissales* 3 (1950), pp. 97–102.
179 Rock, D. (ed. Hart and Frere), *The Church of our Fathers* 1904.
180 Salmon (no. 20) ch. 1 and 5.
181 — 'L'Office divin au moyen âge', *LO* 43 (1967).
182 Swete, H. B., *Church services and service-books before the Reformation*, 1930.
183 Taft (no. 23) ch. 18 and 19.
184 Temperley, N., *The Music of the English Parish Church* (1979), vol. 1.
185 Thompson, A. H., 'Song-schools in the Middle Ages' (Church Music Soc. occasional papers, no. 4, 1942).
186 Wordsworth, C., *Notes on Medieval Services in England*, 1898.
187 Wordsworth, C. and Littlehales, H., *The Old Service-books of the English Church*, 1904.

Personal prayer

188 Bishop (no. 142) ch. IX, 'The origin of the prymer'.
189 *DACL* (no. 6), 'Livres d'Heures'.
190 Heinz, A., 'Lob der Mysterien Christi', in *Liturgie und Dichtung* (ed. E. Becker and R. Kaczynski – Kompendium I, 1983), 609–40.
191 — 'Der Engel des Herrn: Erlösungsgedächtnis als Volksgebet', in *Heiliger Dienst* 33 (1979), pp. 51–8.
192 Hoskins, E., *Horae Beatae Mariae Virginis, or Sarum and York Primers . . .* 1901.
193 Jungmann, J., *Christian Prayer through the Centuries*, New York 1978 (no footnotes); German edn., *Christliches Beten*, Munich 1969 (with footnotes); French edn., *Histoire de la prière chrétienne*, 1972 (with footnotes).
194 Leclercq, J., 'Culte liturgique et prière intime', *LMD* 69 (1972), 39–55.
195 Schnitzler, T. 'Stundengebet und Volksandacht', in no. 16, pp. 71–84.
196 Stadlhuber, J., 'Das Laienstundengebet vom Leiden Christi in seinem Mittelalterlichen Fortleben', *Zeitschrift für Katholische Theologie* LXXII (1950), pp. 282–322.

197 Ühlein, H. and Gensler, E, 'Liturgie und Parodie', in no. 190, pp. 641–4.

Britain

198 Abbey, C. J. and Overton, J., *The English Church in the 18th Century* (2 vols.), 1878.
199 Addleshaw, G. W. O., *The High Church Tradition*, 1941.
200 Best, W., Essay upon the service of the Church of England, considered as a daily service, 1746.
201 Blom, J. M., 'The post-Tridentine English Primer', Catholic Record Society (monograph series), vol. 3, 1982.
202 Clarke, W. K. L., *Eighteenth-century Piety*, 1944.
203 Crichton, J. D., 'The Manual of 1614', Catholic Record Society: *Recusant History* (Jan. 1984), pp. 158–72.
204 — 'The liturgy and the laity from *c.* 1600 to 1900', *Worcestershire Recusant* 43 (June 1984), pp. 1–14.
205 Hoskins (no. 192).
206 Legg, J. W., *English Church life from the Restoration to the Tractarian Movement*, 1914.
207 — 'London Church services in the reign of Queen Anne', Transactions of St Paul's Ecclesiological Society vi (1906–10), pp. 1–34.
208 Overton, J. H., *Life in the English Church (1660–1714)*, 1885.
209 Staley, V. (ed.), *Hierurgia Anglicana*, part iii, 1904.
210 Vaux, J. E., *Church Folk Lore*, 2nd edn. (enlarged), 1902.

France

211 Bäumer (no. 1) vol. ii, pp. 324–71.
212 Brémond, H., *Histoire littéraire du sentiment réligieux en France* (1932), vol. x.
213 *DACL* (no. 6), 'Liturgies Néo-gallicanes'.
214 Collette, A., *Histoire du Bréviaire de Rouen*, 1902.

Germany

215 Bäumer (as no. 211).
216 Jungmann, J. A., 'Liturgische Erneuerung zwischen Barock und Gegenwart', *Liturgisches Jahrbuch* 53 (1962), pp. 1–15.
217 Popp, F., 'Studien zu liturgischen Reformbemühungen im Zeitalter der Aufklärung', in *Freiburger Diözesan-Archiv* 87, 1967.
218 Schnitzler (as no. 195).
219 Trapp, W., *Vorgeschichte und Ursprung der liturgischen Bewegung* (Regensburg 1935), pp. 306–11.

Transylvania

220 Roth, E., *Die Geschichte des Gottesdienstes der Siebenbürger Sachsen*, Göttingen 1954.

Poland

221 Adamski, R., 'Unbekannte Volksliturgie', *Der Seelsorger* 6 (1930), pp. 379–83 and 427–30.
222 Anon., 'Powstanie godzinek o Matce Bożej', *Ruch Biblijny i Liturgiczny*, Rok 5, Nr. 2 (1952), pp. 177–9.
223 Gloger, Z., *Encyklopedia Staropolska*, Warsaw 1958.

224 Gulden, J., 'Polnische Volksliturgie', *Liturgisches Jahrbuch* 4 (1954), pp. 149–86.
225 Kopeć, J. J., 'Męka Pańska w religijnej kulturze polskiego średniowiecza', *Textus et Studia*, vol. 3, Warsaw 1975.
226 Schenk, W. (ed.), *Studia z dziejów liturgii w Polsce* III (Lublin 1980), pp. 77–81: 'Niedzielna Służba Boża'.
227 Słownik Języka Polskiego, Warsaw 1958.
228 Śpiewnik Kościelny, Warsaw 1947.
229 Wojtkowski, J., *Powstanie Godzinek o Niepokolanym Poczęciu Najświętszej Marii Panny z modlitw Wacława, Roczniki teologiczno-kanoniczne* (Lublin) 2 (1955), pp. 23–8.

The components of daily prayer

230 Apel, W., *Gregorian Chant*, 1958.
231 *DACL* (no. 6), 'Antienne', 'Antiphonon', 'Cantique', etc. See also no. 150.
232 Fischer, B., 'Litania ad Laudes et Vesperas: Ein Vorschlag ...' *Liturgisches Jahrbuch* (Trier) 1 (1951), pp. 55–74.
233 Gelineau, J., 'Les Formes de la psalmodie chrétienne', *LMD* 33 (1953), pp. 134–72.
234 Lamb, J. A., *The Psalms in Christian Worship*, 1962.
235 Martimort (no. 17) section III, ch. 3 and 4.
236 Mearns, J., *The Canticles of the Christian Church*, 1914.
237 Schneider, H., 'Die Biblischen Oden im Christlichen Altertum', *Biblica* 30 (1949), pp. 28–65, 239–72, 433–52 and 479–501.

Praying the Psalms

238 Crichton (7), ch. v.
239 Flannery, A. (ed.), 'Making the most of the Breviary', Supplement to *Doctrine and Life* 13, nos. 56/57 (Dublin, no date), pp. 28–74.
240 Lewis, C. S., *Reflections on the Psalms* (1958).
241 Martimort (18) section 3, ch. 3.
242 Neale, J. M., *A Commentary on the Psalms: from Primitive and Mediaeval writers*, 2nd. edn. (1869)
243 Salmon (20) ch. 3.

Index

Numbers in **bold type** refer to *Part V : Sources*.
Patristic and other references from that section, being easy of access, are not included in this index.

Mateos, J. 70
Mather, F. C. 260 n. 155
meditation 112f., 168, 179
memory, performance from 96f., 104, 105f., 126f.
Merton, T. 6, 30, 113f., 189
micro-climate 199f.
minster 86f.
monastic office:
  general 54–9;
  Jerusalem 63;
  Byzantine 77f.;
  imitation of 91, 94, 96, 145;
  and people's office 187f.;
  characteristics 55f., 156;
  hymns in 159;
  contribution to contemporary Church 197
monasticism:
  tradition in prayer 43;
  general 54–59;
  psalmody 62;
  in Rome 85;
  Franciscans 100;
  influence on Anglicanism 115;
  readings in 163, 166f.;
  and the priest's life 207;
  eucharist in 57;
  in Egypt 22, 54f., 149, 163, 36, 37
morning prayer chapel 120
Mowinckel, S. 20, 29
Mozarabic office 85, 92, 157, 30
Mühlen, H. 21
music:
  in people's office 55f., 71f., 85, 150;
  in middle ages 90;
  lay participation 94, 135f., 139;
  English cathedrals 116;
  France 131;
  Transylvania 139;
  Poland 142f.;
  and psalmody 161;
  in Church of England 194;
  in the parish today 201, 206;
  in cathedrals today 209f.
Muslims 52
Myers Briggs workshop 35
mysteries see themes

Neale, J. M. 159
Niceta of Remesiana 156, 25
night prayer 51
noise in church 85, 118f.

obligation 95f., 181f., 189f., 207
Origen 52, 7
Otloh 13
Oxford Movement 116, 120, 122, 202

Pachomius 54f., 149, 37
Paelz, W. 22
Pambo, abba 56
parallel observances: 103ff., 121, 179f.;
  via content 105–10, 123, 131f., 208;
  via times of prayer 105, 110–12, 208
parish clerk 89, 103, 204
parish priest, life of 91, 206f.
parish system 87
paroissien 131, 135
paschal vigil 10, 62
peace, kiss of 66, 71, 149
people's and monastic offices: 55f., chs 10–14
  passim, 163, 187–9;
  mutual influence 55, 57, 91, 94, 145
people's office:
  characteristics 55f.;
  beginnings 52f.;
  Jerusalem 63;
  East Syria 68;
  in the east 71, 73, 80;
  Byzantine 71;
  in the west 84ff.;
  and the primer 110;
  Germany 134;
  Transylvania 137–41
Pepys, S. 119
personal prayer 26, 39f., 51, 82, 104f., 123f., 150,
  158, 180
Phos Hilaron 74, 80
play 31–3
Plove, N. de 258 n. 96
poetry 81, 124, 141f., 156
Poland 107, 141, 180, 209
popular devotions, characteristics 263 n. 10
prayer at night 51
preces 104, 117, 132, 170f., 195
prescribed prayers 52, 5, 7, 8
primer see Hours, books of
private recitation 95f., 100f., 112, 128, 145
procession to cross, tomb or baptistery 63, 68, 70,
  85, 149f., 267 n. 45b
Procter, F., and Frere, W. H. 98, 202
Prudentius 84
psalm breviary 108
psalm collects 59, 70, 81, 155f., 170, 173, 201,
  262 n. 8
psalmody, preliminary 62, 66, 73f.
psalm references:
  ps. 51 in the morning office 153, 257 n. 45,
    262 n. 5;
  ps. 51 known by heart 104f.;
  ps. 51 Jerusalem 60;
  ps. 51 East Syria 70;
  ps. 51 Byzantine chanted office 74;
  ps 51 Byzantine 81;
  ps. 51 dark ages in the west 85;